The Man
Who
Ran London
During the Great War

The Man
Who
Ran London
During the
Great War

The Diaries and Letters of
Lieutenant General Sir Francis Lloyd
GCVO,KCB,DSO (1853-1926)

By Richard Morris OBE

Pen & Sword
MILITARY

First published in Great Britain in 2009 by
Pen & Sword Military
An imprint of
Pen & Sword Books Ltd
47 Church Street
Barnsley
South Yorkshire
S70 2AS

Copyright © Richard Morris 2009

ISBN 978 1 84884 164 2

A CIP catalogue record for this book is
available from the British Library

Printed and bound in the UK
By the MPG Books Group

Pen & Sword Books Ltd incorporates the Imprints of Pen & Sword Aviation,
Pen & Sword Family History, Pen & Sword Maritime, Pen & Sword Military,
Wharncliffe Local History, Pen & Sword Select, Pen & Sword Military Classics,
Leo Cooper, Remember When, Seaforth Publishing and Frontline Publishing

For a complete list of Pen & Sword titles please contact
PEN & SWORD BOOKS LIMITED
47 Church Street, Barnsley, South Yorkshire, S70 2AS, England
E-mail: enquiries@pen-and-sword.co.uk

Website: www.pen-and-sword.co.uk

Contents

List of Illustrations and Maps

29. Aston Hall, near Oswestry, west and north fronts (2008).

30. The Grand Staircase at Aston Hall (1923).

31. Sir Francis Lloyd's Coat of Arms, 1913. 'Supporters' were added in 1919 after he was awarded the GCVO.

32. Lieutenant General Sir Francis Lloyd's funeral cortege leaving the Guards Chapel, Wellington Barracks, London, 4 March 1926.

MAPS

Northern Sudan 1898.

South Africa – Orange Free State 1902.

Lloyd estates at Aston Hall near Oswestry, Shropshire 1921. © Cassini Publishing Ltd.

Acknowledgements

This book is based mainly on the diaries and letters of Lieutenant General Sir Francis Lloyd. In the former respect it is fortunate that Lloyd bequeathed his diaries covering the years 1886-1925 to his old regiment, the Grenadier Guards, where they can be found today in the archives at the Regimental Headquarters. The first twenty years of the diaries are written in Lloyd's own handwriting, but thereafter his manuscripts were typed and bound into annual volumes, together with press cuttings and other ephemera relating to his activities. I am most grateful to the Grenadier Guards and in particular to Lieutenant Colonel Conway Seymour, LVO, for allowing me to spend many hours in the Regimental Archives at Wellington Barracks, reading the diaries and viewing the photographic archive.

During the Sudan campaigns of 1885 and 1898, and part of the Boer War, Francis Lloyd wrote many letters to his wife Mary. They contain extensive details of the military aspects of Lloyd's part in the campaigns, and also much of a personal nature. Lady Lloyd retained the letters, although the replies that she sent to many of the letters from Francis have not survived. Almost 300 of the letters from Sir Francis Lloyd were inherited by his nephew Nigel Gunnis, who bequeathed them to the National Army Museum where they may be studied today.

Andrew Lloyd, Sir Francis Lloyd's nephew, inherited Aston Hall and Rolls Park on the death in 1940, of his father Rossendale, the brother of Sir Francis. In 1949, Andrew Lloyd deposited with the National Library of Wales, a very considerable archive of Harvey and Lloyd family letters and deeds, and the collection was later purchased by the NLW. I have been able to quote from some of the letters in this collection which refer to Francis Lloyd's childhood.

I am most grateful to Derek Williams of Shropshire Libraries at Oswestry who has been able to provide catalogues containing details of the Lloyd home at Aston Hall which give an insight to the time Sir Francis and Lady Lloyd spent there.

A number of the illustrations are reproduced by kind permission of the Trustees of the Imperial War Museum. In the IWM film archive there are twenty clips from newsreels produced during the First World War which show Lieutenant General Sir Francis Lloyd at various events in London between 1915 and 1918.

After the end of the Great War, Sir Francis Lloyd was in great demand for the unveiling of Memorials to the fallen. I have traced eighteen memorials which he unveiled and others where he accompanied members of the Royal Family. At the ceremonies Lloyd was always asked to give an address. I received much assistance from churchwardens, local historians and archivists in finding the memorials, and the associated newspaper reports of the ceremonies.

Loughton, 2009

Foreword

General Sir Francis Lloyd served in the British Army for forty-four years, during which time he saw great change. He joined an Army which still had many veterans of the Crimea and whose background and training were very different from those he was to command in the Great War. Commissioned into the Grenadier Guards, like many officers of Queen Victoria's Army, he saw much active service. His 'Baptism by Fire' was at Suakin. He was awarded a DSO at Omdurman and was seriously wounded in the Boer War at Biddulphsberg. He had a reputation for hard work and being an excellent administrator. He was a strict, but fair, disciplinarian and was an unusually good public speaker. He was conscious of his appearance and many thought he was an epitome of what an Officer from the Brigade of Guards should be.

Lloyd was a serious career soldier who had ambition and rose through merit. He was undoubtedly the right man for the job as GOC London District during the Great War. He had great power and earned the nicknames given him by the press 'The man who ran London' and 'Military governor of London'. He would have liked a field command during the war in France but his contribution at home was of great importance and this was widely recognised.

Fortunately, Francis Lloyd and his wife, Mary, were prolific letter writers during his service in both Sudan and South Africa. Almost 300 of the letters he wrote to Mary have survived and are held in the National Army Museum collection. He also kept a diary from 1886 and by the time of his appointment as GOC London District they had become substantial volumes, which are now in the archives of the Grenadier Guards. We are fortunate that the distinguished military historian, Richard Morris, has had access to them and other material and has been able to produce a fascinating story of a great Guardsman and distinguished General. He has produced a book which tells us much about soldiering, the society and the background that Lloyd came from and the man himself.

General the Lord Guthrie of Craigiebank GCB LVO OBE DL

London, 2009

Introduction

Historically most generals in the British Army have earned their reputations on the battlefield, but although Francis Lloyd served with distinction in the Sudan campaigns, and in South Africa where he was severely wounded, he will always be remembered for his time as GOC London District throughout the First World War.

What qualities did he have that led him to be seen, at least in the eyes of the public during this period, as 'the man who runs London'? His ancestors had come from North Wales, and while he had been born an Englishman in the Welsh borderlands, Francis Lloyd was often still described as being Welsh, and he was proud of this.

He had the gift that so many distinguished men from Wales have, of oratory. The hundreds of speeches that Lloyd made during the war helped to boost the population's flagging morale when news of setbacks on the battlefield reached London. Even after the war he was in constant demand, not only in metropolitan London, but throughout the country, to unveil war memorials, and of course this would involve making a speech.

By early 1915 it had become clear that any hopes for a quick end to the war would not be fulfilled and the need for more troops became vital. Kitchener's early efforts at recruitment had produced an additional 200,000 men, but now many more were needed. Lloyd was able to put to good use his previous experience as the Commander of a Division of the Territorials, and he toured London and the Home Counties encouraging men to sign up voluntarily. He was against conscription and only gave in when Lord Derby's volunteer scheme failed to produce sufficient men by the end of 1915. His value to the raising of 'Volunteers' was recognized when he was put in charge of all the London Volunteer Regiments as well as continuing as GOC London District.

Lloyd's responsibilities throughout the Great War extended far beyond command of the troops in London. He had responsibility for over 200 hospitals and also for the main railway termini. He constantly visited the military hospitals in the metropolis, often accompanied by Lady Lloyd. If on any visit he noticed a problem with the running of the hospital, he

1

would ensure that steps were taken to improve the situation and, importantly, would return to the hospital a month later to see if things had improved.

The Defence of the Realm Act, passed by Parliament in August 1914, effectively put Britain under martial law, with many civil rights suspended and individual freedoms subject to military law. One newspaper correspondent went as far as describing Francis Lloyd as the 'Military Governor' of London, which was possibly a slight exaggeration, but the point was that military courts were able to dispense a form of justice more quickly that their civil counterparts.

The need for specialist treatment for those soldiers returning from the front with limbs amputated had been recognized by May 1915, and through voluntary efforts the first hospital for such men was opened at Roehampton. Sir Francis Lloyd was invited to become Chairman of the Trustees of what became known as Queen Mary's Convalescent Auxiliary Hospital, Roehampton. He was still Chairman at the time of his death almost eleven years later, despite some of the frustrations he endured in his dealings with the Ministry of Pensions and other government departments.

The welfare of those under his command was always a first consideration, and if he had the reputation as something of a strict disciplinarian there is no evidence to show that he used his authority unfairly. His office at Horse Guards was forever filled with people from both the military and civilians seeking interviews, and officers and staff continuously going in and out with some order or paper requiring signature. He therefore needed to be good at administration.

These qualities may have led the Minister of Food in November 1919 to invite Lloyd to take on the job of Food Commissioner for London and the Home Counties. However, he soon became frustrated with the bureaucracy and interference, as he saw it, by the civil servants in the Ministry, and resigned after fifteen months.

It is a little puzzling that his abilities as an organizer and administrator were not in some respects also reflected in the management of his estates in Shropshire and Essex. In his defence it must be said that the agricultural recessions before and after the war did not help, but for much of his later life he was in debt, although his banker commented that difficult as his situation was, he was not in as much trouble as others at the time. It was a wrench for him to have to sell much of the furniture, pictures and family heirlooms from Aston Hall in 1923, in order to pay for the cost of modernising Rolls Park at Chigwell, the ancestral home of his grandmother and her Harvey ancestors, when he and his wife decided in 1920 to live there.

The decision after his retirement to live within easy reach of London, having sold his house at Great Cumberland Place, was possibly taken not only because he was still involved in many activities linked with the capital, but also because of the social lifestyle he enjoyed, and latterly his interest in politics. With regard to the former, the caricaturists had portrayed him since his appointment as GOC London District as something of a 'dandy' while still acknowledging his reputation for discipline. The social columns in newspapers included references to him as 'naturally fastidious about his clothes and an authority on what new fashions are fashions', and commented that his 'uniforms are the neatest and nattiest I have ever seen'.

Sir Francis Lloyd was for many years a member of the Carlton, the club of 'High Tories', and served on its Committee. His political views were in sympathy with his fellow members, and when his time as GOC London District came to an end in October 1918, he thought of entering Parliament but had little time to find a seat before Parliament was dissolved and a General Election called in December. Soundings were made of party organizers and constituency chairmen but no seat was offered. However, his interest in politics continued and he stood successfully as one of the members for East Fulham in the LCC elections of March 1919, when he was in his sixty-sixth year. He spent three weeks treading the streets of Fulham canvassing support for his party and speaking at meetings in the evening.

This probably epitomizes the character of Lieutenant General Sir Francis Lloyd. From the day he joined the Grenadiers, to the day he finally succumbed to his illness, there was no harder working soldier and retired General in the country.

1

Early Life

Francis Lloyd was a descendant of an ancient family from North Wales related to the last Prince of Powys. Several of his ancestors were High Sheriffs of Denbigh, where they owned much land.

Andrew Lloyd, a Captain in Cromwell's army and MP for Shropshire in the time of the Commonwealth, was the first recorded member of the family to reside at Aston Hall.[1][2] He married Margaret, daughter of Thomas Powell and they had two sons: Thomas, the eldest, and Richard. The latter was knighted and became chancellor of Durham and a judge in the Admiralty Court. In 1646 Thomas married Sarah, daughter and co-heir of Francis Albany of Whittington, a few miles from Aston, and brought into the ownership of the Lloyd family the manor of Whittington and Middleton and the Albany estate, including the advowsons of the churches of Whittington and Selattyn.

Thomas and Sarah produced a son, Robert, and a daughter, Elizabeth. Robert was an MP for Shropshire and married Mary, eldest daughter of Sir John Bridgeman, by whom he had one son, also called Robert, who followed his father into Parliament and represented the Jacobite interest. However, their son died unmarried in 1734, and the Aston estates were inherited by the sons of his aunt Elizabeth.

Elizabeth had married Foulke Lloyd of Foxhall in the parish of Hellnan, Denbigh. He was descended in the male line from William Rosindale, grandson of Henry Rosindale of Rosindale, Lancaster. Subsequent generations of Lloyds were to use Rosindale (later Rossendale) as a Christian name. Elizabeth and Foulke had three sons, two of whom succeeded to Aston. John succeeded his cousin Robert, but died without issue in 1741, and was succeeded by his brother, Thomas, who died unmarried in 1754. The third brother, Rosindale, had died in 1734, but had earlier married Jane, daughter of Robert Davies of Llannerch Park, by whom he had one son, William, who inherited the Aston and other nearby estates.

This William Lloyd took holy orders and married Elizabeth, daughter of William Sneyd of Bishton, Staffordshire, and they had an only son and heir, John Robert Lloyd. He also took holy orders and was rector of

Whittington and Selattyn. It was this Lloyd who, as we shall see, commissioned James Wyatt to prepare drawings for the 'new' Aston Hall which was built between 1789 and 1793, the Palladian front of which remains today.

John Robert Lloyd married Martha, fourth daughter of John Shakespeare of London, and they had three sons and two daughters by the marriage. The eldest son William (1779-1843) married Louisa, eldest daughter of Admiral Sir Eliab Harvey (1758-1830) of Rolls Park, Chigwell, Essex. Harvey, who was Captain of the *Temeraire* at Trafalgar, came from a distinguished family whose wealth had been made as successful merchants in the City of London. His ancestors also included Dr William Harvey (1578-1657) who discovered the circulation of the blood in 1628, and two generals in the British Army: Daniel Harvey (1664-1732) who served with William III in Flanders, and Edward Harvey (1718-1778) who was Adjutant-General and acting Commander-in-Chief of the British Army when the Marquis of Granby resigned during the American War of Independence.

Sir Eliab Harvey's two sons predeceased him, and estates in Essex and several other counties were divided between his six daughters, Louisa inheriting the estates in Essex including Rolls Park. William Lloyd and Louisa had six children: four sons and two daughters. The eldest son, Edward Harvey Lloyd, (1811-69) was apparently, due to a family dispute, excluded from inheriting the Aston estate, although he received some financial compensation. The second son, Richard Thomas Lloyd (1820-1898), in due course inherited the Lloyd estates in Shropshire and the Harvey estate in Essex. In 1839 he received a commission in the Rifle Brigade, but in 1843 he transferred to the Grenadier Guards, where he became a Captain. He left the Grenadiers in 1853 and joined the King's Own Rifle Regiment of the Staffordshire Militia. Later, in 1875, he was gazetted as Lieutenant Colonel of the Shropshire Yeomanry Cavalry. His father, William Lloyd, died in 1843, but his mother, Louisa, appears to have continued to live at Aston Hall until her death in 1866.

In 1852 Richard Lloyd married Lady Frances Hay, third daughter of the 10th Earl of Kinnoull. They had ten children, five sons and five daughters. The eldest son, Francis, was born in August 1853, and in celebration of the event, his parents planted two Orecavia Trees (Monkey Puzzles) between the Long Walk and the Grove at Aston Hall.[3] Francis and his parents, together with some of his younger brothers and sisters, may have first lived at Aston Hall with their grandmother, however, much of each summer was spent in Scotland on the Kinnoull family estates. In September 1858, Francis, then just over five years old, wrote to his sister Eva from Cromlix Cottage at Dunblane:

How many Guinea Pigs are there? I am going to send you some white stones from the top of the hill of Cromlix. There is one for you, one for Selina and one for Edith [two of his younger sisters]. You shall have the box on your birthday.

From your affectionate brother, Frankey.

[The letter is in the handwriting of his mother].[4]

The childhood upbringing of Francis followed the normal path for an ancient family of the landed gentry who also had a tradition of service in the army. Rural pursuits predominated, with riding and shooting the principal ones. Writing to her son from Melton Mowbray where she was staying with Lady Stamford, also in 1858, Lady Frances thanked him for making her a fan. She added: 'The toy that Lady Stamford has sent you is such a pretty one. It is a [model] garrison town and there are soldiers and three little cannons, which will shoot peas, only you must mind and not hurt your sisters with them'.[5]

A year later Richard Lloyd and Lady Frances had moved to a house, Abbots Moss, near Northwich in Cheshire, which Francis referred to as 'our new house'. By 1860 Francis was writing short letters in his own handwriting and in one to his father in March, he thanked him for 'all the nice things you have sent us. We like the play of *Pizarro* very much, but not *Othello*. May we change it for another?'[6] Francis was to become an avid reader of books throughout his military campaigns.

A month later the Lloyds had moved closer to Aston Hall, this time to Felton Grange, near Shrewsbury, about which Francis told his father 'we like this house very much and think it all very pretty'.[7]

Shortly after his tenth birthday in 1863, Francis was taken by his father to school for the first time, to Mr Essex's at May Place, Malvern Wells. In 1924 Sir Francis recalled his arrival at Malvern Wells:

Sixty-one years ago today I went to school at Malvern Wells. I remember very well my Father taking me and I blowing the horn on the bus crossing the Common. I was a very sad little boy of ten – I remember it perfectly! It was a very smart School of many Lords, but the man who kept it, named Essex, was I always thought a pompous old ass. I do not think that we were very well treated, although ostensibly there was a good deal done for show.[8]

What form of education he had received before this is not known, but after a little over three years at Malvern Wells, Francis was sent to Harrow, the school of his great grandfather, Admiral Harvey. He started at Harrow in January 1867, and was placed in the Rev T H Steel's house, 'The Grove', but he only spent two years at the school, leaving Harrow in December 1868. He did, however, return to the school on at least one occasion, when in June 1912 he and his wife were among the guests at the Harrow Speech Day which King George V and Queen Mary attended. Francis and Mary had lunch with the headmaster, together with many other guests, and attended the school singing, which Lloyd thought was excellent.[9]

Ten days before Francis left Felton Grange to go to school at Malvern Wells in September 1863, his brother Rossendale had been born. He may have been considered the intelligent member of the family, and was educated at Winchester and Jesus College, Cambridge, before entering the church. He became rector of St Mary's Church at Selattyn, four miles north-west of Oswestry, of which the Lloyd family held the advowson, and remained there for thirty-seven years.

For the first thirteen years of his life Francis's grandmother Louisa Lloyd was still alive, and a note written by her dated 23 February 1866, which Francis pasted into one of his diaries, records that: 'I bequeath to my grandson Francis my diamond ring and wedding ring'. The Lloyds moved to Aston following the death of Louisa in 1866.

Living at Aston Hall, one of the oldest county seats in Shropshire, Francis Lloyd no doubt took part in the social and sporting activities of the estate. The 'coming of age', in August 1874, of the heir to the estate was celebrated with 'great rejoicings', as the announcement in the local Oswestry paper put it. The bells of the parish church of St Oswald 'rang merry peals in celebration' on 12 August, and the *Oswestry Advertizer* commented that the event is to be 'further commemorated in a short time by public rejoicings'.[10]

Tuesday 8 September was the day chosen for the celebrations, and the young Francis Lloyd was going to need a good deal of stamina to complete the day. The tenants and friends of the Aston Hall Estate met at the gates to the Hall at about half-past ten that morning and, led by the Oswestry Mechanics Brass Band, marched to the front of the mansion, where Major Richard and Lady Lloyd, with their son Francis, stood to receive them. Speeches followed and Francis Lloyd was presented with a large silver punch bowl, suitably inscribed. The domestic staff at the Hall had previously presented him with a silver cup. The presentations over, the company made their way to a marquee which had been set up in the grounds where lunch was provided for friends and the workmen employed on the estate.

At two o'clock the sports commenced, the principal one being the Aston Hall Stakes, a programme of horse races with the course situated on land opposite the Aston entrance gates. There were five races in all but it does not appear that Francis rode in any of them. Other rural sports included bicycle races, foot races, high and long jumps, sack races and donkey races. The wives and children of the workmen on the estate were invited to tea

7

and it was estimated that about 350 people sat down. In the evening a public ball was held at the Victoria Rooms in Oswestry, with tickets one shilling each and refreshments at 'moderate prices'.

On the next day, Wednesday, Major Richard and Lady Lloyd gave a ball to a large number of guests at Aston Hall. Marquees had been erected in the grounds in which the 300-400 guests could dine and dance. However, a few hours before the ball was due to start, torrential rain fell, swamping the whole grounds in a very short space of time. Arrangements were quickly altered so that the dancing and the supper could take place in the Hall itself, but it was noted that supper was not taken until soon after midnight. A servants' ball was given on the next night, and this brought the rejoicings to a conclusion.

In the same year Francis Lloyd joined the army, where his first regiment was the old 33rd (Duke of Wellington's). However, he soon transferred to his father's regiment, the Grenadiers, with which he was to be closely associated for forty-five years.

In August 1881 Francis Lloyd, aged twenty-eight, married Mary, eldest daughter of George Gunnis of Leckie, Stirlingshire. The marriage took place at St Peter's Church, Eaton Square, London, known for its 'society' weddings. Judging from the number of people attending the wedding it must have been one of the highlights of the London summer season. Many of Francis Lloyd's colleagues in the 1st Battalion of the Grenadier Guards were invited, and the church portico leading to the principal door was lined by the non-commissioned officers and men of the flank company of the 1st Battalion. After the wedding service, the guests adjourned to 43 Rutland Gate, the home of Mr Francis Gunnis, the bride's brother, for the wedding breakfast.[11] Newspaper reports of the wedding were numerous and lengthy, including a long list of presents. It was reported that the honeymoon was spent at Aston Lodge, Bournemouth, the home of one of Francis Lloyd's sisters.

Locally in Shropshire, the event was appropriately celebrated at Aston Hall in the then time-honoured fashion of giving a tea, followed by rural sports, to all the cottagers and labourers on the estate, and over 400 attended.

With Francis a young Guards officer based in London, the newly-weds probably rented accommodation in the capital. However, it was not until the middle of October 1881 that they paid a visit to Aston Hall, where further celebrations took place. They were met at Rednal station, which was decorated with flags and evergreen and the motto 'Prosperity to Aston Hall'. Outside the station, on the road to Aston, an arch of evergreens and flags had been erected, with 'Happy may the future be' on one side, and 'Welcome' on the other. Two other arches were passed along the road to the

Hall. At the station salutes were fired and answered from Aston Hall. They were met at the Hall by 200-300 friends and workers on the estate. A few days later Colonel (he had been promoted in 1875) Richard and Lady Frances Lloyd entertained the tenants on the estate to dinner in honour of their son and daughter-in-law. Francis Lloyd was presented with a framed illuminated engraved address from the tenants, and many speeches were made and toasts drunk.[12]

Francis and Mary Lloyd were to receive one further gift in celebration of their marriage. At the end of February 1882, a presentation took place at Aston Hall at which the town of Oswestry presented a pair of massive silver bowls which had been subscribed for by the townsfolk of Oswestry.[13]

On the death of his father in 1898 Francis inherited Aston Hall, and this became his home for much of his married life, but as we shall see in 1920 Francis and Mary came to live at Rolls Park at Chigwell, Essex, the ancestral home of the Harvey family, which the Lloyd family had inherited in 1830. However, following his death in 1926, Sir Francis Lloyd was buried in the family graveyard adjoining the chapel at Aston Hall.

2

The Sudan Campaigns

In 1820 an Egyptian-Ottoman force conquered and unified the northern part of the Sudan. Although Egypt claimed all of the present Sudan during most of the nineteenth century, it was unable to establish effective control over the area, which remained a region of fragmented tribes. In 1881 a religious leader Muhammad Ahmad proclaimed himself the Mahdi and led a nationalist revolt.

The Suez Canal opened in 1869 and quickly became Britain's economic lifeline to India and the Far East. To defend the waterway Britain sought a greater role in Egyptian affairs. Although Britain had been ruling Egypt indirectly for years it was not until August 1882 that British troops landed at Alexandria, marking the beginning of British occupation of the country. As a result Britain was also involved fully with the future of the Sudan and Egypt's attempts to develop it. Although Gladstone insisted that the Sudan was purely an Egyptian problem, and it would be wiser for Britain to remain uninvolved, something had to be done about the Mahdist rising and the Egyptians alone could not handle it.

A British officer, Colonel William Hicks, was appointed Chief of Staff to the Egyptian Army in the Sudan, but after some initial success, an army of 10,000 soldiers was annihilated by Mahdist forces in the province of Kordofan in September 1883.

This latest disaster caused great dismay in London. The advice given by Gladstone to the Egyptian government was that Egypt should abandon the Sudan and give up all attempts at controlling the Nile south of Wadi Halfa. A new Egyptian government took a more pragmatic view and proposed that the Egyptian garrisons should be extracted from the Sudan, although Egypt would maintain a claim to the country which could be enforced at some later date, when the Mahdist storm had passed. General Charles Gordon was given the task of withdrawing the garrisons.

The destruction of Hick's army was not the only defeat suffered by the Egyptians in 1883. On the Red Sea coast, the Mahdi's local lieutenant, Osman Digna, was in arms raiding the Suakin to Berber caravan route and besieging the garrisons of the coastal ports. A force under the command of General Sir Gerald Graham was sent in February 1884 to restore British prestige in the area. Graham's force fought well and British honour had been satisfied, but very little of use had been achieved. By April 1884 Graham's force had been withdrawn to Cairo.

The government's attention now turned to General Gordon in Khartoum where, by May, the city was under blockade by the Mahdi forces. Concerned by this news, the British government was forced reluctantly to agree to send a column to get Gordon out of Khartoum. General Sir Garnet Wolseley was to command the force. The 'Desert Column' set out from Korti on 30 December 1884 and a 'River Column' fought its way up the Nile, but it was too late: Khartoum had fallen on 26 January 1885, two days before the relief forces reached the city.

The expedition then pulled back to Dongola to await further orders, and on 11 May 1885 they were ordered to evacuate the Sudan entirely and retire behind the Egyptian frontier. While the River and Desert columns were at Dongola, another expedition had been setting out from Suakin under the command of General Sir Gerald Graham, and among the officers in the Guards Brigade was Francis Lloyd.

SUAKIN

Promoted to Captain in April 1885, Francis Lloyd served in that year as signalling officer to the Guards Brigade on the Suakin Expedition to the Sudan, and was Mentioned in Despatches after the Battle of Hashin. He spent about three months in the Sudan and details of his part in the campaign are recorded in letters to his wife Mary.[14]

Khartoum had fallen in January 1885, but March saw the arrival at Suakin of a new expeditionary force under General Sir Gerald Graham, to protect the construction of a projected military railway from Suakin to Berber. Captain Francis Lloyd had sailed from England with part of this force aboard the SS *Australia*. His wife also made arrangements to go to Egypt and they subsequently met at Suez, before Mary went on to Cairo to stay at the Shepherds Hotel.

The convoy carried on through the Red Sea in weather Lloyd described as 'melting hot', arriving at Suakin on 10 March. The port was crowded with naval vessels, troopships, transports and hospital ships, with special vessels for condensing (desalination) 85,000 gallons of water daily. Nearly 13,000 men made up General Graham's force.

In the first letter to his wife following his arrival at Suakin, Lloyd reported that his Brigade 'marched to our camp two and a half miles off, which we found pitched – a great luxury. We dined with the Coldstream and had a good dinner which I also did not expect'. He was immediately busy with signalling and expected 'heaps of hard work'. Although no one knew when they were to advance, it was not expected to be long before

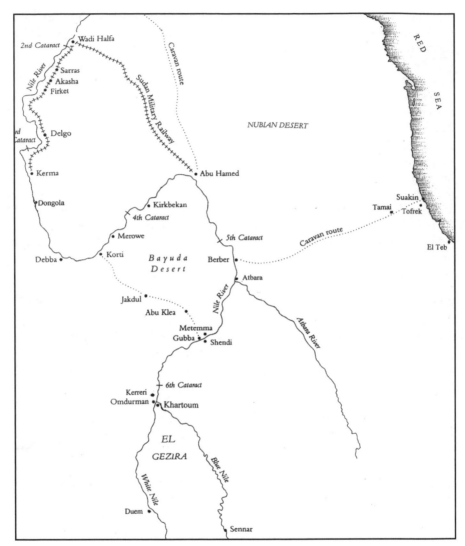

Northern Sudan 1898

they were on the move. One of Lloyd's first actions was to buy himself two horses, but one turned out to be unsatisfactory and he only completed the purchase of a single mount, which he called BP ('Blotting Paper'). In another letter written only four days after he arrived in Sudan he asked his wife in Cairo if she could send him some soap – 'you would not know me if you saw me; dirt, beard and filth'. Dust and sand storms were a recurrent problem.

General Graham's first task was to seek out and destroy Osman Digna's force of about 10,000 in the area of Hasheen-Tamai. Osman Digna was a former slave-dealer who had a substantial following among the tribes in the Suakin region, and remained prominent in the Mahdiyya hierarchy. The rebel chief was able to threaten both the British position at Suakin and the Suakin-Berber railway route, and the tribes were in a dangerous and aggressive mood.

Lloyd could hear constant firing on the evening of 14 March but 'with what result was impossible to say as they always take their bodies away with them'. Ten days after his arrival Lloyd was to write to his wife in Cairo giving details of his first time in battle as a soldier:

Suakin Camp 10pm 20 March 1885.

You will before you read this little scrap, have heard all about today's performance – [communications between the expeditionary front and Cairo were surprisingly good for 1885]. I wrote to you last night to tell you that possibly today would see us under fire and of course by now you will know what happened. Of course I have never been shot at before and therefore am no judge of it but we certainly lost a good lot for a reconnaissance or whatever they may call it.

The bullets whizzed about a bit and I was horrified on going back to look for some signaller or something to see an officer on a stretcher. Poor Dalison [Scots Guards] shot through the heart! I had only been talking to him quite cheerful a few minutes before and we shall bury him tomorrow! The Brigade behaved well as the Brigade are accustomed to… . I did a great deal of signalling with variable success. Tomorrow we have a quiet day. I shall finish this tomorrow as I am dead tired. I now find that our fight was a much bigger performance than I dreamed of, sixty-two men having been killed and wounded.

Lloyd's description of a battle refers to what has become known as the Battle of Hashin (Hasheen). Graham's forces had left Suakin camp and marched to a deserted village where Arabs fleetingly revealed themselves as the reconnaissance was carried out. The force camped for the night and the next morning the troops were deployed in an open square with the Guards forming the right. On a very hot day, marching over rough ground littered with boulders and prickly mimosa-bush, the force moved and fought for nine and a half hours, both cavalry and infantry being repeatedly engaged. The enemy were driven off Dihilbat Hill, but they still fought on, banners waving and weapons flashing. Estimates of their losses vary from 250 to 1,000 killed. When Graham's force got back to their prepared *zaribas* (stockades) after the action, they counted their losses as twenty-two officers and men killed, and forty-three wounded.[15]

On the next day (22 March), General Graham sent out a strong force to build and garrison two *zaribas* as intermediate supply posts between Suakin and Tamai. The force, under Major General Sir J McNeill, included units from the 5th Lancers, the Naval Brigade, the Royal Engineers, the Berkshire Regiment, the Royal Marines and the Indian Brigade. The Guards Brigade, to which Lloyd was attached, remained with Graham at the Suakin Camp. By midday the force had only reached Tofrek, six miles from Suakin, and it was decided to build the first post there. Three *zaribas* of mimosa-thorn were begun, placed diagonally in checker-board fashion, the larger central one to house the animals and stores, the two smaller ones to hold the fighting troops and Gardner guns.

At 2.30pm a cavalryman galloped in and reported that a large force of the enemy was approaching rapidly. McNeill's troops were totally unprepared for a sudden attack. Half the Berkshire Regiment were south of the *zariba* cutting brushwood, while their arms were piled inside the *zariba*, and other units were eating their lunch. All too soon thousands of Arabs were swarming among the expeditionary force. The enemy had few firearms so their only method of fighting was to charge to close quarters with swords and spears, which they did with almost total disregard for their own lives. McNeill's force gradually regrouped and repulsed several attacks. At last, unable to cope with the concentrated fire of the Berkshires and Marines in their *zaribas*, the surviving Arabs slowly and sullenly retreated into the bush. More than 100 British and Indian soldiers had died, with a further 179 wounded, and 500 camels had been killed. Estimates of the Arab casualties vary but up to 2,000 may have been killed.

Francis Lloyd visited the battlefield on the next day and wrote that the action 'was as near a disaster as possibly could be through mismanagement'. He told his wife that 'a battlefield is not an edifying sight but I am not going to explain'.[16]

For some days after the Tofrek action military operations were confined to marching and counter-marching, convoy escorts and skirmishes with bands of belligerent Arabs. Lloyd commented in a letter dated 29 March, that 'we have a great many sick and wounded already; it will be a very expensive "little war" as regards life I fear'. On 2 April 1885, Graham marched with a strong force, which included Lloyd, from Suakin to attack Osman Digna at Tamai, reaching there on the following day only to find the place deserted and the wells almost dry. Lloyd described the action as a 'fiasco'.

On 2 May Lord Wolseley arrived at Suakin to warn Graham that his force was to be broken up because the government had decided to abandon Suakin and discontinue construction of the railway. Writing to his wife on 14 May from HMS *Queen* in Suakin harbour, Lloyd thought that it would not be very long before he would be back in England, possibly by mid-June. The British forces were moved to Egypt where Francis Lloyd was reunited with his wife. Francis and Mary remained together in Cairo for just over a month, after which Mary returned to England, but it was another ten weeks before Lloyd sailed in the SS *Poonah*, arriving back in the UK in early September 1885.

INTERLUDE

Four months after his return from the Sudan, Francis Lloyd's mother died after a short illness. Francis and Mary were living at Rutland Gate in London at the time, and both of them went down to Aston Hall for the funeral on 6 February 1886.

Life in London for a young officer in the Guards was a mixture of training and inspections at Wellington and Chelsea Barracks, with field days held either in Hyde Park or Battersea Park, as well as participating in the social life of the capital. In August, Francis and Mary travelled by train up to the Kinnoull estate at Gordonbush in Scotland, where Francis did some fishing. He stayed on this occasion for a month, but left his wife with her relatives for another six weeks. A short holiday in Paris followed in October.

Occasionally Lloyd visited Rolls Park at Chigwell, the ancestral home of the Harveys. On one visit he was joined by his wife Mary, together with Harvey Bramston and Willy Pigott, both descendants from the Harvey side of the family. The party took lunch at the mansion and later had tea at the King's Head Inn in the village High Road, which had become well known through Dickens' novel *Barnaby Rudge*.

In December 1886 Lloyd's Battalion was posted to Dublin. Francis and Mary left London travelling from Euston on the Irish Mail. On arrival at Westland Station on the south side of Dublin, they walked up to Richmond Barracks and later went house-hunting. Lloyd returned to London briefly in June 1887 to take exams for Staff College, and although he did well in most of the subjects, he failed in Military Topography and Mathematics. The Battalion returned to London in September, shortly after which Lloyd was granted three months leave to allow him and Mary to visit the USA. During their tour they visited West Point Military Academy, Saratoga Springs (where one of Lloyd's Harvey ancestors had been killed in 1777), Niagara Falls, Chicago, New York and Washington.[17]

Francis Lloyd reported back to barracks on 16 January 1888, and at a ceremony a few weeks later he received the Khedive's Star for his part in the Suakin Expedition. Captain Lloyd was now commanding No.1 Company of the 2nd Battalion of the Grenadiers. He had under him eight officers, six sergeants, two drummers, and eighty-seven men.

As usual in the summer Mary went up to Gordonbush, and Francis joined her at the end of August. He went stalking in Dunrobin Forest and killed a good stag: 'eight points, weighing 16 Stone 1 lb', but there were heavy showers and Francis 'walked home wet through'.[18] He only stayed in Scotland for a week.

When his military commitments allowed, Francis Lloyd spent much of the time between November and May each year hunting in Shropshire and other counties well known for the sport. In his diary for 1889, he records that he had hunted fifty-two times during the season with six different packs and had ridden seven horses. On one occasion in that year he had a bad fall when his horse fell in a small brook, and on getting up the horse struck Lloyd on the temple knocking him out. He was taken to Swindon Hospital with a nasty cut which bled a good deal but, as he put it, 'nothing more serious'.[19] The Grenadiers also took part in point-to-point Races with other Guards regiments.

On 1 May 1889 Lloyd was appointed Regimental Adjutant of the Grenadiers. He quickly took up his duties with a field day in Bushey Park. The routine of training, inspections and ceremonial parades continued, interspersed with hunting, holidays in Scotland and the social scene of London. However, Francis Lloyd's diary for Monday 7 July 1890 includes the curt statement 'mutiny in the 2nd Battalion'.

At Wellington Barracks that morning the 2nd Battalion were due on parade at 8.30. The officers and NCOs paraded as usual but when the fall-in sounded only five soldiers answered it. The incident was widely reported in the newspapers but with many of the facts either incorrectly stated or exaggerated. The background to the unprecedented event appears to have been that Lieutenant Colonel Maitland, the commanding officer of the Battalion, had issued instructions on the previous Saturday that a general parade in marching order was to take place at 0830 hrs on the following Monday. That day also happened to be the day on which the Battalion was due to mount guard. Previously to Maitland taking over command of the Battalion it was always the rule that the men should have no other parade on guard-mounting days than that at which they formed up to go on duty. It was also alleged that owing to the sergeant-major's being ill, the orders for the additional parade, instead of being, as usual, given out on Saturday, were not issued until Sunday afternoon. This delay caused problems for those men on pass over Sunday, as well as those who spent the Sunday afternoon with friends out of barracks. There were suggestions that on entering the barracks in the morning, Maitland had been greeted with hisses and groans and hooted at and that there were other grievances. The officers and NCOs went into the barrack rooms and persuaded the men to fall in and they came on parade at once and fell in quietly.

Whatever the circumstances, and there were a number of other issues, the Battalion was guilty of a serious breach of discipline in not falling in at once when the bugle sounded. An investigation was immediately mounted by HRH the Duke of Cambridge, the Colonel of the Regiment, and a Court of Inquiry formed, over which General Mansfield Clarke presided, supported by Colonel Stracey of the Scots Guards and Colonel Wilson of the Northamptonshire Regiment. The Lieutenant Colonel commanding the Regiment, Colonel Trotter, gave evidence and was examined twice, together with Colonel Thynne and several others. Major General Philip Smith, GOC Home District, inspected the 2nd Battalion on 12 July, and spoke to all the officers in the Adjutant's Room at Wellington Barracks. Trotter then addressed the sergeants and corporals, with Lloyd the only other person present.

Following the report of the inquiry it was decided that the longest serving private soldier from each of the six Companies in the Battalion based at Wellington Barracks (two companies were quartered at Kensington) would be tried at a District Court Martial. They were found guilty and sentenced to between eighteen months and two years imprisonment with hard labour. Maitland was succeeded as Battalion commander by Lieutenant Colonel Eaton. A decision was taken to send the Battalion overseas, and at first South Africa was suggested. However, by 18 July Bermuda was the agreed destination. A further inspection of the Battalion by HRH the Duke of Cambridge took place on 21 July and the next day Captain Francis Lloyd, the Regimental Adjutant, accompanied the Battalion on its journey from Wellington Barracks to Chatham, where they embarked on the *Tamar*. On the following day Lloyd went down to Portsmouth to see the wives and children join the ship at Spithead.

On a visit to Shrewsbury in 1891 Lloyd was sworn in as a magistrate for Shropshire. He was following the family tradition in doing so, but how frequently he was able to sit in Court is questionable.

The lease of 43 Rutland Gate in Kensington was first taken on by Francis Lloyd in December 1886, for a period of fourteen years, although with a break clause at the end of the first seven years. The annual rent was £340 with other outgoings of £122. Stables for Lloyd's horses were also rented in nearby Ennismore Gardens at a cost of £80 p.a.

The month of May each year saw rehearsals for the Queen's Birthday Parade (Trooping the Colour) on Horse Guards Parade. In 1892 Colonel Trotter was in command of the Regiment, with Hatton the Major, and

Lloyd the Adjutant at the ceremony, which according to Lloyd went well. A week later the Regimental Dinner was held at the Hotel Metropole where 124 dined. By this time Lloyd had been elected a member of the Carlton Club, and he was to become an active member in later years. At the General Election on 5 July 1892, Lloyd voted for Burdett Coutts, who was elected for the Westminster constituency.

Lloyd was promoted to Major in September 1892, but did not relinquish his duties as Adjutant until May in the following year. In August of that year he was attached to the 3rd Battalion of the Grenadiers based at Pirbright, where he was in command for a month, after which he sat on a Court Martial Board in London. A new posting followed at the beginning of 1894 when he was appointed Commandant of the School of Instruction for Officers of Militia and Volunteers at Chelsea Barracks.

As he was staying in London for the foreseeable future, Francis took the opportunity to determine (end early) his lease of 43 Rutland Gate and to seek a larger house. After viewing several properties, he and Mary decided on 22 Cadogan Square, and signed a lease on the house in March. Their recreational activities included attending lectures in the nearby Chelsea Town Hall on a variety of subjects from philosophy to literature, with lectures on Wordsworth and Tennyson in the programme. Francis also often rode a bicycle as a sporting pursuit, and as we shall see later he proposed their use for military reconnaissance. His own recreational use of the bicycle took him one day to Chislehurst via Norwood, Sydenham and Bromley. 'After having lunch with Mr Firbank I went on to Woolwich and rode home'.[20] The Lloyds also spent some time in Europe, with a visit to Bordighera and Monte Carlo in February 1895, but Francis had to be back in time for the inspection of all three Battalions by the Colonel of the Regiment, HRH the Duke of Cambridge, in Hyde Park in April. 'I marched past in command of No.5 [Company] of the 3rd Battalion'.

When Francis and Mary went on holiday to Norway in August and September they took with them their bicycles, which must have been adventurous to say the least. They came back via the Netherlands, which should have allowed them more suitable areas for riding, but how much of the journey was taken by train is not clear.

Lloyd's association with Rolls Park at Chigwell and that part of south-west Essex which leads into London led him to ride down to Chingford by bicycle. He had lunch there and then rode on to Epping and about the forest in the afternoon. He slept that night at the Forest Hotel. The next day he rode round Rolls Park, the Beehive at Chigwell Row and to Epping where he had lunch, before returning to the Forest Hotel. In the evening he went to Waltham Cross returning to sleep at the Hotel. His diary notes that he left the Hotel at 5.00am on the next morning and that he was back at 22

Cadogan Square by 6.40 am. He had obviously become an enthusiast for the sport of cycling, which he took seriously – he carried a repair kit with him![21]

This was reflected in January 1896 when he was appointed District Cycling Officer for Westminster. Although Mary joined him on some of his excursions, she was possibly more at home on visits to the theatre. Throughout their time in London the Lloyds were regular attenders at the West End theatres, where they saw plays including *The Prisoner of Zenda* at the St James's Theatre, and came to know the leading actors and actresses of the day.

A short visit was made to Paris in May 1896, but events over the following four months were to restrict any social activity. Mary Lloyd became ill in June while staying at Aston Hall, but the correct diagnosis was not made for a week when it became apparent that she had suffered from a perforated vein in the stomach. During the following month Mary was thought to be 'very, very near to death' on several occasions, but by 12 July she was pronounced out of danger. However, it was another two months before she was well enough to leave Aston and to travel to London. In the meantime Francis had become involved with organizing the annual Royal Tournament, which at that time was held at the Agricultural Hall, Islington. Lloyd was appointed Treasurer and remained closely involved with the organization for many years.

While Mary was still recovering from her illness *The Times* announced on 11 August 1896 that 'Major Francis Lloyd, Grenadier Guards, has been selected for the appointment of Commandant of the Guards Depot at Caterham'. The appointment brought with it accommodation at Caterham, and the Lloyds temporarily let 22 Cadogan Square while they lived at Caterham. Mary had recovered sufficiently to return to London by the middle of September.

Francis Lloyd's career was to receive further impetus when in March 1897 a District Order was published saying that he had been passed for Lieutenant Colonel. It was also at about this time that an article appeared in a newspaper commenting on his efforts to use cyclists for a military purpose:

> The full and well thought-out Orders just issued from the Home District Office relative to Volunteer Cyclists are a reminder of the excellent work done in that connection by Major Lloyd of the Grenadiers, Home District Cycling Officer. Major Lloyd long ago grasped the capabilities and the limitations of the military cyclists. He clearly detected that for each man or section to go careering about 'on its own' was a distinct waste of good material. The different units required welding into one whole. Portions might be

detached, parts temporarily disjointed, and individual practice and training carried out; but a general connection and supervision was called for in order to produce progressive results. In short, organisation was necessary. That quality Major Lloyd brought in play. An enthusiastic wheelman himself, and the best type of the Guards Officer, he has been eagerly supported by the cyclist-volunteers in the Home District. His soldier-like straightforward comments on the work done, combined with a suave charm of address, make him just the man for getting all he wants out of those who are only occasionally under his direct control. His conception and execution of the Brigade reconnaissance on the Windsor road last year showed him to possess the real gifts of the highest soldiership.[22]

The article probably says more about Lloyd's character than the extent of the use of cyclists in the army.

The Diamond Jubilee of Queen Victoria was celebrated in June 1897, but an inspection of the Guards Depot at Caterham in July by Major-General Lord Methuen, left a somewhat sour taste. It was considered that the turn-out of the Guards was not up to their usual standards, but how much of the blame Lloyd took for this is not clear. He certainly expressed his own displeasure to his junior officers.

At the end of July Francis Lloyd was appointed second in command of the 1st Battalion of the Grenadiers, although the post did not carry any promotion in rank. One newspaper reported that:

Major Lloyd has been gazetted second in command of the 1st Grenadiers. 'Franky', as he is called by his friends is forty-four but looks at least 10 years younger. He is probably best known outside the select Guards' circle for the interest he takes in military cycling, holding the peculiar post of Home District Cycling Officer. It was at the initiative and by the organisation of Major Lloyd that the scattered fragments of Volunteer cycling sections in the metropolitan corps were welded into one compact body.

Last year he conducted a reconnaissance in force from London to Windsor, when the potentialities for practical warfare were demonstrated to the most sceptical.

In August, Lloyd joined the 1st Battalion at Pirbright under the command of Hatton. There must have already been some indication that the Battalion was to be posted to Gibraltar, as Francis noted in his diary that he needed to buy some clothes for Gibraltar. However, there was still time for some leave and Francis and Mary went down to Stratford-upon-Avon for a few days where they visited Shakespeare's house, the church and memorial, and Anne Hathaway's cottage. The holiday also included visits to Oxford and Worcester, but they were back in Cadogan Square by 24 August.

GIBRALTAR

The decision that the Battalion was to go to Gibraltar was confirmed and on 28 September they left Pirbright for Southampton and embarked on the P&O Transport *Simla*. There were 1,050 men of all ranks, including some women and children, and the troopship was very full. A heavy swell made almost everyone seasick, but Lloyd was unaffected. The Battalion arrived at Gibraltar on 3 October and spent a long and tiring day sorting out their equipment at Buena Vista Barracks. Lloyd lunched at the Bristol Hotel where he set up his temporary quarters. Mary had by now left London to join him.

A week later the Governor of Gibraltar, Sir Robert Biddulph, inspected the Battalion. Francis and Mary settled down to what appears to have been an enjoyable posting. They were not confined to the 'Rock', and often visited Algeciras. The Grenadiers formed part of the garrison at Gibraltar with the Northumberland Fusiliers and the South Wales Borderers. One of the highlights of the posting was when the Channel or Mediterranean Fleet 'came in', and the senior officers went on board the flagship. Lloyd took some Spanish lessons and he and Mary often rode into Spain on horseback. At the beginning of December the Grenadiers held a race day in beautiful weather. The *Gibraltar Chronicle* reported that the attendance was 'a very large one, and large fields were the order of the day'. Lloyd rode, unsuccessfully, in two races.

A new C-in-C arrived in the middle of December, when Major General Sir Frederick Carrington took command of the Brigade. The Lloyds spent Christmas in Tangier with a party of Grenadier officers and their wives. On their return to Gibraltar they heard that the Northumberland Fusiliers were to go to Egypt to join Kitchener's forces in the re-conquest of the Sudan. Lloyd sent telegrams to the Prince of Wales and Duke of Connaught among others, 'begging' them to have the 1st Battalion Grenadiers also sent to Egypt.

Although a reply was received from the Regimental Adjutant saying that the Battalion was not going to Egypt, they were still ordered to be ready for active service. Francis Lloyd went on leave in February, when he and Mary visited Malaga, Seville and Granada. They were back in Gibraltar in April and a month later they moved into 'The Grange', a house which they had had their eyes on for some time. Henry Goulburn arrived in June with the news that the Battalion was to go to Egypt but this appears to have been only one rumour among others, including the suggestion that

21

Lloyd was to take command of the 3rd Battalion. In between this uncertainty Francis and Mary found time to attend a bull-fight in Algeciras and to visit Cadiz. They were in Cordoba on 12 June when Francis received a telegram from the Regimental Adjutant advising him to immediately return to Gibraltar as the Battalion had received orders to go to Egypt, but that Lloyd was to take command of the 2nd Battalion. On his return Lloyd found that nothing had yet been settled and the confusion continued for another month, although on 5 July, Lieutenant Colonel Crabbe was gazetted to command the 3rd Battalion. However, orders arrived in the middle of July for the 1st Battalion to sail immediately to join the forces in the Sudan. On 19 July 1898, the Battalion embarked on the British steamer *Jelunga* with 857 men of all ranks, with Colonel Villiers Hatton in command, Major Francis Lloyd second in command, and Lieutenant Gascoigne as Adjutant.

OMDURMAN AND KHARTOUM

In 1895 the British government authorized Kitchener to launch a campaign to re-conquer the Sudan. The campaign started in March 1896 and by September Kitchener had captured Dongola. The British then constructed a railway line from Wadi Halfa to Abu Hamed and an extension parallel to the Nile to transport troops and supplies to Berber. Anglo-Egyptian units fought a sharp action at Abu Hamed, but there was little other significant resistance until Kitchener reached Atbara, where the Anglo-Egyptian army destroyed a large Dervish force.

Kitchener decided not to advance immediately to Khartoum but to wait while the railway was extended to Fort Atbara, and more British, Sudanese and Egyptian forces could be brought up to the Fort, including the 1st Battalion of the Grenadiers from Gibraltar.

During the voyage from Gibraltar, Lloyd wrote several letters to his wife, who stayed at 'The Grange' in Gibraltar.[24] He was able to post the first letter when the ship 'coaled' at Malta. He reported that 'this ship is most comfortable and as far as I can see they do us a great deal better than a P & O. My cabin is small but still I have it all to myself which is everything'. Two days later the ship passed the Mediterranean Fleet: '15 battle ships – a magnificent sight'.

The Battalion arrived at Alexandria on 27 July and after two days hard work unloading they proceeded by train to Cairo. Lloyd complained that it was very hot and that he lived in a 'bath of perspiration'. They were billeted in the Kasr-el-Nil Barracks and by the following Saturday Francis Lloyd had time to describe the conditions in a letter to his wife:

> At last I have a moment to sit down and write. I have a great deal to tell you. On the 27th (Wednesday) we arrived at Alexandria. That

night I dined with the General [Henderson], a charming old fellow. The right half of the battalion marched off at 2.00pm. I am now left in command of the other half. We have had very little trouble with the men so far but of course I have got a difficult job these last two days to keep them from getting into mischief. Tomorrow I propose taking them for a walk halfway towards the pyramids and then letting them go to sleep and give them lots of mineral water to drink so as to keep them employed. Tonight I dine with the General [Grenfell].

You would not know Cairo it is so altered and improved. Shepherds has been rebuilt and it really is a beautiful town. They have started electric trams which rather spoil the place.

We are soon finding out who are the useful officers and who are the duffers.

Two days later on 2 August, the remaining half of the battalion left Cairo for the front. The first part of the journey was by train to Luxor, with twenty-eight men to each 3rd class compartment in very hot and dusty conditions. At Luxor, with temperatures of 110 degrees in the shade, they changed trains and went on to Shellal. Here they embarked on the Nile Boat *Ibis* and continued up the Nile, which Lloyd thought much pleasanter than the train. The flotilla consisted of an 'indescribable' stern wheel steamer something like an American river steamer with two large barges on the starboard and one on the port side. The 6 August was Francis and Mary Lloyd's wedding anniversary which 'we never spend together by any chance. Last year I was at Pirbright and you were in Scotland. This year I am on the Nile between Korosko and Halfa and you are at Gib. Seventeen years and it has gone like a day. I trust that our next one will be spent together'.

Progress was slow owing to the rapid rise of the Nile and the strong currents, however, a highlight of the river journey was when they passed the Temple of Abu Simbel, 'one of the finest in Egypt – the figure of Ramesses II about sixty-five feet high with three others standing at the entrance of the Temple which is cut out of the solid rock'. They reached Wadi Halfa on the following Monday and after a four or five hour rest there, the next stage was a forty hour rail journey across the desert. The Battalion arrived at Fort Atbara on 14 August, where Lloyd found a telegram from his wife wishing him 'many happy returns' for his birthday, which he had celebrated in the desert two days earlier.[25] The camp was situated at the great junction of the Atbara and the Nile.

At his base at Atbara, Kitchener's goal was in sight and he did not intend to squander the years of preparation. After taking Khartoum back in 1885, many of the Mahdi's relatives had occupied houses there, but on the Mahdi's death his successor, Khalifa Abdullah el-Taaishi [known simply as the Khalifa], fearing it would become a focus of opposition, had ordered the evacuation of the town, moving everyone across the river to Omdurman. Khartoum had been a ghost town ever since. By 1898 Omdurman was a walled city, much larger than the small village it had been in Gordon's time.[26]

Kitchener's advance on Omdurman would be supported by a flotilla of ten gunboats and five steamers. The railway had reached Atbara on 3 July 1898 and it soon began to ferry up reinforcements. A fourth Egyptian brigade was the first to arrive, followed by a second British brigade with four infantry battalions: the Grenadier Guards, the Lancashire Fusiliers, the Northumberland Fusiliers and the 2nd Battalion of the Rifle Brigade. They brought with them more heavy artillery and a British cavalry unit, the 21st Lancers.

On 19 August the Grenadiers embarked on the Stern Wheeler *Dahl*, and continued up the Nile to Wadi Hamed where they disembarked and unloaded their equipment. By the end of August some 26,000 troops of the Anglo-Egyptian forces were mustered at Wadi Hamed ready for the final advance and assault on Omdurman.

Lloyd was unable to write to his wife for three weeks after his arrival at Atbara, but on 5 September he wrote a long letter from Khartoum:[27]

> The nut is cracked and the whole thing over. I telegraphed as soon as I could to say that I was alright but the wire is cut and all telegrams had to go down by boat and you consequently would not get mine till about now. We have had a short but very hard time, and at one time I thought that there would be no fight. Of course you now know that there has been a big battle and that the Sudan fighting is over probably for ever. I landed at Wadi Hamed [Fifty-eight miles north of Omdurman] with the half-Battalion on 23rd August (Friday).

The final advance began on 24 August but it took three days for all the troops to leave Wadi Hamed. The going was bad from the start, with intense heat, 'loose stones and sharp flints which slashed through the soles of boots, constant dry water courses, tussocks of rough grass, stunted mimosa and other thorny bushes'.[28] Progress was slow but by 1 September Lloyd's Battalion was within a few miles of Kerreri, where a battle had been expected, but in the event it was found unoccupied. After a ten minute halt the Grenadiers moved on to Shakrat and occupied a village, put up their shelters and had dinner:

> The gun boats had been up to Omdurman and fired some shot. I was field officer and had posted the picquets and was coming back to

luncheon when the news came in that a large dervish force was advancing to attack. I crammed some stuff down and out we all moved and formed a line. Here we sat waiting attack in a blistering sun. I never felt anything like it.

At about 1630 hrs we sent for food and made our *zariba*. So we slept more or less expecting attack as we knew a force was about two miles from our front. We afterwards heard that they expected us to attack. Had they come on, we should have had a very heavy time. As it was we were glad of the rest for it had been our hardest day and we were tired. At 0400 hrs Reveille and we were in our place and breakfasted.

Soon after 0600 hrs, word came that they were advancing and at 0620 hrs we saw a long line of great depth with many banners and flags advancing about a mile or one and a half miles off making their *suviom* noises [tribal warrior chants]. A little nearer and they opened fire but the range was too great to do much harm. At 0640 hrs the Battery on our left opened, then the Maxims on our immediate left and then we began at 2,700 yards.

Such a hell of fire you never dreamt of and we could see great bunches of men dropping. Bullets now began to come in, not many but more than we thought at the time. An officer of the Warwicks close to us was shot dead, four of our men were wounded. Bagot was hit on the chin by a spent ricochet, Frankie Rhodes was shot through the shoulder. It was wonderful why we lost no man as the forces were drawn up and there was no reason why one part should have lost more than the other but we were fortunate. After about an hour the dervishes began to draw off leaving many dead, in fact yesterday they counted 4,000 in one place on a front 200 yards long, caused not only by us but by the combined force. The men were as steady as if they had been on the N Front [at Gibraltar].

At 0715 hrs, the enemy began to move back and at 0733 hrs we ceased fire completely. At 0820 hrs the Brigade moved forward and marched for about a mile and a half when we changed front half right and after some delay came into action on the left of a Sudanese Brigade. We kept on advancing till they were completely driven into the desert and then marched on Omdurman.

When two or three miles below, we halted on the Nile and put up shelter. Here we remained from 1300 to 1600 hrs when we fell in, and as we expected marched to assault Omdurman.

In the meantime there had been very heavy fighting by the Sudanese, some very gallant work done by the 21st Lancers and a breach made in the wall by the Howitzer Battery from Tuti Island.

The Mahdi tomb had also great holes knocked in it. Eddy Wortley who was moving up the other bank with the Friendlies [an irregular force of about 2,500 reputedly well-disposed Arabs] had also had a fright the day before. When we moved forward some black battalion with Maxims preceded us and as they reached the tomb they heard the Khalifa call to arms to which no one responded. He had been out in the morning and returned early. His flag was taken; the blacks then entered the town and with the Maxims cleared the *Baggara* [horsemen] who came out in force. As they assaulted the front of the Khalifa's house he escaped at the back and made off. It was at the moment that Hubert Howard (Lord Carlisle's son – do you remember him standing on his bicycle that night at the Grosvenor) was killed by a shell from one of our guns, he having gone into the town. He was out as a correspondent [*The Times*]. This practically ended the battle.

We moved through the outskirts of Omdurman and into bivouacs which we reached at 1900 hrs. Here we lay down for the night without water except what we carried. Slatin went on with some cavalry but the horses were dead beat and although he got within ten miles he could not catch him [the Khalifa]. Neufeld was found in his chains and was brought out and his chains knocked off after a lot of trouble. I had them in my hand, a tremendous weight.[29]

So ended what I suppose has been the biggest battle of the Sudan as regards numbers and manoeuvring and everyone is loud in praise of the *Sirdar* [Kitchener]. Numbers have been variously estimated against us as from 30,000 to 60,000. I should say 50,000 was a fair estimate. Of course whenever the dervish had a chance he mutilated the men. Every 21st Lancer down was cut to pieces and mutilated. Of course also every wounded dervish that could played the old game trying to shoot anyone who helped him or did not.

The morning after the fight we marched off passed the *Sirdar* and cheered him. We then marched on to the Nile getting there about 2100 hrs and drunk.

Yesterday (Sunday) a proportion of men and most of the officers were taken up to Khartoum where we hoisted the British and Egyptian flags over the palace where Gordon died with much ceremony. We also saw the spot where he died. I have got you some things from the spot. In the evening I went with Simon into Omdurman where we went into the Mahdi tomb which had been properly knocked about and also into the Khalifa and his son's houses, the Armoury etc. There was no furniture at all except the son's bed which was a good one. There was any quantity of rifle ammunition and guns of all sorts. If you can send any extracts from this to 72 Princes Gate (Sammy) and a little to my Father do, as I cannot write more now. The day of the battle was a tremendous hard day for all, and the men have justly earned great praise. The Warwicks go off today and troops are to be sent down as quickly as possible this place is most unhealthy. It will be some time before we can get off; I daresay ten days as very rightly they are sending down first the regiments that have been longer up.

I am afraid this is a bad letter to read as I have got nothing but thick pencil. I have been very well except at the Atbara when I was bad with sickness and diarrhoea and again on the march when I had a slight go of fever but took both in time and was able to stave them off without going on the sick list. There have been very few sick comparatively.

Since Wadi Hamed we have slept in our boots, clothes, swords and revolvers every night till last night. In fact we have had a rough dirty time what with some wet sand-storms but it has been short and it has been well worth it all to have seen the battle of the 2nd September. I shall never forget seeing them come on.

Oxborough went sick some marches back and has gone down. I don't think very ill but rheumatism. So far as I am concerned a good riddance of the worst servant and stupidest man I ever saw. Greenwood could not have done better and is fit and well.

In an Order of the Day on 2 September, General Rundle praised the action of all the forces involved in the battle:

The *Sirdar* [Kitchener] wishes to congratulate the troops, British and Egyptian on their excellent behaviour during the general action today which resulted in the total defeat of the Khalifa's forces and which has worthily revenged Gordon's death. The *Sirdar* regrets the loss that has occurred and in warmly thanking the troops for their service wishes to record his admiration for their courage, discipline and endurance.

The outcome of the battle had probably never been in doubt, largely because of superior British firepower. During the five-hour battle, about 11,000 Mahdists died, whereas Anglo-Egyptian losses amounted to forty-eight dead and fewer than 400 wounded. Correspondents had been unanimous in citing the extreme conditions that the expedition had to endure: the burning heat and baking sun, the parched throats and unslakeable thirst, the sandstorms and absence of shelter.

Four days after the long letter to his wife, Francis Lloyd wrote a shorter letter from Khartoum to his father at Aston Hall, the family home in

Shropshire. In it he hoped that his father had seen the earlier longer letter but Lloyd still repeated that 'the sight before we opened fire I shall never forget – the long line of dervishes, there must have been from 40,000-50,000 waving banners and the singing was most extraordinary'. On the same day Lloyd wrote his last letter from Khartoum to his wife:

> We ought to be in Cairo in a fortnight or three weeks. I hear rumour that I am to be dropped off at Gib., but I think not. Anyway I must go home to get clothes for another year.
>
> I have got a good many things, spears etc. for you, which will make a trophy. He [Kitchener] I believe is going to Fashoda to hoist our flag and to ascertain the rumours about the French.

Two weeks later Francis Lloyd had arrived at Alexandria from where he sent his wife a brief letter on 23 September 1898. He had received a telegram from Mary advising him that she was returning overland from Gibraltar to England. This was the first intimation that Lloyd was not going to be stationed at Gibraltar, and a day later this was confirmed in a letter from the Regimental Adjutant. He was to travel back to England on the *Delwara* and arranged for his baggage and servant to join the ship at Gibraltar. Before leaving Omdurman, Lloyd had another bad attack of diarrhoea which lasted about ten days. His sickness worsened during the rail journey across the desert and there was a moment when it was thought that he would have to be left at Halfa, but as Lloyd put it:

> I was in command and Kilkelly pulled me round. I am right now as I telegraphed to you. I was tremendously reduced and you would have sworn at my appearance but I am right now and by the time you see me shall be as fit as ever. I am afraid you will be very uncomfortable in London but I am afraid I can do nothing till I get to 22 [Cadogan Square].

On 6 October the 1st Battalion of the Grenadier Guards arrived back in England and marched through huge crowds from Waterloo Station to Wellington Barracks. Major Francis Lloyd was one of five officers to be awarded the Distinguished Service Order for their part in the battle of Omdurman/Khartoum. In the following June the Regiment was awarded Khartoum as a battle honour.

A BATTALION COMMAND

Francis and Mary returned to Cadogan Square. It was over a year since Francis had left England with the Battalion, first for Gibraltar and then Egypt and the Sudan and they had much to catch up with in London. Lloyd noted in his diary that he did a great deal of shopping in the immediate weeks following his return.[30] Visits to the theatre resumed and they saw performances of the *Runaway Girl* at the Gaiety, *The Liars* at the Criterion, and the *Belle of New York* at the Shaftesbury – all within three weeks of returning to London.

On 26 October 1898, Francis Lloyd was promoted to Lieutenant Colonel and given command of the 2nd Battalion of the Grenadiers, replacing Horace Ricardo. This good news was tempered with his father being diagnosed as having cancer. Francis arranged for him to have an operation in Wimpole Street to remove the tumour, but there was no post-operative care, his father returning to his hotel on the same day as the operation, where he died from shock that evening. Colonel Richard Lloyd's body was taken to Aston Hall where it lay in the drawing room under a 'Grenadier Union Jack'. With his father's death on 4 November, Francis inherited the estates at Aston Hall in Shropshire and at Rolls Park in Essex.

The 2nd Battalion was still based in Gibraltar and Lloyd arranged to take some leave in November to allow him and Mary to visit Paris and Madrid on their way to Gibraltar, but they were back at 'The Grange' by the end of the month and Lloyd took up his new command on 1 December. Life was much the same as his time in Gibraltar a year earlier, with field days for the Battalion, and visits by the Channel Fleet. The Governor, Sir Robert Biddulph, presented medals for the Sudan campaign and later presented Francis with his DSO. Christmas was spent on the 'Rock', and Francis and Mary dined in mess with the officers and their wives.

The New Year (1899) started uneventfully – Point-to-Point races were held, Francis and Mary took a holiday in Granada, and the Grenadiers played the Coldstreams at cricket and beat them – but soon the question everyone was asking was whether the Battalion would be going on active service to South Africa. Training included physical drill, and Francis was weighed in the gymnasium and found to be 10st 10lbs, and his height 5ft 10 1/4 in. In August the Manchester Regiment which formed part of the garrison left for South Africa. A telegram from the ROR on 21 August indicated that if the 2nd Battalion was to be sent to the Transvaal, this would include reserves, who would be called out, to form a total of 1,112 of all ranks[31]. Two days later Major Gordon Gilmour arrived to assume second in command of the Battalion. Lloyd went to see the Brigade Commander to see if he could clarify the rumour that the 3rd Battalion was coming to Gibraltar. Within a month the 3rd Battalion had arrived in Gibraltar on the *Nubia* to relieve the 2nd Battalion, which returned to England on the same ship to mobilize for South Africa In fact the 3rd Battalion very soon after left Gibraltar for South Africa.

The 2nd Battalion arrived at Southampton on 3 October, from where they went by train to Waterloo, and marched to Wellington Barracks. The remaining months of 1899 were spent preparing for South Africa. The reservists were called up and training and inspections continued. Lloyd went to see HRH the Duke of Cambridge to see if he could get a date for the Battalion's posting to South Africa. News came of the 3rd Battalion's successful and gallant action at Belmont where they lost twenty-four killed, and 113 wounded including their commander Colonel Crabbe.

The Lloyds temporarily moved out of Cadogan Square while the house was redecorated, and took a short lease on a house in Chester Terrace. In early December a visit was made to Aston Hall, which Francis was now responsible for maintaining. Later in the month Lloyd went to Windsor to receive the Queen's Sudan Medal from the Prince of Wales.

January 1900 brought official confirmation that the Battalion was to be part of the 8th Division but no date was given for the departure of the Division to South Africa. A day later Lloyd received the order to mobilize but not to draw clothing. Training continued with a field day at Wimbledon, and at the end of the month he took the Battalion to Clapham Common where they were drilled in attack. Bar Campbell, who was to be Lloyd's immediate superior in South Africa, was appointed Brigadier to 16 Brigade.

Francis took the opportunity to go down to Rolls Park. This involved taking a train from Liverpool Street to Chigwell, a journey of about eleven miles, and then by horse and carriage to the house. On this visit he was entertained by Arthur Lobb, the tenant, but Lloyd only spent a couple of hours with him before returning to London.

Another month was to pass before, on 27 February, the Regimental Adjutant arrived with the news that the Battalion was to embark for South Africa as part of the 8th Division at an early date. Lloyd drilled the Battalion, about 800 of them, on Horse Guards Parade, prior to an inspection by the HRH Duke of Cambridge at Wellington Barracks on 9 March when 1,035 men of all ranks were on parade. On the next day the Battalion, together with the 2nd Battalion Scots Guards, were inspected by the Queen in the Garden of Buckingham Palace.

The 2nd Battalion Grenadier Guards, under the command of Lieutenant Colonel Francis Lloyd, paraded at 0500 hrs on 18 March and then marched from Wellington Barracks to Nine Elms Station where they entrained for Southampton. Lloyd noted in his diary that 'a very large crowd accompanied us to the station, very orderly and well behaved. Mary and Selina [Lloyd's sister] went down with me in the troop train'. It was to be two and a half years before Lloyd returned.

3

The Boer War

In May 1899 the British government arranged a conference at Bloemfontein in a last ditch attempt to resolve the differences between the Transvaal and Britain. The meeting predictably failed, and by August Britain was preparing for war. So thorough were British preparations for the looming conflict in South Africa that several weeks before the outbreak of hostilities in October, over 10,000 British and Imperial troops were stationed in South Africa and soon after the war began another 50,000 were on their way under the command of General Sir Redvers Buller.[32]

The last three months of 1899 saw humiliating defeats for the British forces. 'Black Week' in December saw General Gatacre defeated at the Battle of Stormberg, General Lord Methuen defeated at Magersfontein and Buller, who had arrived in Capetown at the end of October, repulsed at Colenso. The British government needed to move swiftly to address the rapidly deteriorating situation, and they decided to remove Buller from his command and to replace him with Field Marshal Roberts, supported by General Kitchener.

Roberts was determined to strike quickly and boldly. He and Kitchener arrived in Capetown in mid-January 1900, and on 8 February Roberts summoned his senior officers to his camp on the Modder River in the Orange Free State. A week later the relief of Kimberley was achieved by General French, and on the same day the Boer forces under Cronje had abandoned the Magersfontein hills and headed east towards Bloemfontein, but were trapped at Paardeburg where Cronje surrendered. By the end of February Ladysmith had at last been relieved and on 13 March the British forces occupied Bloemfontein. It was now clear that the tide of war had turned.

On 18 March 1900, Francis Lloyd sailed for South Africa with the 2nd Battalion of the Grenadiers in the troopship SS *Dunera*. She carried twenty-nine officers and warrant officers, and 1,082 Grenadiers of other ranks, a total of 1,111 men. His wife Mary watched from the quay as Francis Lloyd's ship moved out slowly from Southampton, passing the Isle of Wight. It was the third time that she had seen her husband leave on active service. In a letter written to Mary two days later, Lloyd complained of bad weather (it had been so rough that the ship anchored off the Needles and did not sail finally until some time during the night) with sea sickness all round. They appeared to have recovered forty-eight hours later when he commented that: 'The food is excellent – quite the best I have seen on a trooper'.

Lloyd noted in his diary for the 20 March a list of clothing and equipment that each Guardsman had with him:

1 red serge jacket	1 clasp knife with lanyard
2 khaki jackets	1 towel
2 pairs blue trousers	1 cardigan jersey
2 [pairs] khaki [trousers]	1 field dressing, sewn in coat
1 great coat	1 haversack
1 helmet and pugaree	1 pair braces
2 pairs boots	1 clothes brush
1 pair canvas shoes	1 comb
2 flannel shirts	1 table knife, fork & spoon
2 pairs socks	1 tin of grease
1 worsted cap	1 razor
1 field service cap	1 mess tin
2 pairs puttees	1 clothes bag
1 pipeclay sponge	1 black infantry bag
1 hold all	

The ship arrived at St Vincent on 26 March, which Lloyd described as 'the most god forsaken hole that I have ever been in, a place I never wish to set foot in again'.[33] He called on the Consul, who had lived 'in this horrible hole' for twenty-seven years. However, they did find time to play the telegraph station at cricket.

One distressing part of the voyage had been the number of cases of death from typhoid on the ship. Over 500 of the troops were inoculated, which gave them some protection, but Lloyd 'could not believe that a simple thing (inoculation) could have made one so ill – fever and feeling like bad influenza'.[34] By 8 April the hot steamy tropical weather had gone and beautiful fresh breezy weather replaced it.

The troopship arrived in Capetown Harbour on 11 April to 'coal', before proceeding to Port Elizabeth, from which Lloyd inferred that the Battalion's destination was Bloemfontein. Easter Monday, 15 April, was 'a nasty wet morning … it is raining hard', and disembarkation was deferred until the next day. There were 1,000 men in eight companies under Lloyd, and the Battalion served in 16 Infantry Brigade in General Rundle's 8th Division.

The next part of the journey was by train to Edenburg, via Springfontein, during which Lloyd commented on the beautiful country. From there the

Battalion set out on a rapid march on half rations to Reddesburg and Rossendal, arriving on 20 April. They caught up with the Scots Guards at the tail of the 8th Division, and by the following Saturday the Battalion was marching towards the front, with Lloyd expecting to be in action the next day: 'My ambition has always been to command a battalion in action'. Writing from Dewetsdorp on 25 April, Lloyd was able to say: 'I am now in the proud position of having been under fire with all three Battalions of Grenadiers, as we came under shell fire at dawn this morning'. The fight continued for the next two weeks. The 30 April found Lloyd sitting on top of Thaba'Nchu Mountain:

> We have been fired at all day and at intervals heavily by shell. Only two men were wounded by bullets. This is 3,000 feet high and very cold at night. By day fairly warm, sun hot, but cold wind. We were to have had two days rest after our twenty-two miles march but were turned out the next day. The Boer seems very difficult to round up; he always appears to slip off. I look forward to a very hard campaign and a long one.[35]

A week later they were six miles east of Thaba'Nchu but little had changed:

> We have had a very rough time of it during the three weeks since we landed. It seems to me that Rundle is gradually driving the Boer from these parts and sweeping up this end of the Free State. Of outside news we know nothing. Queen Victoria may be dead for all we know! We do not know if Mafeking is relieved, all we know is whether the Boer are in front of us and whether it is Bully Beef or cold mutton for dinner – we have bread occasionally. I don't expect a big battle but I do expect a good deal of desultory fighting.[36]

The Battalion continued to move north and by 27 May had reached Senekal, where Lloyd was put in charge of the township while the army was in occupation. Two days later, a few miles beyond Senekal, General Rundle ordered the Battalion to advance and capture a Boer gun which was holding up the advance from a flank. Lloyd had developed a method of deploying his Battalion when in extended order by half companies:

> I had always determined never to form for attack again with a single Company in firing line supported by other single Companies, as the extension is too great for one Captain to look after, and I had my half battalion formed up in column of section, so that each Captain should command in depth rather than in breadth. Gilmour knew this, but not having bivouacked in column of section as I had done, he had no time to do it.[37]

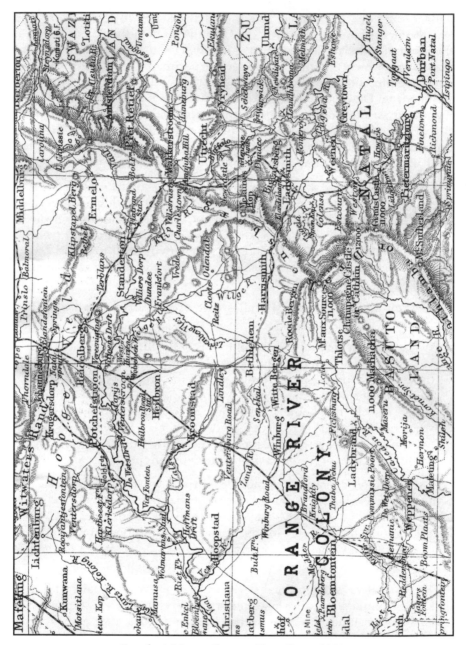

South Africa – Orange Free State 1902

The Battalion advanced initially through mealie fields to a low flat ridge in column of Companies on a frontage of about 1,000 yards. When thus committed to the open it was ordered to turn half right to gain the shelter of what was thought to be a lightly occupied *kopje* (small mountain). Under cover of this hill it was intended to assault the gun position. In order to effect this change of front Lloyd himself decided to ride forward to the right half company of No.6 in the second line and order them to alter their line of advance, hoping the following six companies would conform while he rode forward to the firing line to change their line of march. The *veldt* (open plain) had already caught fire from shelling by artillery as he rode forward:

> When I was about midway I came under such a hail of bullets that I jumped off my horse and let him go. As I did so I was hit in the thumb, rifle and wallet. I then ran to No.5 and led them. I prolonged the line to the right with half a Company of No.6 under Seymour. It may not have been more than a section.[38]

Down on the ground in the long grass visibility was nil, the noise terrific, and a fire had started. The Companies that had received the order to change direction now attempted to carry the *kopje* by short rushes of half-companies, alternately led by Lieutenant Seymour and 2nd Lieutenant Murray. The advance continued for about 300 yards when mounting casualties in the officers, including Murray, caused loss of control and Lloyd himself was hit again.

The smoke and flame from the increasing fire in the *veldt* added to the confusion. The leading company appeared to be almost wiped out and the momentum thus lost was never regained. Lloyd told everyone their best chance was to lie still:

> There were a few ant heaps but they were rotten and useless. I was behind one on my back with Drummer Haines and Fruin of No.6. Drummer Haines had got his arm over me drawing me to him for protection I suppose, when bang came a bullet that hit me bang in the stomach, but it was covered by his arm, which it broke, and only bruised me fearfully. He absolutely saved my life. I tied him up with a handkerchief and he put some stuff on my wounds and there we lay.
> Soon after this an ammunition carrier belonging to No.8 came sloping up as if nothing were happening, in fact had it been in Hyde Park I should have taken his name for moving in slow time! He was bringing up ammunition he said, and did not seem to care a straw. I made him lie down pretty quickly, but he was twice hit immediately. His name was [Private Bevan]. I have sent it in [for a bravery award].[39]

With the wind on that hot day constantly changing direction the flames in the grass ran this way and that, and then began to advance towards where most of the wounded from the front line were lying. After three hours in this growing inferno of bullets and flame it was clear that further advance was impossible, and that the smoke might be used to cover a withdrawal. Lloyd had intended remaining until dark, but the fire coming towards them eliminated that possibility. About 3pm the order was passed to withdraw. Not all got the order but Lieutenant Quilter and a few men from No.1 Company went forward through the fire to drag back some of the wounded. Lloyd himself tried to crawl back:

> I did not think I could move, but they pulled me to my feet and I stumbled thro' the flames, mercifully getting nothing more than a singeing.
>
> I managed to struggle for 300 yards or so, when Colour Sergeant Morgan came up and helped me. He was one of the few unhit. Bullets were falling thick, but I reached a wire fence where I lay down behind a stone post for a minute or two. Colour Sergeant Morgan and a man then came and insisted on pulling me along, and others did the same, ie, those who could walk helped those who could not. Further on, I was put on a Scots Guards stretcher. I was very silly by now, and was carried past Rundle, who gave me some whisky and told me we had done all that was possible. At the collecting station we were all quickly dressed and then I was taken to the dressing station, where I asked if I was mortally hit; they said they thought not. As soon as they could we were put into ambulances and then began the long weary jolt to camp.[40]

The total losses in the battle were 148, of which forty-one were killed or burnt to death, ninety-nine were wounded and eight missing (taken prisoner). The Battle of Biddulphsberg, as it was known, was by far the worst experience of the 2nd Battalion in the war.[41]

After the war Christian de Wet, the Boer Commander in the Orange Free State, included a note on the battle in his memoirs of the three years he spent as a commando:

> General de Villiers followed the English to Senekal and Lindley, and at Biddulphsberg, near the first named village, he again engaged them successfully, killing and wounding many of them. But a grave misfortune overtook us here, for the General received a dangerous wound on the head.
>
> There was still another most deplorable occurrence. In some way or other the grass caught fire; as it was very dry, and a high wind was blowing, the flames ran along the ground to where many of the

English wounded were lying. There was no time to rescue them; and thus in this terrible manner many a poor fellow lost his life.

General de Villiers' wound was so serious, that the only course open was to ask the commanding officer of the Senekal garrison to let him have the benefit of the English doctors' skill. The request was willingly granted, and De Villiers was placed under the care of the English ambulance. Sad to say, he died of his wound.[42]

Lloyd was taken to hospital in Senekal, from where he wrote several letters to his wife at Aston Hall, in which he played down his injury and forecast that he 'hoped to be up and fit in a week or nearly so – you never saw such a mass of bruises as I am, all the colours of the rainbow'.

He was obviously in much pain and could only lie on his back. This was in part due to the fact that although it was clear where the bullet had hit Lloyd, there was no evidence of its exit, and it was almost two weeks before the Doctors located the part of Lloyd's anatomy where it resided. They found it: 'in the left cheek of my bottom, which bullet they all say now must have passed down my penis through that part of my body and lodged there. I am told that it was unique and I should think it was. I was very considerably cut about'.[43] Lloyd was operated on under chloroform on 18 June, twenty days after he had been wounded, and the bullet was successfully removed. He kept the bullet with the intention of giving it to his wife.

Francis Lloyd's only consolation was that: 'I have taken a battalion of Grenadiers into action and been wounded at their Head. What more can be asked for?' Lloyd was full of praise for the Grenadiers: 'the 2nd Battalion have behaved magnificently', and was equally fulsome about his Divisional commander, General Rundle: 'I only hope that Rundle gets full credit for his actions. He has been kindness itself since I was hit, and I never wish to serve under a better General'.[44]

General Clements decided to evacuate Senekal and to remove to Winburg. After one false start when they had to return to Senekal, Lloyd arrived at Winburg on 25 June. It was clear that he could not return to his Battalion at the front and arrangements were made for him to take the next hospital train south. There was some delay, and on 4 July he took an ordinary train to Bloemfontein. By 8 July he had arrived at the Mount Nelson Hotel in Capetown. Francis Lloyd was to spend six weeks in Capetown recovering from his wounds, and with little to do he spent much of his time writing letters to his wife Mary, in which more details of the Battle of Biddulphsberg and his injuries were explained.

Lloyd spent the first week of his convalescence at the Mount Nelson Hotel, which he likened to 'living in luxury'. He saw a physician who pronounced him 'quite sound' and said that he would soon be fit to go back to the front. In a letter to his wife, Francis told her that he would not go back until 'I feel perfectly well, as a sick Commanding Officer is worse than useless'. The letter also contained references to Drummer Haines: 'He saved my life trying to take care of me and ease the pain but there was no especial act of gallantry. I am glad that you wrote to him. I owe him much but a commission is out of the question'.

On his way down to Capetown from Winburg, Lloyd had picked up a chill and was 'full of quinine'. His wife asked if his face was burnt in the *veldt* fire, to which Francis replied: 'My eyebrows, moustache and hair on my body (my breeches were open) were all singed, but marvellous to relate, got off with nothing worse'. This understatement probably reflected his wish to get back to his Battalion, but in reality he knew that he was in no fit state to do so. 'I am getting on as well as possible', he wrote on 15 July, adding 'but I am still stiff in my back'. It transpired that the bullet had broken his pelvis in two places, in addition to the damage caused by the route it had taken.

Throughout the time that Lloyd was on active service in South Africa, Mary regularly sent various small items to him, and by the time of his arrival in Capetown he had most of what he needed, except for the regular request for 'chocolate and brandy which I shall be grateful for if we remain up Country'.

At the beginning of his second week in Capetown, he was invited to stay at the house of General Sir Frederick Forestier-Walker. Mary Lloyd sent him a copy of the report of the Battle of Biddulphsberg that appeared in the *Daily Telegraph*, and he thought it mostly to be true. Other letters from Mary recounted events in England, and in particular at the family home at Aston Hall in Shropshire that Francis Lloyd had inherited just over a year before he went to South Africa. He always encouraged his wife to stay at the large mansion and it appears that considerable improvements were made to the house and gardens under the supervision of Mary, with the knowledge of Francis in South Africa.

The Lloyds still rented the house in London at 22 Cadogan Square, and on the occasions when Mary was in London for any events during the 'season', she stayed there. In July she told Francis that she had attended a garden party at Buckingham Palace. She also continued to visit her relations and friends in Scotland, often staying at Blair Castle.

The year 1900 was yet another when Francis and Mary spent their wedding anniversary apart: 'Monday is our wedding day, we never or rarely spend it together', Francis wrote on 4 August. A week later Lloyd was able to report that the Doctor had passed him fit and he started to make plans to return to the front to join his Battalion. He left Capetown on 21 August and travelled by rail to Port Elizabeth, from where he went on to East London. His train was delayed and he missed the sailing of the *Moor* to Durban, with the result that he stayed at the Beach Hotel in East London for over a week. Lloyd eventually arrived at Harrismith on 8 September in search of his Battalion, but they were out in the *veldt* on 'trek' trying to clear the Orange Free State of the Boer guerrilla forces. He moved to Ladysmith on 18 September but returned to Harrismith ten days later still not having located the Grenadiers.

He received orders to move to Standerton, over the border in the Transvaal, and was there by 8 October. The following day Lloyd joined a convoy which was going to Vrede, and he found his Battalion about fourteen miles east of Reitz. 'I had a tremendous reception when I rode into camp and from every company on outpost duty as I went round. I believe the men were really glad to see me'. It was not long before Lloyd was in action again:

> Next day we went out and had what might have been a very nasty affair. We came under considerable fire at one time and I lost five men wounded. I fancy that it is the biggest job they have had since I was hit. It was necessary and good work well done and I think a certain amount of fear was put into the sniping Boer. We are now devastating the country. It is the only way to stop it.[45]

Lloyd's comment about devastating the country referred to the policy of farm burning, begun by Roberts in the Orange Free State and extended to the Transvaal by Kitchener. The object was to enable the British forces to track down the commando leaders, and to punish those who aided them, but it aroused bitter resentment among the Afrikaners and mixed feeling among the British troops who actually set fire to the homesteads.[46]

On 27 October the Grenadiers found themselves in another skirmish near Vogelsfontein, which Lloyd described in a letter to his wife:

> We had a very ticklish day yesterday. I never had any doubt as to the result. I feared at one time we should have very heavy loss. The Boer must have been in very considerable force and held what should have been an impregnable position but mercifully for us they evacuated or we must have lost heavily. It was a picturesque fight too, covering a very considerable area and was unexpected. We are going to Harrismith being short of ammunition.[47]

The plan was to go to Harrismith to replenish stores and for ten days rest and recuperation, and then to go out on another of 'these jaunts' clearing the country. Lloyd noted that 'the rainy season has started and I am sitting in a tent with a thunderstorm going on and torrents of rain. Every night there is a thunderstorm with the most vivid lightning you ever saw'.

Two weeks later the Battalion was at Reitz with a supply convoy, but Lloyd had returned to Harrismith by 16 November, 'safe with my convoy and harem of 50 Dutch ladies'. While at Harrismith, Lloyd went before a medical board so that he might be recommended for compensation for his wounds. Four months later he was informed that he had been awarded £145 16s 3d, the equivalent of three months pay, which he thought appropriate, and was 'very well satisfied'.

Kitchener visited Harrismith briefly on 17 November to confer with Rundle, the Divisional Commander, and for a short while Lloyd acted as Brigade Commander in place of Bar [Campbell], who was ill. After another trek lasting a fortnight, Lloyd went to Durban for a few days rest. He claimed that he was perfectly fit but tired more quickly than he used to. He returned to Harrismith on 22 December to find that the Battalion was out in the *veldt* on a trek, but he was able to join them at Bloomfield in time to celebrate Christmas. Lloyd had managed to order plum pudding for the Christmas dinner and the men seemed very happy. The only complaint was that at this time of the year a wind, almost half a gale, blew incessantly on the high *veldt*, 'which is disagreeable'.

The Grenadiers continued moving slowly in a circle of about twelve miles radius from Harrismith, clearing all up in the country. On 24 January 1901, they heard that Queen Victoria had died. Lloyd speculated as to the title of the new King: 'Is he to be Edward VII, or Albert Edward I, or Albert I?'

By mid-February Lloyd's Battalion had moved to Standerton in the Transvaal where the trekking routine was the same. A month later Francis Lloyd noted that it was now a year since he had sailed from Southampton in command of a Battalion of the Grenadiers. Heavy rain and the consequent high level of the rivers, making it impossible to cross them, delayed the Battalion's return to Standerton from one of their treks. They had been informed that they were to return to Harrismith by train, but three days after arriving at Standerton on 25 March, Lloyd developed a fever which at first was thought might be enteric (typhoid) and he was admitted to hospital. The fever was subsequently diagnosed as 'stink' fever, but Lloyd was to remain in hospital at Standerton for over a month, during which time his Battalion had returned to Harrismith.

At the end of November 1900, Kitchener had succeeded Roberts as C-in-C South Africa. Roberts returned to England in December to succeed Wolseley as C-in-C of the British Army. Brodrick succeeded the Marquis of Lansdowne as Secretary of State for War in 1901, and he put forward proposals for the reorganization of the army. During his stay in hospital in April 1901, Lloyd wrote a letter to his wife which was one of the few in which he commented on the politics of the day and the leadership of the

British Army. Wolseley had recently made a speech on his retirement which Lloyd considered:

> ... is that of a patriotic soldier and gentleman. Lansdowne's was that of an incompetent and angry man who descended to personalities. I always did believe in Wolseley as the best man we have ever had. It is a question as to whether the army is to be commanded by a soldier or a civilian. Brodrick's scheme for army reform seems a good one. I have no faith in this government. There are far too many relations of Lord Salisbury and too many Peers. I do not much trust Arthur Balfour and the Duke of Devonshire and Lord Salisbury are getting very old.[48]

Francis Lloyd received a telegram from his wife on 16 April the contents of which were not very clear, but from which he inferred that Mary had been ill. It appeared to be a recurrence of her serious illness in 1896, and Lloyd was obviously concerned, but it was difficult for him to establish the details, being thousands of miles away.

One piece of good news came on 24 April when he heard that he had been appointed a Companion of the Order of the Bath and Mentioned in Despatches. 'Needless to say I am as proud as Punch', he wrote to Mary, adding: 'After all, wounded in action, CB and DSO, no one can say I have absolutely failed so far'. Lloyd had sufficiently recovered from the fever by the end of April to allow him to travel to Durban, arriving at the Royal Hotel on 5 May 1901. He spent the next three weeks enjoying the 'lovely climate', which with 'good food and comfort have done more for me than all the Doctors could do'. However, on 30 May, Lloyd developed an attack of dengue fever. He commented in a letter to Mary that: 'It is not in the least dangerous but makes you feel most horribly ill. It does not I believe last long but is very reducing'. He had intended to go back to Harrismith in the following week, but this had to be put back by a fortnight.

In the end it was 19 June before he left Durban, travelling first to Ladysmith, of which he always spoke disparagingly, and then on to Harrismith. His Battalion was spread out on outpost duty around the town and he did not join them immediately. Lloyd pressed his superiors locally and in London for more men to join the 2nd Battalion of the Grenadiers, which had been reduced to 650 from the original 1,000 he could put in the field.

Lloyd lived in very considerable comfort in Harrismith, 'quite sufficient' as he put it. He was appointed President of a Military Court to try a Dutch lady for sending supplies to the enemy. The lady was Mrs Dina Wessals of Harrismith and she was accused of sending cigarettes, cocoa etc. to her son Laurens who was on commando with the Boers. Lloyd had sat on many Court Martials but never before on a Military Court. Wessals was fined £100 or in default six months imprisonment. He was also appointed President of the Board of Compensation Claims for the Harrismith District. This was hard work which seemed to go on interminably as the Board found it difficult to obtain the necessary evidence.

The 2nd Battalion left Harrismith on 8 August without Lloyd in command and it is clear that Rundle wanted to be sure of Lloyd's fitness before allowing him back in action. A little news filtered back about the Battalion's manoeuvres; they had passed through Bethlehem without any fighting. He was very sorry not to be with them as he only had one year and two months more to command the Battalion, 'and I should have liked to have been with them, but of course I have to do what I am told'.

At the beginning of 1901 Kitchener had come to the conclusion that a massive series of barbed wire fences must be built across the *veldt*, with at intervals blockhouses which became mini fortresses, with sandbags and barbed wire surrounding the blockhouse itself. The 2nd Battalion of the Grenadiers had by the end of October reached the Brandwater Basin in the north-eastern part of the Orange Free State, and were involved in building a line of blockhouses as well as clearing the country.

Lloyd remained in Harrismith carrying out administrative work, which he found frustrating and may not have fully occupied him. In addition to the usual requests to his wife for chocolate, tea, soap, ink and writing paper, and a weekly supply of 200 cigarettes, he asked for a constant supply of books, mostly English literature, to be sent to him.

General Rundle arranged for Lloyd to be relieved from his work on the Claims Commission, and on 4 October he left Harrismith to join his Battalion. This involved a five day rail journey to Bloemfontein and then a ten day trek along a line of blockhouses to Brindisi, 'a charming little town', eighty miles from Bloemfontein. From this base he moved into Basutoland and stayed briefly at Rantuma where the chief of the village, Jonathon, a great personage in his own right, came to see him. Jonathon was a sub-chief under the paramount chief of Basutoland, which Lloyd thought was a beautiful country. Lloyd and a colleague stayed with the village chief for about an hour and were given some tea and local beer.[49] A few days later Lloyd, amid the destruction of war, rode over to Bute Buta with several of the Imperial Yeomanry to see a cricket match between Brindisi and Bute Buta. He had 'a nice ride in a pretty place' and acted as one of the umpires.

Colonel Lloyd caught up with his Battalion on 7 November and found them fit and well although very ragged. There was a general shortage of supplies, including clothing, and delays in replacing stocks. Lloyd noted in a letter that 'The Battalion has had a hard rough time in this out of the way part of the world'.[50] When little was happening, Lloyd's letters to his wife included comments on the political scene locally and at home. He had little time for politicians but thought that although Winston Churchill was 'a bumptious young devil he has his opinions and is not afraid of his party'. Over twenty years later Sir Francis and Lady Lloyd were to entertain Churchill at Rolls Park, Chigwell, when he stood for parliament in the local constituency. While Lloyd agreed that some reform of the army was necessary he considered Brodrick's proposals too much.

The building of blockhouses was now the main activity, but there was still the occasional sighting of the Boers, as on 6 December when about fifty were seen in the distance near Retiefs Nek. However, General Dartnell's mounted column was attacked by De Wet with a considerable force in the middle of the month, and Lloyd had to gather every man that he could muster and race out from Bethlehem to cover the withdrawal of the Yeomanry. The decision was taken to pursue De Wet with a force of 700 men made up mainly from the Imperial Yeomanry, but not including Lloyd's Battalion. A battle took place at Tweefontein, twenty-five miles from Bethlehem, on Christmas Day, the result of which was a disaster for the Yeomanry. They lost fifty-seven killed, eighty-eight wounded and 200 taken prisoner.[51] There was some subsequent criticism of the Yeomanry when it was alleged that their sentries has been asleep in full view of the Boers.

With the lines of blockhouses nearing completion, the plan was for them to be garrisoned by the forces. This left relatively few men of Lloyd's Battalion at Bethlehem, which had become his headquarters. Lloyd had spent Christmas Day sitting on a *kopje* above a deserted town, 'but one might be in worse', he thought, oblivious of events at Tweefontein. Divisional Commander General Rundle returned to England at the end of February 1902 and was succeeded by Major General E S Brook. Major General Campbell, who had commanded 16 Brigade under Rundle throughout the war, and who was Lloyd's immediate superior, also returned to England in March 1902. In the last year of the campaign Lloyd had become increasingly disillusioned with Campbell's performance, and many of his letters to his wife were very critical of him. He was not alone in his views, for as early as May 1900 Lieutenant M Gurdon-Rebow from the 3rd Battalion Grenadiers had commented in a letter to Mary Lloyd that 'General Bar Campbell is worse than useless'. However, in fairness to Campbell, when Francis Lloyd was severely wounded at Biddulphsberg, he had written to Mary Lloyd praising her husband's action:

> I cannot tell you how well and gallantly Lloyd led his Battalion into action, the wonderful coolness, steadiness of all ranks and the discipline maintained was past praise.[52]

A rare excitement occurred on the evening of 25 February when Lloyd's column was at Stenekamp. Just after they had finished dinner at about 8.30pm, the Intelligence Officer came in to say that there was a large force of Boers advancing on the camp. Very soon tents were taken down and the ground cleared for action, but it appeared that when the Boers saw that the Grenadiers were ready to fight, they disappeared into the night. The column continued to seek out the Boers in the now barren *veldt* and a few weeks later they came across a deserted farm where there was a grove of peach trees simply laden with ripe fruit. Lloyd wrote that this was 'a good thing for the men but conducive to stomach-ache as they eat them in all stages of ripeness'.

Lloyd rode into Bethlehem, a distance of twenty-eight miles, on 6 March to say goodbye to Campbell, who was to be succeeded by Colonel Slaney.

His column was back in Brindisi before the end of the month and remained there for a couple of weeks. He used some of the time to catch up on his reading and to respond to a letter from Mary. His wife had been to see a play in London on an evening when there had been a terrible fog in London. However, it appears that some streets were now lit by electric light, on which Lloyd commented: 'You don't mean to say that London has at last tumbled to the fact that electric light is a good thing!'

The Boers were making desperate attempts to cross the blockhouse lines and a strong force captured three blockhouses, with three men killed and five or six wounded, from the Leinsters. Lloyd's column had been reinforced with sixty mounted infantry and a further 200 Yeomanry.

By the middle of April 1902, Francis Lloyd was in Bethlehem and everybody was very excited about the prospects for peace. On 23 April, De Wet crossed the blockhouse line at Tweefontein with a pass to visit Longburg. Lloyd recorded subsequent events in his diary:

> April 25th (Bethlehem) – At nine o'clock Percy came to tell me that a flag of truce was reported at No.25 blockhouse having come from the direction of Longburg [Langberg]. In about half an hour it arrived and proved to be Christian De Wet, his secretary Potgeiter, and about five others mounted. General Elliot and his staff went out to meet him. I went also. He was taken to Colonel Slaney's hut where he and his Secretary had breakfast. The remainder went to the Grenadier's Mess. They had left Lonburg at daybreak and all did themselves well at breakfast.
>
> I had a good deal of conversation with De Wet, who seemed a good fellow, and he certainly looked a personality and a leader of men. A man of 5 foot 10, not more, with an enormous chest, a strong face and most determined chin. His hair, of which he had plenty, was black and he wore a beard. He was dressed in a blue serge coat, cord

breeches, field boots and a felt hat. He told me he was forty-eight. He spoke very little English and said that he had only been to school for three months in his whole life when a boy and that he had learnt it from a Dutch woman. Some of the others seemed good fellows, and some stolid sort of stupid Boers. We gave them some British warm coats and a few things they wanted. At about eleven o'clock they inspanned and went on to Kaffir Kop, going down to Omdraai line. General Eliot and Colonel Williams, his Chief Staff Officer, dined.

At the beginning of April the British government and the Boers had resumed peace negotiations and it was agreed that the elected delegates of the Boer states and the governments would meet at Vereeniging on 15 May. An order was issued on 13 May that Boers were not to be fired on unless they committed acts of aggression. The conference lasted for two weeks and Lloyd thought that 'the Transvaal want to finish [the war] but the Free State wants to go on'. On 1st June a telegram arrived to say 'Peace is signed' and two days later an order arrived for Lloyd to nominate one officer, three NCOs and seven men, who were immediately to return to England to represent the 2nd Battalion at the coronation of Edward VII.

The peace treaty required the Boers to lay down their arms by 17 June and Reitz was appointed as the local town for this. Lloyd subsequently heard that 3,000 Boers had surrendered at Reitz. Lloyd's column moved to Harrismith, which was to be the centre where troops would concentrate before going home. Within ten days six battalions were in the township, made up from 3rd Dragoon Guards, Grenadiers, 1st Battalion Black Watch, 2nd Battalion Black Watch, 4th Battalion Kings Royal Rifles, and the Manchester, Staffords and East Yorks Regiments. News reached South Africa of the King's illness and that the Coronation was put off. The troops could now begin to relax and think of home. The Grenadiers defeated the 2nd Battalion Black Watch at football and there was also a Polo tournament.

Events now began to move quickly. It was decided that the reservists in Lloyd's Battalion, about 600 men, would go home first, leaving about 320 Grenadiers in Harrismith. The reservists left for Pietermaritzburg on 30 June, before embarking for England at Durban in the *Sicilian* and *Mohawk*. Lloyd went down to Durban to see them off. Back in Harrismith the remaining garrison gave a ball to the town which Lloyd organized. It seemed to be well appreciated by the local residents who danced from 9.00pm to 3.30am.

It was the first week of September before the remaining part of the 2nd Battalion Grenadiers and other regiments left Harrismith for Pietermaritzburg on the first stage of their journey home. Lloyd thought

Pietermaritzburg was 'a rank bad place for men, a lot of drink flying about. I had a man killed (probably murdered), the cow-catchers of a tram killed him'. Francis Lloyd received a telegram asking if he wished to go on half or retired pay from 23 October – he replied 'Half pay'. His final letter to his wife from South Africa was written on 10 September from Durban:

> Leaving next night and embark on 12th on the *Galeka*. I cannot realise that I am actually on the road home. It is too good to be true, almost.

The journey back to England took four weeks. Lloyd noted on 29 September that it was 'The hottest night I ever remember'. The ship arrived at Las Palmas on 2 October to 'coal', where Lloyd heard that they were to go to Chelsea Barracks on their return. The *Galeka* arrived in fog off the Needles on 8 October. They landed at Southampton at about 1.30pm, where Lloyd was met by Mary, and were taken to London by a special train arriving at Nine Elms at 6.00pm from where the Battalion marched to Chelsea Barracks to be met by friends and large crowds. The men had dinner in the recreation room, and were dismissed and allowed to go out of barracks. Francis and Mary went to Cadogan Square.

A week or so after his arrival in London, Lieutenant Colonel Francis Lloyd was invited to visit HRH the Duke of Cambridge, the Colonel of the Regiment, who asked him many questions about the war. A few days later Lloyd was invested with the CB by the King at Buckingham Palace. The King also inspected the Battalions of the Guards Regiments which had been in South Africa at Horse Guards' Parade:

> 2nd Battalion Grenadiers under Lieutenant Colonel Lloyd.
>
> 3rd Battalion Grenadiers under Lieutenant Colonel St. Aubyn.
>
> 1st Battalion Coldstream under Colonel Codrington.
>
> 2nd Battalion Coldstream under Colonel Henniker-Major.
>
> 1st Battalion Scots under Lieutenant Colonel Harbord.

The 2nd Battalion Scots Guards were not there as they had not yet arrived back from South Africa.

After the parade all the Commanding Officers and the Seconds in Command went to luncheon with the King at Buckingham Palace. In the evening 203 of the officers past and present of the Grenadiers attended a dinner at the Whitehall Rooms, Hotel Métropole.

Lloyd saw a consultant about his war wounds, who confirmed that there was some damage to the bottom of the urethra. Social life recommenced with a visit to Daley's theatre to see *The Country Girl*. On 25 October Lloyd was gazetted a Brevet Colonel. A few days later Francis and

Mary returned to the family home at Aston Hall in Shropshire, where they received an enthusiastic welcome. The tenants and friends on the Aston Hall estate had subscribed towards a handsome silver salver which was presented to Francis as 'a token of their esteem and in appreciation of his noble services'.

Much of Francis and Mary's time was now spent at Aston Hall. In November the Mayor and Corporation of Oswestry held a banquet in honour of all those from the town and district who served in the Boer war.[53] Francis Lloyd, who was among the 150 guests, was presented with a sword of honour on the silver hilt of which was the mark of the Grenadiers, while on the blade were inscribed the wars in which he had taken part. In his speech of welcome, the Mayor in referring to Colonel Lloyd said that he would like to quote the words of a London newspaper:

> There are few better or more devoted soldiers than Lieutenant Colonel Francis Lloyd, who has been in command of the Battalion of Grenadier Guards in South Africa. Colonel Lloyd, from the day that he adopted soldiering as a profession, has never relaxed in his energy. It would have been therefore to him a great disappointment not to have ridden at the head of the splendid battalion at the King's review of his own Guards.

Lloyd attended a Magistrates' Meeting at Oswestry. It was the first time that he ever sat on the 'bench', although he had been a magistrate for nearly twelve years.

4

Aldershot and the Welsh Marches

1ST BATTALION GRENADIER GUARDS

New Year's Eve saw Colonel Lloyd in his role as Lord of the Manor of the Aston Hall estate. To welcome in 1903, Francis and Mary entertained the tenants and their wives to dinner at Aston Hall. Several members of the Lloyd family were present in addition to the hosts, including Rossendale Lloyd and his wife Kate, and Selina and Ada, Francis' sisters. After dinner the party adjourned to a tent which had been erected in the back yard, where they held a ball and danced until 3.00am. The weather was bitterly cold, however, with eight degrees of frost.[54]

Francis Lloyd's enjoyment of hunting included the social side as well as in the field, and he was among a party of friends who attended the Hunt Ball at Shrewsbury on 15 January when it was even colder, with sixteen degrees of frost, although a slow thaw set in before long.

Francis and Mary's interest in the more serious cultural and educational activities of the social programme has already been seen in London, but Oswestry also had its series of lectures. Francis was in the chair at the first Oswestry Town Lecture, which was held in the Public Hall. The subject of the first monthly lecture was 'Marvels of the Nile', some of which were familiar to Lloyd from his time in the two Sudan campaigns. The lecture was illuminated by the 'Oxy-Hydrogen Lantern'. According to Francis it was a 'most excellent lecture' at which there was 'a very large attendance'. The subjects of other lectures provided a very eclectic programme and included: 'The South Pole and those in search of it', 'Vegetable appetites and how satisfied', and 'Fads, hobbies and eccentricities of all sorts and conditions of men, women and children'.

Before returning to London at the beginning of February, Francis Lloyd entertained the Mayor and Corporation of Oswestry at Aston Hall, when twenty-eight sat down to dinner.

Francis always showed an interest in new inventions and innovations. It was not to be very long before he purchased a motor car. He went to the motor car exhibition at the Crystal Palace, no doubt to survey the alternatives. Slightly lower down the scale, but relevant to his and Mary's interest in the theatre, Francis purchased a phonograph.

While staying at Cadogan Square in February, Lloyd was asked to visit the Adjutant General, who asked him if he would be interested in taking command of the 1st Battalion of the Grenadiers. 'I of course accepted and was marched before Lord Roberts, who confirmed the offer, but pointed out that it must first be approved by the King'. The approval came the next day, and Lloyd left London for Aldershot to take over command. He reported to General Paget, the Brigade commander, and later Mary joined him to look over the house that came with the command. The official notice of his new command appeared in the *London Gazette* and indicated that it was effective from 14 February. Lloyd's appointment was for one year and much of his time at Aldershot was spent on training and inspections, not only for the Battalion, but as part of larger manoeuvres for the Brigade and Division. On occasion Lloyd acted as Brigade Commander during these exercises.

As a keen huntsman, Lloyd attended the Household Brigade Steeplechases at Hawthorn Hill while staying at Padworth. London was within easy reach by train from Aldershot and visits often included staying overnight at 22 Cadogan Square after an evening at the new Music Hall in Chelsea. On one occasion Francis and Mary went to His Majesty's Theatre to see Herbert Beerbohm Tree in *Richard II*, and Lloyd noticed that the King was in the audience.

In October 1903 the Battalion moved to Chelsea Barracks, where a month later they were inspected by General Oliphant. Before the end of the year Lloyd had purchased his first motor car for £550.

Lloyd still needed to visit Aston Hall to ensure that the house and estate were being maintained. He discussed the installation of a new heating system for the Hall, the estimate for which was £478, a considerable sum in 1903. For many years Alfred Savill's firm had acted as his land agent. Savill came from Essex where the firm looked after Rolls Park and the other estates inherited from the Harvey family, but also had offices in London. However, Lloyd felt that with his inheritance of the estate in Shropshire, he needed someone closer to hand, and he appointed Mr Williams of Oswestry to act as his agent for the Aston Hall estate. Lloyd regularly went down to Aston to meet Williams, and as a good landlord he toured the estate with his agent looking to see what needed to be done. It was agreed that a silver fir, about eighty feet high, near the Chapel at Aston Hall needed to be felled as he thought it was not safe. During a visit to Whittington, where the Lloyd family had owned the Castle for many centuries, they went round thirty-five cottages for which Lloyd was the landlord, seeing what repairs were required.[55]

Lloyd was in London at the beginning of February 1904, for the State Opening of Parliament, where as Field Officer in Brigade Waiting, he attended the King. However, it was a pouring wet day and the troops got soaked.[56] Lloyd's term as commander of the 1st Battalion formally ended on 14 February, when he was to be placed on half pay. A week before his retirement he went to see Lord Esher and Sir George Clarke at the War Office. The discussion must have been informal as nothing came of it immediately, but it was indicated to Francis that they proposed giving him either a Brigade at Aldershot, the Chief Staff Officer of the 4th Army Corps, or the Regiment. Lloyd told Lord Esher that he would prefer a Brigade but he was ready to take anything.[57] On 16 February Lloyd was gazetted out of the Grenadiers and put on half pay.

He returned to Aston Hall to deal with more routine matters: an inventory was taken of the stock of wine in the cellar. Francis and Mary, together with his brother Rossendale and his wife Katie, walked over to Decoy Wood where they counted 1,437 trees. The house in Cadogan Square in London continued to be used during their visits to London to attend various functions. HRH the Duke of Cambridge, the Regimental Colonel of the Grenadiers, died in March, and Lloyd attended the funeral at Westminster Abbey where the King was the chief mourner. Two days before the funeral Francis Lloyd had completed thirty years service in the army, having been gazetted to the 33rd Regiment (Duke of Wellington's) on 17 March 1874.

While in London Francis and Mary visited the Wallace Collection, and Francis took the opportunity to go to the motor show at the Agricultural Hall. The motor car provided the means to travel around England more easily and quickly and visits to friends and relations became more common. Francis often kept a record of both the distance travelled by car and the time it had taken on these journeys. On a visit to Hardwick, they joined the house party attending the Grand National at Aintree.

A BRIGADE COMMAND

Shortly after returning to London, Lloyd received a letter from Lieutenant General Sir John French, Commander-in-Chief of the 1st Army Corps at Aldershot, saying that he was to be appointed to command the Guards Brigade at Aldershot. This was formalized in a letter from the War Office on 23 April confirming his 'appointment as a Brigadier General (Temporary) on the Staff, to command the 1st (Guards) Brigade, in the 1st Division of the 1st Army Corps, for a term of three years'. Francis was requested to proceed to Aldershot to take up his duties. Four days later Lloyd took command of the Brigade. Mary came down from Cadogan Square on the same day and they went house-hunting and subsequently took a lease on Farnborough

Park, a few miles north of Aldershot.

Although now a brigade commander, much of Lloyd's time was still taken up with training and inspections of the troops. Lieutenant General Sir John French called a meeting of all the General officers at Aldershot to discuss the arrangements for the visit of the King to one of the field days – nothing could be allowed to go wrong. Similar days were held in the presence of the Prince and Princess of Wales. HRH the Duke of Connaught who had succeeded HRH the Duke of Cambridge as the Colonel of the Regiment paid the first of many visits during the thirty-eight years that he held the post. Each September a major tactical exercise was held involving several Divisions and Corps. In 1904, the Guards Brigade first moved to Southampton, from where they were taken by ship to the Essex coast and disembarked at Wivenhoe near Colchester. They spent the next two weeks 'fighting' a simulated battle in manoeuvres across much of the county with Brigades from other Divisions, before returning via Clacton to Southampton and Aldershot.

Lloyd went on leave for two months from the middle of November, when he and Mary visited Paris, Naples and Rome. The use of the motor car also encouraged Francis to take holidays in Europe, and during a week in Paris in the spring of 1905, he motored 500 miles in four days.[58] Ceremonial duties sometimes brought the Brigade to London, as in June when they lined the streets for the visit of the King of Spain.

Later in the year Lloyd became involved in a proposal which caused some consternation in the higher reaches of the Army. The four Lieutenant Colonels of the Guards Regiments wrote a letter appealing to the GOC London District to do away with the Guards Brigade at Aldershot. A draft of the letter was sent round to all Commanding Officers, including Lloyd, who thought that it sounded like incitement to disaffection. Lloyd saw Sir John French and General Paget about the 'seditious' letter, and Paget subsequently discussed it with the King. However, nothing came of the proposal and when Lloyd saw French again a week later he was told that General Oliphant had been left to 'close the affair'.[59]

Francis Lloyd always showed interest in the history of both the Lloyd and Harvey families from which he was descended. The 21 October 1905 was the hundredth anniversary of the battle of Trafalgar, and Mary, Francis and his sister Maudie went to Westminster School:

…where we heard a lecture by Sir Clement Markham on Sir Eliab Harvey and Trafalgar. Sir Eliab Harvey having been an Old Westminster boy. This being the hundredth anniversary of Trafalgar, a tablet was put up to him in the school. I brought some relics such as his GCB, his miniature medals, his watch, his miniature [portrait] and two of Lady Louisa.[60]

In the evening Francis took Mary to the Lyceum Music Hall where they saw a 'fairly good ballet'.

While he was based at Aldershot, Francis and Mary met the Empress Eugénie, the widow of Napoleon III, who lived nearby at Farnborough Hill. They visited this remarkable lady at both her home and at the Benedictine Abbey that she had built as a memorial to her husband and her son, the Prince Imperial, who died in 1879 while serving as a British cavalry officer in the Zulu War. The Empress died in 1920 at the age of ninety-four, and all three lie buried in the crypt of St Michael's Abbey.

Lloyd purchased a new motor car in November 1905, which after various alterations to the bodywork cost him the considerable sum of £926. However, their next major journey was by train when they joined the Orient Express at Brussels on 17 December, and four days later arrived in Constantinople. Lloyd described the journey as excellent with a warm train, good sleeping carriages and a good restaurant car. He was less happy with Constantinople where he found 'the town in a state of slush and indescribable dirt from the melting snow'.[61]

Francis and Mary stayed at the Pera Palace Hotel in Constantinople where they paid £2 14s 0d per day for a sitting room, bedroom, dressing room and maid's room. Three weeks were spent in the city, during which they were entertained by officers in the Turkish Army and government ministers. On New Year's Eve they were among thirty people who dined at the British Embassy. Lloyd took the opportunity on many of his overseas travels to visit military establishments in friendly countries, and he visited the Master General of Ordnance in Constantinople.

In the middle of January they sailed from Constantinople to Smyrna and Piraeus, from where they drove into Athens. For the next couple of weeks they were tourists before returning to Constantinople. The Lloyds left the city on the Orient express on 12 February but did not travel straight back to England. Vienna was the next city where they were 'wined and dined' and went to balls, although Francis did find time to visit the barracks of a local Infantry Regiment. They finally arrived back at Farnborough Park on 1 March after a rough crossing of the Channel from Calais.

Three days later Lloyd was out training with the Brigade at North Camp in Aldershot, but managed to attend the final of the Household Brigade football Cup at Stamford Bridge between the 2nd Battalion Grenadiers and the 1st Battalion Scots Guards, which the Grenadiers won 2-0.

Francis Lloyd's reputation for insisting on high standards of performance in the Guards Brigade was reflected in the reports he made after inspections of the Regiments. The Irish Guards came in for some criticism during training in March 1906, when Lloyd thought their performance was very indifferent. Later he examined them in their winter work in the barracks, which he said could not have been worse, but the Coldstream Guards performance was excellent.[62] A case of 'Ragging' in the Scots Guards received much unwanted publicity and took up much of Lloyd's time, and led to Courts Martial and a Court of Enquiry by the Army Council.

Francis was, as we have seen during his active service in the Sudan and South Africa, a heavy smoker. In April 1906, 1,000 Turkish cigarettes arrived from Constantinople for which he paid seven shillings and four pence per hundred. However, he gave up smoking at the end of July 1907.

Lloyd continued to make periodic visits to Aston Hall, where he met his land agent Williams, and on one occasion in May 1906 they settled the tenancy of the White Lion public house in Whittington, for which there had been thirty-nine applicants. Rolls Park at Chigwell received a visit in the same month when Francis and Mary stayed with their tenants Vivian Hugh Smith, later Lord Bicester, and Lady Sybil, daughter of the 6th Earl of Antrim. They spent three days at Chigwell and paid a visit to the Tudor mansion at nearby Hill Hall. Lloyd noted that 'we found the place [Rolls Park] in very good order, the Smiths evidently having taken to it'.

Paris appears to have been one of the European cities that Francis and Mary enjoyed most and they were there in June for a week. On his return to Farnborough Park and North Camp at Aldershot, Lloyd went to see General Sir John French, the Divisional commander, to talk about a proposed reduction of two battalions from the Guards Regiments. Haldane, the Secretary of State for War, was also at the meeting and Lloyd had a long talk with them about the possibility of continuing the Brigade at Aldershot even if two battalions were done away with. He suggested that there should be three Battalions of Guards at the west end of London (Wellington and Chelsea Barracks), one at Windsor and four at Aldershot. It had previously been suggested that a reduction of three battalions should come from the Coldstream and Scots Guards, but nothing was decided immediately.

Two weeks later another meeting was called by Haldane which Lloyd attended together with HRH the Duke of Connaught, Lieutenant General Sir John French, Lieutenant General Sir Lawrence Oliphant (GOC London District) and the Adjutant General. It was practically decided to do away with three battalions from the Coldstream and Scots Guards. 1 Brigade at Aldershot would be made up of two Battalions from the Guards Regiments and two from Line Regiments, instead of four Battalions of Guards. This would be known as 1 Infantry Brigade, under Lloyd's command.[63] In between these meetings Francis and Mary managed to attend some days at

Royal Ascot Week, and later they were invited to Buckingham Palace to see the presentation of new colours by the King to the 3rd Battalion Grenadiers.

During their visit to Vienna Francis and Mary had met the Hungarian artist Philip de Laszlo, and in July Lloyd arranged for him to paint portraits of himself and Mary. In addition to the two portraits in oils, de Laszlo also made a sketch of Francis in chalk. A curious incident occurred in August when Francis had an accident by 'washing' his head in petrol which ignited and burnt his forehead. Luckily there was no more damage beyond singeing his eyebrows and moustache. Lloyd thought himself fortunate, but no details of how he came to douse himself in petrol are known, and he was confined to his home at Farnborough Park for a week.

With two large houses to maintain, notwithstanding the rents from the estates, Francis Lloyd's level of spending on motor cars, china, and visits to Europe appears at times to have exceeded his income. In August 1906 he found it necessary to give his bankers, Cox, a promissory note as security for a loan of £1,250 with which he paid de Laszlo for the portraits and a tiara that he had bought for Mary. The loan was to be repaid within eighteen months. However, they still found time to go on a short motoring holiday visiting Cambridge, Peterborough, Lincoln and York.

The shortage of money may have contributed to the decision to let Aston Hall, first to a Mr Parker and later to Mr and Mrs Baines. The house was probably let furnished or partly furnished, but the Lloyds were soon to want to resume their occupancy of the Hall. In the meantime when Francis wished to visit the Aston Estate he had to stay elsewhere and during a visit in September he stayed at the Wynnstay Arms in Oswestry. Not unexpectedly he was critical of the accommodation. He and Williams went to Aston Hall to see his tenants, who he described as 'not a very high class but likely to do'! Lloyd thought the place looked well but Parker, the previous tenant, had neglected the gardens for which he would have to pay. Lloyd and Williams went on to Whittington to look at work on the castle.

Later in the month Lloyd was occupied with the annual manoeuvres involving a large part of the British Army. The visit of King Haakon and Queen Maud of Norway in November involved the Brigade in ceremonial duties lining the streets of London.

Francis Lloyd was always mindful of opportunities for promotion and a new command, as his term as commander of the Guards Brigade at Aldershot was due to end in May 1907. He went to see General Sir John French in December and talked to him about 'my promotion'. French was supportive but it was not within his authority to offer anything.

Lloyd went on leave, travelling with Mary to Paris and then on to

Naples where they spent Christmas, and the New Year was celebrated in Palermo. Much of the time during this European tour was spent in Rome visiting its antiquities, and the Lloyds did not return to Farnborough Park until late February.

The term of Lloyd's appointment as commander of the Guards Brigade had originally been for three years, however, it appears that by April 1907 he had been asked to continue for another year in the command. This was probably at the time of the reorganization of the 1st Division when the number of Guards Battalions was reduced and the Brigade became known as 1 Infantry Brigade. He asked Colonel Carlyon, his landlord at Farnborough Park, if he would extend the lease by a year at the same rent. Carlyon replied that he would only extend the lease if Lloyd agreed to an increase from £400 to £500 per annum. Francis rejected this and threatened to leave the house on 24 June if Carlyon did not change his mind. He and Mary went as far as to look at Frimley Park as an alternative, but in the end he stayed at Farnborough Park.

The routine for Lloyd at North Camp at Aldershot continued in the first half of 1907 with Brigade training and visits by the King and Prince and Princess of Wales to field days. However, on 31 July Francis had retired to bed, only to wake during the night with 'a most disagreeable heart seizure'. Mary sent for Doctor Winter who prescribed a mustard leaf and an injection of strychnine. The diagnosis was a 'tired' heart, and the remedy was simply that Francis had to rest in bed. The problem continued over the next few months and several physicians were consulted, each giving a different diagnosis. While staying in Florence in September, Francis saw a physician and was told that nothing was wrong with his heart but that his nerves were completely out of order owing originally to his wound, and that had reacted on his heart. He commenced a course of electrical treatment for his nerves, but in the long term this did not solve the problem, which was later diagnosed as a more simple disorder of the stomach.

Francis had travelled to Italy with Mary and his niece Ivy Pigott, daughter of his sister Edith, and Joey Gunnis, accompanied by a valet and maid. They visited Genoa, Florence and Milan before returning via Paris, where they spent a week, arriving at Farnborough Park in November.

Lloyd resumed command of his Brigade, but his Divisional commander, Sir John French, told him that he was trying to get him one of the Territorial Divisions. Francis suggested the Welsh Border Division which included Shropshire, and French said that he would do his best. The Brigade lined the streets of London for the visit of the German Kaiser in November, for which Brigadier General Lloyd, among others, received the Emperor's 'Red Eagle Order, Second Class with Star'. Christmas was spent at Shipley Hall, Derby, as guests of the Miller Mundy family.

Lloyd was eager to pursue the possibility of commanding the Welsh Territorial Division and in the New Year he saw General MacKinnon, Director of the Territorial Army, when he was told he had the support of Haldane, the Secretary of State for War, but that there were difficulties. Francis had to think about where he was going to live after his Brigade command at Aldershot ended in May, and he spoke to Peake his solicitor in London about going to live at Aston Hall. Peake thought that the tenancy of the Baines could be terminated and Francis and Mary settled on a return to Aston.

Financial matters reared their head again as Francis wished to make some improvements to the Hall including installing electric light (run off batteries) and a new heating system. His solicitor thought that there would be difficulties but that the necessary money could be found. Meetings took place at Aston Hall with a consulting engineer from Birmingham and Williams. The cost was estimated as over £4,000, but this did not deter Francis from signing another promissory note for a loan of £900 to pay for a new Nordenfeldt motor car and repairs costing £150 to the old Durkopp. Gales in March at Aston had blown the Dutch barn down and felled ninety trees.

Francis Lloyd met Haldane at a Dinner party at the Grosvenors where 'he was most agreeable and practically promised me a Territorial Division'. 1 May was his last day in command of 1 Infantry Brigade at Aldershot, and Brigade Orders for the day included a farewell from him:

> Brigade Orders by Brigadier General Lloyd CB, DSO, Commanding 1st Infantry Brigade, Marlborough Lines, Aldershot.
>
> Friday 1 May 1908.
>
> Farewell Order.
>
> Brigadier General Lloyd thanks all ranks of the Brigade for their support during his tour of duty. The work has been hard but it has always been cheerfully, and successfully done.
>
> His four years of duty at Aldershot will ever be a memory of pleasure to him entirely owing to the efforts of those who have so generously served under him.
>
> F Gathorne-Hardy, Major.
>
> Brigade Major, 1st Infantry Brigade.

Lloyd also gave a farewell dinner at Farnborough Park. He was now on half pay again, but his immediate concern was to have the new electric light and heating system installed at Aston Hall, so that he and Mary could return to live there. It was decided to turn six stall stables into an engine room and to convert the laundry into a battery room. The Board of Agriculture sent an inspector to Aston to see whether they would give leave for the lighting and heating system to be installed, and Peake subsequently heard that they had agreed to the spending of £2,700 on the systems.

It was to be another couple of weeks before Francis finally left Farnborough Park, and during this time he took some house guests to Aldershot Races – he had seven staying in the house and another nine to dinner. On 14 May, Lloyd and his niece Ivy Pigott left Farnborough for good. Mary stayed behind for a few days to arrange for furniture and other furnishings to go into store. Progress on his promotion seemed to be being made, with a letter from Haldane saying that he had recommended him to succeed Brigadier General Hill in command of the Welsh Division of the Territorial Army from January next [1909], with the temporary or local rank of Major General.

When in London at this time, the Lloyds stayed at 35 South Eaton Place, the sub-lease on 22 Cadogan Square not yet having expired. Francis and Mary went to Buckingham Palace on 1 June to see the King present new colours to the 2nd Battalion Grenadiers under the command of Bill Cavendish, and in the evening Lloyd attended the Regimental Dinner.

Reports in the *Western Mail* and *Oswestry and Border Counties Advertizer* stated that the command of the Welsh Territorial Division had been decided:

> The question of the command of the Welsh Territorial Division has at length been determined. A Welsh Division, commanded by a Welsh General was what the Secretary of State pledged himself that the Principality should have. But it had been recognised that an exclusively Cymric Division would not be formed, the inclusion of a certain brigade of infantry and other units from over the border rendering the idea, admirable as it was, impossible of realisation.
>
> We are now able to state that for the command of the Welsh Division Brigadier General Francis Lloyd, CB, DSO, late Grenadier Guards, who a few weeks ago retired from the command of the 1st (Guards) Brigade at Aldershot, has been selected.
>
> Every Guardsman, whatever his rank, has his familiar name. That of General Lloyd is 'Frankie' – than whom there is nobody better liked or more highly esteemed, both for his personal charm and his high and many-times proved soldierly qualities.

Later reports indicated that the Headquarters of the Division would be at Shrewsbury. This was possibly all a little premature as Lloyd had received no formal letter of appointment from the War Office. The development of the territorial forces throughout the country was progressing rapidly and by 1 July there were 8,326 officers and 173,351 other ranks. Within these figures the Welsh Division had 16,384 men in total against a proposed establishment of 27,073.[65] But the Division was still under the command of General Hill, whose term had another six months to run.

With the disruption at Aston Hall caused by the installation of the lighting and heating systems, in which Francis took a close interest, he decided to rent a house in Oswestry until the Hall was ready for them to move back into, and after some searching Lloyd took a lease on Plas Wilmot (where Wilfred Owen had been born in 1893) at a rent of six guineas a week, his landlord being Mr Drew of the Wynnstay Arms. More expense was incurred when another new motor car was purchased for £500, Lloyd having to borrow the money from his bankers. At the same time new furniture and furnishings including china and glass were purchased for Aston Hall.

Lloyd returned briefly to Aldershot in September, when he was asked to command the 4th (Guards) Brigade during the annual manoeuvres of the British Army. This year they took place near Alton in Hampshire when Lloyd had 2,355 men under his command.

Plas Wilmot in Oswestry was a convenient base not only for keeping an eye on the work at Aston Hall, but also allowed Francis and Mary to visit Francis's brother Rossendale who was vicar at Selattyn, a few miles north of Oswestry, his sister Selina who also lived near Oswestry, and Eva, another sister who lived at Wrexham. Francis and Mary, who had no children of their own, appear to have been particularly close to Rossendale and his family: Katie his wife, Andrew their son and the two twin girls. Francis often brought toys from London for the children.

Living in north Shropshire also provided the opportunity to renew contact with some of their country pursuits, with Mary going to sheep dog trials in the Vale of Llangollen. The Holbechs, the family of Francis' sister Ada, visited Plas Wilmot and in August Mary went up to Gordonbush to stay with her Scottish relations. Francis Lloyd's love of motor car travel allowed him to drive, in the Nordenfeldt, up to Lake Vernwy to see for the first time the lake that had been constructed to supply Liverpool with water. Installation of the electric light was completed at Aston Hall in October and the first trial went well. Francis attended the Oswestry Petty Sessions and sat on the Bench – as chairman for most of the time.

THE WELSH TERRITORIALS

At the end of October, Francis Lloyd received the formal letter from

Lieutenant General Sir Arthur Wynne, Military Secretary, War Office, about his appointment to command the Welsh Territorial Division:

Dear Lloyd,

Will you be so good as to inform me confidentially whether it would be agreeable to you to be appointed to command the Welsh Division of the Territorial Force with the temporary rank of Major General.

The vacancy is due to occur on the 26 January 1909.

Yours sincerely,

[signed] A Wynne[66]

The War Office wrote again to Lloyd on 9 November confirming his appointment:

Sir,

I am directed to inform you that sanction has been given for your appointment as General Officer Commanding the Welsh Division of the Territorial Force with the temporary rank of Major General whilst holding that appointment to fill the vacancy which is due to occur on the 26 January, 1909, and I am to request that you will proceed to Shrewsbury and take up your duties accordingly.

You are requested to acknowledge the receipt of this letter.

I am,
Sir,
Your obedient Servant,
[signed] G F Brown
Major General.
Director of Personal (sic) Services.[67]

A somewhat discordant note occurred in early November when Francis Lloyd recorded in his diary, while staying in London, that:

I contradicted the absurd rumour which somehow had got about that we were going to be divorced. Dr Percival White gave his opinion that Mary must go to Bath and go through a course or she would be seriously ill.

No indication is given of the nature of the illness or the course of treatment Mary was to undergo. While staying at Aston Hall later in November, Francis Lloyd carried out his civic duties when he accompanied the Mayor of Oswestry to the annual Civic Service, which in 1908 was held at the Zion Church. Francis marched in uniform to the church where 'we heard a very good sermon from the Welsh Calvinistic

Methodist Minister', and then marched back to the Town Hall when the Mayor made a speech and I followed him'.

Although Francis and Mary were now back in residence at Aston Hall improvements continued to be made, including the demolishing of the verandah outside the billiard room, and putting new French windows in the small drawing room. Van loads of furniture arrived every day for about a week at the Hall, together with deliveries of new china and glass that had been purchased recently. Some of the family portraits that had been restored were returned and had to be hung.

Mary was in Bath undergoing treatment and Francis and Ivy visited her. Back at Aston in early December, Francis took Ivy to the Oswestry Ball, where she 'looked well and danced a great deal'. The rumour that Francis was to divorce persisted in London circles, and Francis saw Woolly 'about the ridiculous rumour that I was going to be divorced. I thought that the Lieutenant Colonel of the Regiment [the Grenadiers] was the best man to contradict it'.

Mary returned to Aston in time for the Christmas celebrations, where there were forty-two guests in the house. For the first time in four years Francis and Mary were able to attend the distribution of the Lloyd charity at Aston Hall on 21 December:

> On Monday, General and Mrs Lloyd distributed among the cottagers and workmen on their estate some 500 lbs of beef and a quantity of bread, each recipient in fact receiving an 8lb loaf. This was the first time for four years that General and Mrs Lloyd were able to take part in the annual distribution of their bounty, and it goes without saying that all the recipients were glad to have the opportunity of welcoming them back to Aston once more. General and Mrs Lloyd were assisted in the distribution by Mr Gunnis, Miss Pigott, and Mr C. E. Williams, the agent.

The charity was, Francis believed, instituted by his grandfather William Lloyd (1779-1843): 'It was purely a free gift and there were no obligations whatever. The dole consists of beef and bread and is given to cottagers on the Aston estate alone. It is always given on 21 December which was my grandfather's birthday'.[68]

Before Christmas, Lloyd had distributed the prizes and made a speech on the Territorial Army at the annual 'smoking concert' of the Oswestry Company of the 4th Battalion, Shropshire Light Infantry. He told the meeting that there were three essentials to the making of a good soldier. Firstly he must be able to march well, and to do this he needed a good pair of boots to reach the place required at the right time! Secondly he must be able to shoot well, and perfect marksmanship was essential. Thirdly and most important of all was intelligent discipline. It was impossible to fight 'shoulder to shoulder' without intelligence.

On Boxing Day, Francis went to see Brigadier General Hill at Shelton Oak Priory to talk about the Welsh Territorial Division, command of which Hill was to hand over to Lloyd on 26 January. Reports in the Press continued to support the new commander: 'The command of the Welsh Division of the Territorial Force was most suitable for a man who combined the discipline and precision of a Guards General with the local knowledge of a landlord on the Welsh Marches'.

In the New Year Lloyd still found time to make a short visit to Paris before taking up his new command. He obviously enjoyed the break, which included a visit to Maxims one evening from which he returned to his hotel at 3.15am! On his return to London he visited his military tailor to try on his new uniform. At the War Office he was introduced by Mackinnon to Lord Lucas, the Undersecretary of State for War, who he found 'a very nice young man and very civil'. Lloyd returned to Aston Hall and dined in Shrewsbury with Lord Kenyon, the commanding officer of the Shropshire Yeomanry, together with the officers and NCOs.

On 26 January 1909, Lloyd drove into Shrewsbury and assumed command of the Welsh Division of the Territorial Army. One of his first duties was to inspect the Oswestry and Ellesmere Company of the 4th Battalion, Shropshire Light Infantry at Powis Hall. The weather was bitterly cold and there was skating on the large lake at Aston Hall. The annual tenants' supper, followed on the next day by the one for the cottagers on the Aston Hall Estate were held at the Hall.

Within a week of taking up his command, Francis Lloyd made the first of innumerable visits over the next four years to towns and villages in Wales and the borderlands where he inspected the local Territorial Forces, and made speeches encouraging recruitment: 'making it my first duty to see everybody and inspect all units throughout Wales'. Cardiff was the first city to which he travelled, where he inspected a Brigade of Artillery and had lunch with the Lord Mayor. Newport and Swansea were visited during the same journey. Meanwhile Mary had returned to Bath for further treatment at the renowned mineral springs.

Lloyd wanted people to look upon the Territorial movement from a much higher standpoint than they did in the early days of the formation of the units. He saw the Territorials as a patriotic movement for the defence of the country against invasion. He was also determined to see that the performance of the troops under his command reached a high standard, and within a month he was supervising tactical exercises by the South Wales Territorials. The Headquarters of Western Command was at Chester, only a short drive from Aston Hall. Visits to inspect the Territorials at

Nantwich, Wilmslow and Stockport often included a visit to Western Command to see the C-in-C.

During one visit to North Wales, Francis motored to Llangollen and saw the house at Plas Newydd where the 'Ladies of Llangollen', friends of his grandmother, formerly lived. He was also able to go to the Bangor Steeplechases, which were attended by a large crowd on a beautiful day. Carnarvon and Colwyn Bay followed, with more speeches about the 'people's army'. Lloyd's old commander at Aldershot, General Sir John French, was now Inspector General of the Forces, and he made an inspection of the Welsh Division in May. The ten day tour included a weekend spent at Aston Hall.

Francis took Mary to London to see a consultant physician about her health. Dr Percival White diagnosed problems with her heart and recommended a course of 'Nauheim'. (This was a therapeutic treatment originating from the mineral content of the waters at Bad Nauheim in Germany). The treatment required a stay in London and a flat was rented for Mary at 124 Knightsbridge. Francis returned to Aston Hall and presented long service medals at a church parade in Oswestry, before continuing his travels throughout the principality inspecting Territorial units.

Lloyd had as we have seen received the support of Richard Haldane, the Secretary of State for War, in securing the command of the Welsh Territorial Division. On several occasions during visits to London Lloyd visited Haldane both at the War Office and his home in Queen Anne's Gate, where they talked about the Territorial force, which Haldane had created, and the Army in general.

By the end of July, Mary had finished her course of treatment in London and had gone up to Gordonbush to stay with her Scottish relatives. Francis attended tactical manoeuvres near Brigend, where the mountain sides of the Amman valley were swarming with long lines of Khaki-clad men. The King had presented new colours at Windsor to the 4th Battalion Royal Welsh Fusiliers and they were taken to Wrexham where they were received at a parade attended by Lloyd. The Shropshire Territorials held their summer camp under canvas near Oswestry which was convenient for Lloyd. Also locally, in September, Francis and Mary attended a swimming gala at which the mayor of Oswestry reminded everyone that five members of the Lloyd family had been mayors of the town and he hoped that Francis Lloyd would follow the tradition. Francis replied that this was not possible while he held the command of the Welsh Territorial Division.

The Lloyds continued to spend money, with Francis buying a diamond and sapphire necklace for Mary, and Mary purchasing a Grand Piano. Shooting parties on the Aston estate were an annual event during the shooting season but the estate was not known for its game, compared with some of the larger estates in Shropshire.

At the beginning of December, Francis Lloyd received a letter from Haldane advising that his name had gone to the King and that he was to be promoted a substantive Major General at once. The King visited Chester in the middle of the month when Lloyd was gazetted Major General, and the King personally bestowed on him the 3rd Class of the Victorian Order (CVO) at Eaton Hall.

Francis was able to enjoy Christmas at Aston Hall when he received many congratulations on his recent promotion and personal award from the King. Lloyd paid a visit to Paris for two weeks in January, but returned in time to vote at the General Election, in which he had two votes: one as the owner of Aston Hall, where he voted in the Oswestry Division for the successful Conservative candidate Mr Bridgeman, and at Rolls Park, Chigwell, where he voted for Col Lockwood, the successful Conservative candidate for the Epping Division. The election produced a hung parliament, with the Conservatives led by Arthur Balfour receiving the largest number of votes but with the Liberals led by Asquith returning two more MPs than the Conservatives. A second election was held in December.

On returning to Aston, Francis attended the annual licensing meeting of the Oswestry magistrates at which licences for Public Houses were renewed.

In early 1910 the War Office announced a new scheme for the establishment of local voluntary aid organizations for the sick and wounded of the Territorial forces, and Francis Lloyd attended a meeting in Shrewsbury to discuss the forming of a branch for north Shropshire. Another organization with which Francis was to be closely associated for a number of years was the Boy Scouts, and in April 1910 he was appointed Assistant Commissioner of the Scouts for his part of Shropshire, having formed a division for Oswestry. At Aston Hall, Francis received a note from his agent advising that 44,000 Larch, 2,700 Spruce Fir and 1,200 Oaks had been planted in Decoy Wood.

King Edward VII died on 6 May, and although Lloyd did not attend the funeral in London, he discussed with MacKinnon and Haldane the form of services to be held in Wales on the day of the funeral. This coincided with the annual camp of the Cheshire Infantry Brigade which that year was being held at Bow Street a few miles north-east of Aberystwyth, when for two weeks the Clarach valley was full with 3,808 men from the Brigade. At the end of the camp the whole Brigade marched into Aberystwyth where Lloyd took the salute on the seafront. Lloyd was very well satisfied with the camp, which was important as two months later the whole of the Welsh

Division of 14,000 men were holding their annual camp in the same area. Francis Lloyd made sure that he thanked the local landowners for their cooperation in allowing the troops to use their land for the manoeuvres.

The camp and tactical exercises of the Welsh Division in July and August received much publicity, which was used in the drive for recruitment. Lloyd was impressed by the standard of the Territorials but considered that the final exercise at the end of the two-week camp, which involved a major simulated battle, was 'absolute nonsense everything having been arranged by Thompson as a showpiece'.

Francis and Mary were in London in October for the marriage of their niece Ivy Pigott to Captain Hargreaves Brown of the Coldstream Guards. The marriage ceremony at the Guards Chapel was conducted by the Rev Rossendale Lloyd, Francis's brother.

Lloyd met Haldane again in November and was asked if he would like to command a Regular Division of the Army. Lloyd of course said yes, and Haldane indicated that his name was on the list for one.

Christmas 1910 saw the Lort-Phillips and the Gunnis's (Frankie, Ivy and their children Geoffrey, Rupert and Nigel) as guests at Aston Hall. Rossendale and his family joined them from nearby Selattyn.

Throughout his time as commander of the Welsh Territorial Division, Francis Lloyd sought through his speeches to dispel the public misunderstandings about the Territorial Army. The public's views varied from those who thought the Territorials unnecessary, to others who thought that it did not go far enough and that there should be some form of conscription. Lloyd argued that he was not an alarmist with regard to the threat of invasion, but that the Territorials were essential to the country's defence.

In February 1911, Lloyd heard from Haldane that he had not been selected to command the 4th Division, allegedly because he was a Guardsman, and it appeared unlikely that any other Divisional command would become available in the near future. Lloyd's disappointment was only marginally offset a couple of weeks later when he was elected a member of the Turf Club. At a St David's Day Dinner at the Trocadero, which he attended, Winston Churchill was the chief speaker.

Recruitment of Territorials in Wales continued with the opening of new Drill Halls including those at Llanelly and Welshpool, and later in the year at Cwm and Ebbw Vale. Francis, together with friends, left Aston Hall at 9.30am on 24 March and motored to Birkenhead, where they crossed the Mersey by ferry without having to get out of the car, and then proceeded to Aintree to watch the Grand National. Lloyd's friend Frank Bibby was the owner of the winning horse, Glenside, in a race where it was practically the only horse left standing.

Arrangements for the investiture of the Prince of Wales at Carnarvon Castle took up much of Lloyd's time in May and June, but when in London, Francis and Mary still enjoyed going to the theatre and they saw *The Chocolate Soldier* at the Lyric, *Peggy* at the Gaiety, and later in the year 'a most excellent play' called *Kismet*, starring Oscar Ashe and Lily Brayton.

In mid-June Francis Lloyd received a letter from Haldane, who had been made a peer two months earlier, telling him that he was to be knighted, probably in the following week on the occasion of the Coronation of King George V. The *London Gazette* listed the Coronation honours which showed Francis Lloyd as being created a Knight Commander, Military Division, Second Class, of the Order of the Bath. Francis was in London at the time of the announcement, and on his return to Aston Hall he was met at the gate to the park with the sound of crackers and guns going off and cheering workmen.

On the day of the coronation Sir Francis Lloyd went to church with the Mayor of Oswestry and inspected contingents of Territorials, Scouts and Police. In the afternoon he planted an oak tree in the Little Field at Aston Hall and distributed coronation badges to estate workers. The local school children marched to the park where there was a large attendance of parents and tenants. Tea was provided in a large marquee, and during the evening sports took place. The beautiful gardens and grounds were thrown open to the public during the evening.[69]

Francis and Mary returned to London where they attended a garden party at Buckingham Palace, and a week later, on 6 July 1911, Sir Francis was knighted by the King at St James's Palace. The investiture of the Prince of Wales took place at Carnarvon Castle on 13 July, where Sir Francis Lloyd commanded the troops who lined the route. The King took the opportunity of his visit to North Wales to present new Colours to the 4th Battalion Shropshire Light Infantry and Shropshire Yeomanry, and Lloyd was in charge of the parade at Bangor. Sir Francis accompanied the King who, with Queen Mary, went on to visit Aberystwyth to lay the foundation stone for the new National Library of Wales which had received its Royal Charter in 1907. The occasion was marked by a twenty-one gun salute from an eight warship flotilla in Cardigan Bay. On his return to Aston Hall, Sir Francis and Lady Lloyd gave a garden party for the tenants and cottagers on the estate, which he thought 'went off well'.

After all the celebrations life returned to normal with the annual camp of the Welsh Territorial Division, this year held at Lamphey near Pembroke, which was attended by 15,000 men. Before the two weeks camp had ended the threat of a national rail strike resulted in the recall from leave of all men in the Regular Forces. Nothing much happened for a few days with the threatened strike in the balance, but on 19 August a general strike on the railways began. However, it was short-lived, being settled at 2.00am on the next day.

The C-in-C, Western Command called a meeting at Chester to consider the political crisis in Europe that was supposed to be coming, and what was to be done for the future of the Territorial Army in the way of recruiting, but Sir Francis was optimistic that the proposed number of recruits could be achieved. He took the initiative in discussing with employers in the Llanelly area the terms on which employees could be released for Territorial duty. Lloyd also discussed with Lord Haldane and the Adjutant General the formation of a separate medical corps for active service.

Sir Francis had his first motoring accident in September when a bicyclist ran into his car on the Pershore road and was hurt. He discussed the matter with the police but no action was taken. An eventful year ended with the usual Christmas celebrations at Aston Hall where Frankie and Ivy Gunnis, with their three sons, and two Streatfeild's, the Lort-Phillips, the Ruggles Brises, together with Oey (a family nickname for Lloyd's brother Rossendale) and his family joined Sir Francis and Lady Lloyd.

The new year saw visits to Government House at Chester, where Lloyd saw the C-in-C Western Command, General MacKinnon, and then went on to open a new Drill Hall at Northwich. On this occasion Lloyd included a reference in his speech to the 'Club' at most Drill Halls: 'A Club was the thing that must always appeal to the soldier, and it was a thing which – if he might put it strongly – was the soldier's home. There was no better club than the Army'. In London in the middle of January, Francis Lloyd attended a debate at the United Services Institute on the Territorial Forces and he defended Lord Haldane's optimism with regard to the recruitment programme.

Francis and Mary decided to rent an apartment in London for eight weeks and took a lease on 16 Great Cumberland Place. They went to the Apollo Theatre where they saw *Glad Eyes*, which they thought 'very amusing indeed'. The weather in February was particularly cold, with seventeen degrees of frost at Aston. The Dee was frozen over below Government House at Chester and the Severn was frozen at Shrewsbury.

The threat of a coal strike over the miners' demand for a minimum wage for all underground workers was looming and Lloyd was recalled to Shrewsbury by MacKinnon to take up a strike command. The strike by the miners started on 1 March but by the end of its third week there were some signs of it weakening, with the men at Brynkinalt colliery returning to work. This was not to the liking of the miners at Rhos colliery, who decided to march to Brynkinalt to protest. With the possibility of violence occurring Lloyd decided to send fifty men from Shrewsbury, while at the same time applying for a battalion from London. Haldane instructed Lloyd to go to Brynkinalt and to report to him personally on the situation. Francis reported that troops were an absolute necessity, and the 2nd Battalion Suffolk Regiment with over 500 men arrived at Chirk. Matters seem to have calmed sufficiently by 8 April, when Lloyd was able to telegraph the War Office to say that the troops were no longer required.

The debate on the future of the Territorial Forces continued, and a conference of the C-in-Cs and Territorial Divisional Generals was called at the War Office. The object of the meeting was to ascertain if any inducements could be offered to employers to increase the number of Territorials, but the conclusion was that very little could be done. General Sir John French was now Chief of the General Staff and a meeting was arranged at Guildhall in the City of London which was attended by the Lord Mayor and Mayors from all the Boroughs in the Metropolis, together with leading employers, with the purpose of encouraging recruitment to the Territorial Force. Their total strength was still sixteen percent below the agreed establishment. Lord Haldane's term as Secretary of State for War came to an end in June 1912, after a period of seven years. Apart from creating the Territorial Force, other changes had been made to the organization of the armed forces during this time and *The Times* described his term at the War Office as 'a notable administration'.

The King and Queen visited South Wales in the summer, and Lloyd was in charge of the troops for the visit to Cardiff. He was among the guests at a dinner on the Royal Yacht, *Victoria and Albert*, but the weather throughout the visit had been appalling, with pouring rain throughout.

Many Voluntary Aid Detachments had been formed throughout the country and often they were commanded by women, as was the case for the No. 24 Shropshire Detachment which was led by Lady Lloyd. Francis suffered a recurrence of his heart condition and was told to rest. He and Mary spent a week in Llandrindod Wells, but Lloyd returned to duty in time for the Welsh Territorial Division's annual camp at Carnarvon. At Government House in Chester, he met Colonel Seely, the new Secretary of State for War.

Following the tradition of his ancestors Francis attended the Welsh National *Eisteddfod* at Wrexham, where he presided on one evening when he spoke to an audience of between 8,000 and 9,000 people. David Lloyd George also spoke at a meeting a few days later and Francis joined him on the platform to give him support. Several suffragettes tried to break up the meeting but were unsuccessful. The Hall was packed and Francis thought that there must have been 12,000 in it. At the *Eisteddfod*, Francis Lloyd was made a Bard (Ovate) with an honorary *Corsedd* degree, and given the name of his ancient ancestor, Einion Efell.

For health reasons it was decided that Francis should take a cruise, without Mary accompanying him, to South America, and he left Southampton, with a valet, on the SS *Asturias* at the end of September. Visits were made to Vigo, Lisbon and Madeira before the Equator was crossed on 9 October 1912, and after calling at Pernambuco and Bahia, the ship arrived at Rio de Janeiro. Lloyd described the city as 'The most beautiful thing I have ever seen', even though the weather was wet and foggy. Two weeks were spent at Rio, in a hotel, from where Francis went out riding to see the 'sights'. While in Rio he received a letter from the War Office offering to extend his command of the Welsh Territorial Division by a year, until 25 January 1914, and Lloyd accepted the offer, sending his reply via the HQ of the Welsh Division at Shrewsbury.

Francis Lloyd managed to keep abreast of world events while he was away, and heard by telegram that the Turks had been beaten back with heavy losses and that the Bulgarians were marching on Constantinople. The Great Powers were sending warships to Constantinople to protect Europeans, and Salonika had been captured by the Greeks with 25,000 Ottoman soldiers taken prisoner. Francis arrived back at Southampton in mid-November where he was met by Mary, and it was concluded that the voyage had been good for his health.

It was towards the end of November that Francis Lloyd had the first inkling of his next command. He went to see Sir John French, the CIGS, in London, and in a meeting shortened by French being called to see the Secretary of State for War, he was told that General Codrington, the GOC London District, was likely to continue in command for some time, but that when he did go Lloyd would probably take over the London District. Lloyd noted that French also seemed to think that war was likely, by which he probably meant in the Balkans.[70] At the end of the year the Territorial Force had 264,000 men, still 60,000 short of its proposed establishment.

In January 1913, Francis paid what had become his annual visit to Paris, and shortly after his return to London, took a lease on Lord Mostyn's house at 1 Hereford Gardens, near Marble Arch, for six weeks. He attended the St David's Day Dinner at the Connaught where he proposed the toast of 'Wales'. In consecutive days he and Mary visited the theatre when they saw Hawtrey in *General John Regan* at the Apollo, which they thought very good, and *Oh, Oh Delphine* at the Shaftesbury, which was excellent. While in London in early April, Francis attended his first meeting as a member of the Committee of the Carlton Club. Domestically, both cooks left Hereford Gardens on the same day, but Francis left the problem to Mary as he had to travel to Shrewsbury to attend a staff tour. The King's review of the Foot Guards took place in Hyde Park when nine Battalions of Guards paraded under the command of Sir Alfred Codrington. A total of over 7,000 officers and men, including reservists, took part in the review, which Lloyd attended.

A further meeting took place at the War Office at which Colonel Seely, the Secretary of State for War, met the fourteen Territorial Division Commanders to discuss if anything could be done to improve recruitment to the Territorials. Conscription was considered out of the question because neither the Liberals or the Conservatives would consider it. Seely asked how they would spend more money if the Government agreed to provide additional funds to assist recruitment. On the whole Lloyd found the meeting satisfactory. Following the meeting David Lloyd George wrote to Francis Lloyd about the Territorial Force in Wales:

> Dear Sir Francis Lloyd,
>
> I am anxious to have a talk with you about the position of the Territorial Forces in Wales, as I am convinced that under favourable conditions Wales ought to make an excellent recruiting ground. I have already talked to the Lord Chancellor on the subject and he has evidently communicated with you. I am not quite sure whether I shall be down in Wales during the Whitsuntide Recess. If I can get away I will let you know later on.
>
> Ever sincerely,
>
> [signed] D Lloyd George

Francis Lloyd attended the King's Levée at Buckingham Palace on 2 June, followed on the next day by Trooping the Colour at Horse Guards Parade. At a meeting with General Grierson he was told about his chances for the command of the London District. It was coming up on the following Monday before the Selection Board, and Grierson considered that Francis Lloyd was certain to be appointed. In the meantime Francis and Mary visited an exhibition of portraits by Philip de Laszlo, which included the drawing in chalk of Francis. The Selection Board met on 30 June and Francis Lloyd heard later that day that he had been selected to command the London District.

Lloyd still had two months of his existing command to fulfil, and early in July he attended a review by the King of the two London Divisions of the Territorial Forces, which took place in Hyde Park with about 12,000 Territorials on parade. Mary left London for a cruise to Norway, which her doctor had recommended sometime earlier. Francis Lloyd was summoned to appear before the Committee of National Defence in Whitehall. The Prime Minister (Asquith), the Secretary of State for War (Seely), the Lord Chancellor (Lord Haldane), Lord Roberts, Lord Esher, and Winston Churchill (First Lord of the Admiralty) and others were present. Lloyd gave evidence on the state of the Territorial Forces and was questioned for nearly an hour. Two weeks later Francis received the formal letter from the War Office offering him the command of the London District:

Dear Lloyd,

Will you inform me whether it would be agreeable to you to be appointed to command the London District. The vacancy is due to occur on the 3rd September next.

If you accept the Secretary of State for War would like to see you with regard to the appointment.

Pay – £1,500 a year or £1,300 if quarters are allotted.

Yours v.truly,

[signed]

August was the month when the annual camp of the Welsh Division of the Territorials was held and Francis used his visit to the camps at Haverfordwest and Rhyl to view the manoeuvres and to say farewell. He visited the camp at Porthcawl on his sixtieth birthday and reviewed, in pouring rain and half a gale, the Welsh Border Infantry Brigade, 1 Welsh Howitzer Brigade, and 1 Welsh Ambulance of the Territorials.

At two meetings in London he was given some idea of the discussion which took place at the War Office Selection Board which resulted in his appointment to the London District. The Secretary of State for War (Colonel Seely) told Lloyd that there had been a great set made against him because he had been too hard on the [Guards] Brigade when he commanded it at Aldershot, but Seely told him to behave in his new command exactly as he had done in the past.[71] The second meeting was with Sir John French, who practically repeated what Seely had told him. Lloyd had a fairly good idea of where the allegations had come from, but they had only arisen after he had left Aldershot. French told him that [General] Arthur Paget, Lloyd's Divisional Commander for his first three years at Aldershot had gone dead against him. Francis Lloyd drew the conclusion that had it not been for French and Grierson on the Selection Board, he would have been beaten.

News of Lloyd's new appointment was reported widely in the Press, and many reports included summaries of his career and assessments of his character:

The General of the Dandies.

This is how 'Frankie' has been dubbed by that type of warrior – happily scarce in our Army – who is born a sloven and continues to exist as such in the service.

Major General Sir Francis Lloyd who is a grandson of the 10th Earl of Kinnoull, is to be the new boss of the London District, and being fairly rich, remarkably good looking and fond of society, will compare favourably with certain 'cocked hats' who have not been socially popular in London Society during – well, the last dozen years.

It is not true that Frankie wears stays (*Vanity Fair*, I call to mind, said so when he was commanding the 1st Infantry Brigade at Aldershot) but *en revanche* he has a curious liking for thin lace handkerchiefs and delicate perfumes. And yet there is nothing in the least effeminate about London's new Commander-in-Chief. He saw service in two campaigns under 'K of K' in the man-eating Sudan, and he earned his 'Bath' again under the cold grey eye of Kitchener in the other end of the Dark Continent.[72]

In the week before taking up command of the London District, Francis Lloyd was a guest at Powis Castle, as was Lord Kitchener. Francis had a long talk with him and was told many things he had not previously heard about the Battle of Omdurman and the South African war.

5

GOC London District

HORSE GUARDS

At eleven o'clock on 3rd September 1913, General Sir Francis Lloyd went to Horse Guards and took over command of the London District. His first District Order, issued on the same day, included the statement that:

> Major General Sir F Lloyd KCB, CVO, DSO, having been appointed to command the London District from 3rd September 1913, inclusive, has assumed the command, and is taken on the strength of the District accordingly.

Lloyd had been appointed to the supreme position reserved for Guardsmen, which he was to hold, at the special request of the Army Council, for five years, during which he became the best known military figure in London. He was now sixty, with the expectation of five years more of military life. The outbreak of war might have given him the opportunity of exercising a higher command in the field, to which he would have brought ten years' experience as a brigade and divisional commander at home. But this was not to be, however, for as GOC London District his command grew beyond all possible expectation. During the war years he was not only in command of the units quartered in the London area, and reinforcing the brigades – which became a division – of Household Troops; but in addition the hospitals were brought under him (there were 200 of all sorts in the London District), together with the rail termini.[73]

Mary did not return from her Norwegian cruise until a week after Francis took up his new command, and they lived temporarily at Russell's Hotel in Curzon Street while searching for a house. The annual manoeuvres of the British Army took place in September, and Lloyd went down to Marlow to see the operations between the Aldershot Command and 1 Cavalry Brigade and 4 Guards Brigade combined. At the end of the manoeuvres a conference of about 300 officers under the Presidency of the King was held at which Sir John French summed up the outcome and lessons to be learned from the exercises. Later the Army Council gave a dinner at the Whitehall Rooms for all the senior officers and representatives from Forces overseas, the Dominions, and Foreign Military Attachés.

A month after taking up his command General Lloyd made his first inspection of Brigade of Guards troops when he inspected the 1st and 2nd Battalions of the Coldstream Guards at Chelsea Barracks – he thought both battalions very good. Inspections of the Irish Guards and the Scots Guards at Wellington Barracks, and the 2nd Battalion Grenadiers at the Tower of London soon followed.

He was now a public figure in London and as a result newspapers frequently included articles about how he was settling into his new appointment, including the furnishings of his office:

> General Sir Francis Lloyd has already become very popular at the Horse Guards and is spoken of almost affectionately by his subordinates there. They say that whilst the General is a firm disciplinarian and a man who knows his work and sees that others carry out their duties thoroughly and efficiently, he does so with the least possible friction.
>
> The office of the Commanding Officer of the Forces in London is a very plain affair indeed, a couple of tables, a screen, a chair or two, a few shelves containing records and papers, comprising the whole of the furniture. It is a room measuring twenty feet each way and entirely devoid of any effort at decoration.

In the light of Francis Lloyd's other interests and how he continually purchased furniture, glass and pictures for Aston Hall, it is difficult to believe that his office remained so sparsely furnished for very long. Another newspaper also touched on some of his habits and interests:

> He has a very youthful figure and a very good tailor. He is naturally fastidious about his clothes and an authority on what new fashions are fashions, and what are freaks only to be indulged by eccentrics. On the other hand, in South Africa and the Sudan he seemed to be able to endure hardships without turning a hair that knocked up men who had been apt to regard him as too pretty to be efficient.

By the end of October, Lloyd was ready to start visiting the many Territorial units in the metropolis and this took up much of his time during the following six months. During one of his early visits he encountered the 'worst day I ever remember in London – thick fog and wet'.

Now that Francis and Mary were living in London, a decision had to be made about Aston Hall. Francis asked his agent, Williams, to come up to London for a meeting with his solicitor, Ronald Peake, at Bedford Row. Concern was expressed about the future of the garden at Aston Hall, but the main decision taken was to have a professional valuation made of the house and estate. A house had been found in London at 17 Stratford Place, and some of the servants came up from Aston Hall.

The international political situation was, by December 1913, of increasing concern to the Government. Lloyd dined at the Royal Automobile Club in Pall Mall for the principal purpose of inspecting the Club with a view to it becoming a general hospital on mobilisation. A meeting was called at the War Office on 16 December, which was attended by the Secretary of State for War, Field Marshal Sir John French, and seven other Generals, including Francis Lloyd, who simply noted in his diary that the Secretary of State 'spoke on matters very secret'.

Francis and Mary went to stay at Attingham Park, near Shrewsbury, for Christmas where they joined the Van Bergen, Gunnis and Lort-Phillips families. On New Year's Eve, Francis met his agent in Shrewsbury, when they discussed letting Aston Hall to Mary's brother Frankie Gunnis. He also raised with Williams the possibility of letting the shooting on the Aston Estate.

On his return to London, General Sir Francis Lloyd attended the first of many functions to which he was invited in his capacity as GOC London District. This event may not have had the pageantry of some of the greater occasions he attended, but as a soldier he no doubt enjoyed the Annual Sergeants' Dinner of the Coldstream Guards, which he described as 'very dignified'. Lady Lloyd often accompanied her husband on his visits to review Territorial units, when she presented the prizes for the target shooting and other sporting activities of the units, as she did in January 1914, to the London Irish Rifles, a 600 strong Territorial unit, at Chelsea Town Hall. On most Sundays, when they were in London, Sir Francis and Lady Lloyd attended church at the Guards Chapel in Wellington Barracks, and Francis invariably read the lesson. Mary kept in close contact with her nephews Geoffrey, Rupert and Nigel Gunnis and took them to some of the seasonal and other events in London including the Circus and the Zoo.

At the end of January, General Lloyd presented Meritorious Service Medals at a parade of the 3rd Battalion Grenadiers in Wellington Barracks, including to one Guardsman who had been born in 1840. Lloyd's interest in motor cars continued and he signed a contract with Delaunay Belleville for a new chassis on which he had built the body of the Nordenfeldt, his existing car, making it in his mind a thoroughly new car. It cost him £750, but, probably not surprisingly in these still early days of motoring, breakdowns seemed to occur all too often to Lloyd on his journeys throughout England.

The King's interest in his Regiments of Foot Guards went as far as the details of their dress, and the GOC London District on one occasion visited the King's Private Secretary at Buckingham Palace to discuss the question of Guardsmen wearing the waist belt inside instead of outside the greatcoat. General Lloyd was requested to parade two Guardsmen dressed in the alternative styles.

Francis Lloyd's health must have given both Lady Lloyd and his superiors in the War Office cause for concern, and may have been taken into account by the latter in deciding not to give him a Field Command. In February 1914 Lloyd contracted pneumonia, from which it took him three weeks to recover, and he seemed to be forever suffering from colds and seeking prescriptions from his doctor. Throughout his life he suffered from headaches or migraines, the severity of which often required him to stay at home for the day. Lady Lloyd always denied that any weaknesses in his immune system or his other ailments, had anything to do with his wounds from the Battle of Biddulphsberg, and the many physicians that he consulted were often unable to agree on the causes of his illnesses.

The recovery from pneumonia had been assisted by a week's recuperation with Mary at the Grand Hotel in Brighton, and they returned to London in March in time to see Nijinsky dance at the Palace Theatre, and thought the performance 'very wonderful'. One of the annual events in the City of London, to which Sir Francis Lloyd received an invitation, was the Lord Mayor's Banquet at the Mansion House for the City Livery Companies, which was always held in March. He was also invited by some of the older Livery Companies to banquets in their own magnificent Livery Halls, and in the spring he attended dinners at Drapers' Hall and Armourers' and Brasiers' Hall in the City.

All such social and ceremonial occasions were abruptly, if only temporarily, put to one side in the middle of March, with the threatened resignation of more than fifty officers in the British Army stationed at the Curragh. The 'incident' reverberated throughout the Army and, although short-lived, caused a crisis in the Government. In 1912 Asquith had introduced the Third Home Rule Bill for Ireland, which proposed the creation of an autonomous Irish Parliament in Dublin. Following the passing of the Parliament Act, the House of Lords could only delay by up to two years any measure sent up to them. The Conservative party, now led by Bonar Law, openly encouraged Ulster to arm for resistance under Sir Edward Carson's sincere and dogged leadership.

Sir Arthur Paget, Commander of the Curragh base in Ireland, had been given orders to prepare to march on Ulster should the Ulster Volunteers respond violently to the passing of a Home Rule Bill. Paget misinterpreted these precautionary orders and believed he was to march immediately against Ulster. On his own initiative he offered the officers under his command the option of resignation or 'disappearance' to ensure they would not be forced to fight the Ulster Volunteers. Fifty-seven of the seventy officers of 3 Cavalry Brigade, led by Brigadier General Hubert Gough, threatened to resign their commissions.

Gough was summoned to London for discussions with Sir John French, the CIGS, and Sir John Spencer Ewart, the Adjutant General. It was made clear by Gough that he wished the Government to issue a statement that the Army would not be employed to enforce Home Rule on Ulster under the pretext of maintaining law and order. Ewart, perhaps with French's help, prepared a draft statement which sought to clarify the situation and this was sent to the Cabinet for approval. The Cabinet made some amendments and Asquith handed the revised document to the Secretary of State for War, Colonel Seely, who was not at the meeting, as he had been summoned to Buckingham Palace to brief the King on the crisis.

News of the threatened resignations had spread throughout the British Army, and Haig had told French that the resignation of every officer in the Aldershot Command might be expected if Gough were punished.

When Seely saw the amended draft produced by the Cabinet he decided to add two paragraphs before it was sent over to the War Office to be seen by French, Ewart and Gough. There was one expression in which Gough thought there was a possible ambiguity, and on a separate piece of paper he added the following words:

> I understand the reading of the last paragraph to be that troops under our command will not be called upon to enforce the present Home Rule Bill on Ulster, and that we can so assure our officers.

This was shown to French, who after some deliberation, wrote at the foot of Gough's paper: 'This is how I read it', and added his initials and 'CIGS'.

The nature of Seely's additions to the Cabinet draft and the guarantee given to Gough soon became known and on 25 March, Asquith publicly repudiated the guarantee. This led to the resignations of French, Ewart and Seely. Asquith declared that it was all a misunderstanding, but added a few days later that 'the army will hear nothing of politics from me, and in return I expect to hear nothing of politics from the army'.

General Sir Francis Lloyd had first read reports of events at the Curragh barracks in the newspapers on 21 March and had immediately called a meeting of all Commanding Officers in the Household Brigade. Following the repudiation of the 'guarantee', Lloyd was summoned to a meeting at the War Office of all Divisional Commanders, but within four days the CIGS had resigned. French subsequently sent a letter to all senior commanders including Lloyd:

My Dear Lloyd,

The Adjutant General and I have resigned our appointments and our resignations have been accepted by the Government. The issue was a purely personal one, absolutely unconnected with any political consideration whatever. We should have not taken the step if we had not been quite confident that all officers, non-commissioned officers and men would continue to carry out their duties in the same loyal and whole hearted manner which has ever characterised the Army.

I feel confident, therefore, that I may rely upon you to maintain discipline at the same high standard as heretofore and to allay and remove by your own influence any feeling which may exist in regard to what has recently occurred.

Yours ever sincerely,

[signed] J D P French

A few days later a demonstration took place in Hyde Park, where Unionists protested against Home Rule. Sir Charles Douglas was appointed CIGS, and for the interim Asquith acted as his own Secretary of State for War. At Horse Guards Parade they had other matters to prepare for.

In May a visit by the King and Queen of Denmark required troops from the Household Brigade to line the streets and perform their accustomed ceremonial duties. Sir Francis Lloyd was responsible for ensuring the smooth running of these arrangements and he was subsequently made a Commander 1st Class of the Royal Order of Danneborg by the Royal visitors. As GOC London District, Lloyd took a leading part in the arrangements for the Royal Naval and Military Tournament at Olympia. He had been associated with the Tournament for some years, but it was his duty as GOC London District to receive any important guests who attended the Tournament. The King and Queen took as their guests in 1914 the King and Queen of Denmark during their visit to London. General Lloyd had given instructions for the Danish National Anthem to be played as well as the British National Anthem, but somehow this did not happen. According to Lloyd, King George V was 'not best pleased'. [75]

Another visitor who General Lloyd was due to receive was Winston Churchill, the First Lord of the Admiralty: 'Who did not come and had not the civility to send and say so till the last moment'.[76] However, the annual Trooping of the Colour on Horse Guards Parade was held on a fine day, all went well, and the King expressed his pleasure. Away from the ceremonial in London, Lloyd went down to Pirbright to see the 3rd Battalion

Grenadiers training, and a couple of days later he was at Purfleet inspecting the 2nd Battalion at their camp.

THE GREAT WAR BEGINS

Events in Europe caused the postponement of a court ball at Buckingham Palace, when the Archduke Franz Ferdinand and his wife were assassinated at Sarajevo on 28 June, but Francis and Mary were still able to attend the ball a little over two weeks later. The gravity of the crisis in Europe was appreciated in London, but the attempts of Sir Edward Grey, the British Foreign Secretary, to broker a peace conference were not successful, and on 28 July, Austria declared war on Serbia. When Sir Francis Lloyd went to Horse Guards the next morning, he found that an order had been issued by the War Office putting into force the 'precautionary period' before mobilization. An order was also issued for all officers to return from leave, and the Military Secretary at the War Office wrote to Lloyd telling him to make arrangements for an officer to be at Horse Guards all night.

A war involving Britain now seemed very near and the 2 August was a day of extreme tension in London, with excited crowds walking the streets and cheering the King.[77] At 11.00 pm on 4 August, Britain declared war on Germany, following the failure of the German government to respond to the ultimatum requiring the withdrawal of their troops from Belgium. Two days later the British government authorized the dispatch of the British Expeditionary Force of 150,000 men. Lloyd visited Wellington Barracks and Regents Park Barracks and thought that mobilisation was going very smoothly. His days were now long and busy, and not helped three days after war had been declared, when he received an order to arrest every German and Austrian in London. He saw the Commissioner of the Metropolitan Police and later that evening visited the Home Secretary, who advised that the order had been a mistake!

Within a week he was seeing off to the front the Irish Guards, the 3rd Battalion Coldstream Guards, and the 3rd Battalion Grenadiers. An order was issued that all hospitals should be ready to their utmost expansion and by the beginning of September reports of those killed and wounded started to be received. Lloyd had heard of the death of his old friend General Sir John Grierson who was commanding II Army Corps in France, and had died from heart failure during a train journey to the front. Francis described Grierson as 'a great friend and I believe the best man in the Army'. News also reached London that the French government had moved from Paris to Bordeaux.

It was now vital that the strength of the British Army was increased as quickly as possible, but at this stage recruitment was still to be on a voluntary basis. The first appeal for recruits appeared on the walls of London on 6 August. It was printed in the national colours and within a deep red border, in vivid blue letters on a white background, were the words, 'Your King and Country need YOU'. Another poster said that an addition of 100,000 men to the Regular Army was immediately necessary. Lord Kitchener, who had been appointed Secretary of State for War, was confident that the appeal would be at once responded to, and by the evening a large crowd of young men was queuing at the recruiting headquarters in Old Scotland Yard. Within a month Lloyd was at the Guards Depot at Caterham, where he inspected nearly 4,000 new recruits which he thought 'very fine stuff'.

The Royal Navy decided to raise a Naval Brigade to fight in Europe, and Winston Churchill, the First Lord of the Admiralty was keen to have a second Brigade. He wrote to Francis Lloyd early in September seeking assistance:

> My dear General,
>
> I have a vacancy for the command of a battalion in the second Naval Brigade of the new Royal Naval Division. It is a fine command and I should be glad if you could recommend me the name of a really capable officer from the Guards for the appointment.
>
> Yours sincerely,
>
> [signed] Winston S Churchill

The need for recruits was further emphasised when General Sir Francis Lloyd met the first hospital train at Waterloo, with 300 casualties from the retreat at Mons. There were no bad cases; some had arms and legs in splints; others had bandaged heads, faces and necks. Most of the men were in khaki uniforms – their tunics torn, soiled and without buttons.[78] With hospitals in the capital now under his control, visits to them were a regular part of Lloyd's work. In one week in the middle of September he visited King's College Hospital in Denmark Hill, St Mark's Hospital in the Kings Road, the London Hospital in Whitechapel, and No.3 General Hospital in Wandsworth, where his sister Selina was working as a nurse and he saw 136 wounded men.

The speed with which men were recruited and trained was reflected in a newspaper report of an inspection in Hyde Park:

> General Sir Francis Lloyd, GOC London District, yesterday made an inspection of the 9th (Reserve) Battalion County of London Regiment (Queen Victoria's Rifles) on the Guards' Ground in Hyde Park. This battalion which is 1,050 strong, was raised in the short

space of four days, and the inspection was made after only three weeks' drill.[79]

News from the front in October 1914 was not good, with the fall of Antwerp marking a defeat for the Entente. Some of the blame for this was directed at the Royal Naval Brigade sent out by Winston Churchill, 'untrained, unequipped, with old rifles and little ammunition'.[80] The 100,000 recruits Kitchener had asked for had been obtained, and by the end of September over 478,000 had joined up, far more men enlisting than the War Office could feed, train or even house.

Rumours of German agents in London abounded and the authorities were said to be fully aware of the 'spy peril', although nothing was allowed to be said in the newspapers on the subject. It was the end of October before the first spy was arrested and appeared in Court. Sir Francis Lloyd attended the trial by court martial of Carl Hans Lody, alias Charles Inglis, at the Middlesex Guildhall. Sentries of the Grenadier Guards were posted at the entrance. The military officers constituting the court were in khaki, except for the President, Major General Lord Cheylesmore, who was in civilian dress. The prisoner sat in the dock between two Grenadier Guards armed with rifles and fixed bayonets. According to the evidence, Lody travelled extensively through the British Isles pretending to be an American tourist. He was in fact a senior lieutenant in the German Naval Reserve. Lody admitted that he had been instructed to go to England, and remain there until after the first naval engagement, when he was to supply information of the actual British losses. He was found guilty of spying and sentenced to death. Lloyd made the arrangements for the execution by shooting, which took place at the Tower of London. A coroner's inquest followed and Lody was buried at Bow.

Sir Francis Lloyd's efforts in the recruitment campaigns were not limited to the London area. He had visited Cardiff several times during his command of the Welsh Territorial Forces, and he travelled there in November, when he met the Lord Mayor and made a speech at a luncheon, calling for more men to volunteer. He returned to London on the same afternoon and later that evening attended the annual Lord Mayor's Banquet at the Guildhall. It had been announced some weeks previously that after consultation with the Government it had been decided to be very desirable that the banquet 'as a national institution' should be continued despite the war. The Prime Minister (Asquith), the Secretary of State for War (Kitchener), the First Lord of the Admiralty (Churchill) the French Ambassador, and Arthur Balfour (at this time out of office) all spoke. Lloyd thought that the only really fine speech was Balfour's.

Leaving Guildhall at about ten o'clock, the guests found the streets of the City dark, empty and silent. Very few of the street lamps were burning, and these were so masked that their light fell only at one's feet. The public-houses closed at ten and the City clocks were silent at night and their dials not lighted. Big Ben had ceased to sound the quarters and the hours.

A new session of Parliament was opened on 11 November, but the Household Brigade troops along the route to Westminster were for the first time in khaki instead of in full-dress scarlet. However, great crowds still lined the streets. In his speech from the throne, the King declared that business would be limited to Bills in aid of the war. A week later, Lloyd George introduced his first War Budget in the House of Commons. Income tax was doubled from nine pence to one shilling and sixpence in the pound.

Inspections of new units by Sir Francis Lloyd sometimes drew criticism from him, as when he inspected the 3rd Battalion (Reserve) Scots Guards at Wellington Barracks. There were about 1,300 men on parade and Lloyd considered them 'a very fine Battalion indeed, but not completely clothed and armed'.

Francis and Mary Lloyd spent Christmas in London, but Francis still managed to gather together his sisters Selina and Maudie, Mary's brother Frankie Gunnis and two of his sons, and the Lort-Phillips, for a family dinner. However, meetings on the war effort continued over the holiday, with Francis attending a conference on Boxing Day to discuss the protection of water pumping stations. On the following Monday he was at Poplar in East London to open a Soldiers, Sailors and Wives Club, which received a favourable report in one newspaper describing 'Sir Francis Lloyd's Activities':

> This very popular officer has been actively engaged in helping the various agencies for aiding our soldiers and sailors and their wives and families, and his little addresses on any of his public appearances have been most practical and sympathetic. Sir Francis paid a visit to Poplar the other day to open the new British Women's War Club, organized by Lady Winifred Renshaw and Mrs Albert Rutson, and held in a disused public-house on the premises of the Welsh Ale Brewery Company, and kindly lent by them. Lady Lloyd was not able to accompany Sir Francis, as she had gone to sympathise with Lady Cholmeley, whose husband has been killed at the front. In opening the club, Sir Francis said how much depended on the women of the country and on the influence they could exert if they would use it.
>
> The club activities are numerous, and include excellent cooking and cheap food and many helpers in Poplar will entertain the women, and tell them about the War and about what their husbands and sons are doing at the front.

New Year's Day 1915 brought news of the loss of the *Formidable*, a battleship of 15,000 tons which had been sunk in the Channel by the Germans. Francis and Mary found time to go to the Shaftesbury Theatre where they saw Benson in *Henry V*, but no opportunity was lost to encourage recruitment, and before the performance the Lord Mayor spoke on the stage followed by Lloyd, emphasising the need for every able-bodied male to enlist. On some occasions Sir Francis Lloyd joined Lord Kitchener on inspections of troops: 'I called at 2 Carlton Gardens at 0855 for Lord Kitchener and drove him down to Warley (Essex) where he inspected the 2nd Battalion Irish Guards. He was very pleased with the appearance'.[81]

Lloyd was a good public speaker not only on military subjects, but also when the discussion was about some other issue of the day. Such was the case at the People's Palace in Mile End when he spoke in support of the call which army leaders were making for temperance: 'General Lloyd had a tremendous reception – indeed, apparently the applause which greeted him threatened to continue for the rest of the evening and leave no time for a speech'.

The reputation of Sir Francis Lloyd for discipline and performance was slightly jeopardised on one occasion when he motored down to Windsor for an inspection. His car ran into a van at Colnbrook ('our fault') and bent the radiator, delaying him for about half an hour. But he duly arrived and inspected 1,800 men on parade, and then went on to Caterham where he saw another 1,900.

A New Regiment of Foot Guards

Early in 1915, George V indicated his wish that a Welsh Regiment of Foot Guards should be formed, and Lord Kitchener, Secretary of State for War, was instructed to proceed with its creation. Kitchener decided to give General Sir Francis Lloyd the task of forming the regiment and Lloyd records in his diary for 6 February that:

> At 1130 hrs I had an interview with Lord Kitchener about the formation of a battalion of Welsh Guards. I pointed out the objections which are greatest – I told him if he wished it done it could and should be. He insisted somewhat tyranically and would not listen to any reason so it has got to be done. I sent for Murray Threipland who has got a Welsh-speaking wife and asked if he would command. He said yes.

Later, in 1920, Lloyd wrote a longer version of his meeting with Kitchener, as an introduction to Dudley-Ward's history of the Welsh Guards:

LORD KITCHENER, very abruptly: You have got to raise a regiment of Welsh Guards.

SIR FRANCIS LLOYD: Sir, there are a great many difficulties in the way which I should like to point out first.

LORD KITCHENER, very rudely: If you do not like to do it some one else will.

SIR FRANCIS LLOYD: Sir, when do you want them?

LORD KITCHENER: Immediately.

SIR FRANCIS LLOYD: Very well, sir; they shall go on guard on St David's Day.[82]

It is not hard to imagine that the order to raise the Welsh Guards hit Sir Francis from two opposite directions. As a Welshman he was delighted, as a Grenadier he thought at once of the many fine men his regiment recruited from Cardiff.

Two days later Lloyd had a meeting with the Adjutant General and was told not to proceed until he heard that Kitchener, who had written to the Prime Minister, had received a reply. The go-ahead was soon received and Kitchener saw Sir Francis Lloyd again together with Major Murray Threipland, a Grenadier, whose name was sent to the King for his approval of Murray Threipland as commander of the battalion. Approval of this choice was received later that day. Lloyd noted in his diary for 11 February: 'Birth of the Welsh Guards'.

The task of finding the officers and men for a Welsh battalion started immediately. It had been decided that the battalion should consist only of Welshmen, but as Lloyd put it:

What we have to do is to get trained Welsh soldiers for the Guards, because you cannot begin such a regiment with a lot of recruits. It is going to be a regiment of Guards for the King, not merely a regiment of Welshmen, and we must have the right type of man, and such a regiment of Welshmen will fight, well – like the very devil.[83]

The first step was therefore to call for Welsh volunteers from the Grenadiers, Coldstream and Scots Regiments of Guards to form a trained and disciplined core of the battalion. Colonel Sir Henry Streatfeild, commanding the Grenadiers, gave Lloyd free access to his old regiment, and together with Murray Threipland he went to Chelsea Barracks and spoke to the 4th Battalion Grenadiers and called on all Welshmen to come forward and transfer to the Welsh Guards. Lloyd then went on to see the 3rd Battalion at Wellington Barracks where he did the same thing. The response was some 303 men including about forty NCOs. Later in the day

Murray Threipland was sent for by the King, and Lloyd saw him in the evening to hear about the interview.[84]

The next day was very wet but Sir Francis Lloyd and Murray Threipland, now promoted to Lieutenant Colonel, drove down to Caterham. Lloyd addressed 2,000 Grenadiers in the Recreation Room, calling once again on all Welshmen to join the Welsh Guards, and about 200 came forward. He and Murray Threipland then motored to White City, where 400 Grenadier recruits were addressed. Back at his office at Horse Guards, Sir Francis sat down with Murray Threipland to go through the list of the names of possible officers for the Welsh Battalion. With the core of the battalion now formed, Sir Francis Lloyd wrote to the Lord Mayor of Cardiff and the Mayors of Swansea, Newport and Wrexham, about stage two of the recruitment campaign directed to the Welsh counties, from which several hundred men were required to bring the battalion up to full strength.

Reports now began to appear in newspapers indicating that success was already assured in raising the Welsh Battalion, and quoted Lloyd as saying:

> I am fully satisfied with the men we have got together today as the nucleus for the Welsh Guards. They are all typical Welshmen, and many of them speak the language. They are all Evanses and Joneses and Davieses and Lloyds. We are out, in fact, to make this a characteristically Welsh regiment.[85]

Haste was still the order of the day, and arrangements were made for Lloyd to visit Cardiff on 18 February, where he met the Lord Mayor, and addressed a meeting of 800 people for forty-five minutes on the new Welsh Guards. According to Lloyd he was 'enthusiastically received and so was the topic'.

Some of the finer details in the formation of the Regiment had now to be agreed, and Lloyd saw Kitchener about the badge of the Welsh Guards. Lloyd proposed the Welsh emblem of the leek and, although Kitchener was against it, the leek was adopted as the badge of the Regiment. Lloyd was almost on his home ground when he spoke at a meeting at Wrexham. It was not a large meeting, but he thought a good one, which his sister Eva, who lived at Wrexham, attended. Lloyd returned to London to hear that earlier that day, 26 February 1915, the King had signed the Royal Warrant authorising the formation of a Welsh Regiment of Foot Guards, at the meeting of the Court at St James's Palace.

Sir Francis Lloyd only had three days left to fulfil his undertaking to Kitchener that the Welsh Battalion would go on guard on St David's Day. He was not going to let his reputation falter, and on 1 March, Sir Francis

Francis Lloyd, Grenadier
Guards, in active service
uniform 1885.
Courtesy of the Council of the
National Army Museum, London.

1st Battalion Grenadier Guards boarding train at Cairo en route for Sudan in 1898.
(IWM/HU 093859).

Officers Mess, 1st Battalion Grenadier Guards Omdurman/Khartoum campaign, Sudan, 1898.

Battle of Omdurman: Grenadiers outside tents (1898). (IWM/HU 093917).

Raising the flag on General Gordon's ruined palace at Khartoum, after the re-conquest of the Sudan in 1898. © Imperial War Museum. (IWM/HU 093966).

Major Francis Lloyd and Lieutenant Harvey Bathurst with spears and other relics from battle of Omdurman, Sudan 1898.

The Garden front, Rolls Park, Chigwell, Essex (1918). © Country Life Picture Library.

The Music Room at Rolls Park, Chigwell, showing Harvey family portraits (1918). © Country Life Picture Library.

Aston Hall, near Oswestry, west and north fronts (2008).

The Grand Staircase at Aston Hall (1923).

Sir Francis Lloyd's Coat of Arms, 1913. 'Supporters' were added in 1919 after he was awarded the GCVO.

Lieutenant General Sir Francis Lloyd's funeral cortege leaving the Guards Chapel, Wellington Barracks, London, 4 March 1926.

went to Buckingham Palace to see the 1st Battalion, Welsh Guards mount guard over the King, to the strains of the band of the Scots Guards. The King watched the parade from the palace windows.

Later in the day Sir Francis followed what had now become a tradition when he spoke at a St David's Day meeting at the Central Hall, Westminster, before an audience of, he thought, 3,000 to 4,000 people. That night was the first and only occasion when Lord Kitchener dined 'on guard', and Sir Francis Lloyd joined them after his meeting at Westminster.

On the next day the King sent for both Lloyd and the Battalion commander and agreed to all the proposals which they put forward to him:

The Leek to be the badge of the Welsh Guards.

The Dragon to be emblazoned on the collar.

The motto to be 'Cymru am byth'.

The senior Company to be the 'Prince of Wales Company'.

The Company Colour to be the same shape as the banner carried at King James I's funeral.

The plume to be green and white.[86]

At a further meeting with the King two weeks later, badges for the cap, a cypher, and button were settled. Sir Francis Lloyd continued to visit towns in Wales in the drive for recruits, and meetings were held at Merthyr, Swansea and the Rhondda. The White City became the initial base for training and on 23 March Lloyd inspected the Battalion there, and was introduced to any officers that he did not know. Now that the 1st Battalion was completed so far as numbers were concerned, the formation of a Reserve Battalion was about to begin. The King presented Colours to the 1st Battalion, Welsh Guards, on 3 August 1915, and two weeks later the Battalion left for the front.

Sir Francis Lloyd's close ties with Wales had been further recognized in March 1915, when he was appointed Colonel of the Royal Welch Fusiliers:

Dear Lloyd,

I have much satisfaction in acquainting you that His Majesty has been pleased to approve your appointment as Colonel of the Royal Welch Fusiliers, and a notification to this effect will shortly appear in the London Gazette.

Yours sincerely,

[signed]

Sir Francis visited the Regiment at Wrexham in April – 'my first experience of the Royal Welch Fusiliers – I was very much impressed'. It was also at this time that Sir Francis and Lady Lloyd came to know John Buchan, who as well as working in the Colonial Service, standing for Parliament, and acting as a correspondent for *The Times*, was a well known novelist. Buchan gave a series of lectures on the war which Lloyd attended and thought excellent. They subsequently became friends and met socially. This led to Buchan dedicating his novel *The Power House* to Sir Francis Lloyd when it was published in 1916:

To Major General Sir Francis Lloyd, KCB

My Dear General,
    A recent tale of mine has, I am told, found favour in the dugouts and billets of the British front, as being sufficiently short and sufficiently exciting for men who have little leisure to read. My friends in that uneasy region have asked for more. So I have printed this story, written in the smooth days before the war, in the hope that it may enable an honest man here and there to forget for an hour the too urgent realities. I have put your name on it, because among the many tastes which we share one is a liking for precipitous yarns.

J.B.

Inspections of new battalions of the London Regiment (formed from the Volunteer Force battalions of the Territorial Army) continued and drew the comment in one newspaper: 'The Busy General – Hardly a day passes but finds him scrutinising critically London units in the new Army'.

The *Lusitania* was torpedoed by the Germans off the Old Head of Kinsale in May 1915, with almost 2,000 on board, all non-combatants, including many Americans. This led to an explosion of anger against the Germans. The Members of the Stock Exchange decided to exclude brokers of German birth, even though they might be naturalised British subjects. A procession at least 2,000 strong marched to the Houses of Parliament to press upon the Prime Minister the necessity of interning Germans in London during the war.

The Government was coming under increasing pressure as a result of the shortage of shells, and events at Gallipoli led Asquith to announce after the Whitsun adjournment that agreement had been reached on the Liberals, Unionists and Labour entering into a coalition but still with himself as Prime Minister. Gone were Lord Haldane, the Lord Chancellor, and Winston Churchill had been moved from the Admiralty to the very subordinate office of Chancellor of the Duchy of Lancaster, and replaced by Arthur Balfour. A new Ministry of Munitions was created with Lloyd George at its head.

By the middle of 1915, the sight of tired and hungry soldiers passing through the main London rail termini on leave from the front was common. This led to the setting up of free buffets, organized by volunteers and manned entirely by women. The first such buffet was at London Bridge station but soon similar facilities were in operation at Euston, Victoria, Liverpool Street, Charing Cross and Paddington. Initially no free buffet was set up at Waterloo, as it was considered that the 10,000 men who came through the station on Saturdays and Sundays was more than any buffet could deal with, and many of the men were on local journeys and not from the front. However, pressure from Lady Brassey, who visited Sir Francis Lloyd at Horse Guards, saw a free buffet opened at Waterloo in January 1916, and it was expected to cater for 1,000 soldiers and sailors each day. Lady Lloyd had accompanied her husband to the opening of the free buffet at Waterloo and she became one of the regular helpers at the station. At London Bridge the free buffet was presided over by Lady Limerick, where an average of 1,500 men were served each day in the first week of its opening, but Victoria was to easily surpass this with nearly 25,000 a week.

The success of the free buffets was not surprising when, as an article in *The Times* put it: 'You hand a man, chilled and tired and still covered with trench mud, hot coffee and cake and sandwiches across a buffet counter and watch him visibly cheering up and growing warm and happy before your eyes'.[87] The buffet at Victoria was open day and night with the volunteers working four or five hour shifts. Sometimes the regular staff received unexpected help from casual volunteers. Such a volunteer one day at London Bridge was Queen Mother Alexandra who arrived unexpectedly, took her turn for an hour and a half, and on leaving asked to be allowed to come again.

In addition to the free buffets, a number of rest houses and 'huts' were opened throughout the metropolis for troops returning on leave from the front. The YMCA was predominant in finding, converting and managing suitable buildings for this purpose, and worked closely with the GOC London District in doing this.

Francis Lloyd took a close interest in the free buffets and considered them of great benefit to the travelling sailor or soldier. He would often tour the stations late in the evening, accompanied by Colonel Matthews, who was responsible for their day-to-day running. On one evening they managed to visit the free buffets at Euston, Waterloo and Victoria, the YMCA 'huts' at King's Cross, Waterloo, Victoria and Horseferry Road, and the Earl Roberts Rest Home. Later in the war a booklet was published by the London District giving instructions on meeting and dealing with soldiers on leave from abroad passing through London. Lloyd wrote a short introduction for the booklet, which included sections on instructions for volunteers, transport, workers at clubs, rest houses, overseas reception committees, free buffets, air raids and sickness.[88]

QUEEN MARY'S HOSPITAL, ROEHAMPTON

The increasing number of wounded soldiers returning from the front with limbs amputated showed the need for some specialist treatment and care in the rehabilitation of the men, who could then return to employment and make a fresh start in life. In the early months of the war amputees were sent to general military hospitals and, if they were lucky, fitted with the most basic form of artificial limb. This unsatisfactory situation was noticed by Mrs Gwynne Holford one day when walking through the wards at Millbank Military Hospital and, as she later recounted, 'I then and there made a vow to start a hospital whereby all those who had the misfortune to lose a limb in this terrible war, could be fitted with those most perfect artificial limbs human science could devise'.[89]

In order to turn her vision into reality she first needed a building that could be converted into a hospital. Her attention was drawn to Roehampton House, a large stately pile a few miles south-west of London. The house had been requisitioned by the War Office and was being used as billets for soldiers before they left for the front. The owner was Mr E Kenneth Wilson of the Ellerman Wilson Shipping line, and he agreed, with the cooperation of the War Office, that the house should be used as a hospital for the rehabilitation of soldiers and sailors who had lost limbs in the war.

Having acquired a building, Mrs Gwynne Holford and her close friend, Lady Falmouth, now set about organizing the Hospital and appealing for funds. The owner of Roehampton House had agreed to lend the house and thirty acres of grounds rent free, and a month later Mr Pierpont Morgan, the owner of the smaller adjoining Dover House agreed to lease this building to the Hospital at a rent of one shilling a year.

The first that General Sir Francis Lloyd heard of the proposal was when he was invited to a meeting at Mrs Holford's house in Wilton Street on 13 May 1915. Lady Falmouth, Sir Charles Crutchley and Charles Kenderdine, a London estate agent, were also present. Sir Francis was invited to join a committee to implement and oversee the running of the Hospital, and he was promptly elected Chairman of the Committee. The ability of volunteers to move more quickly than government in getting things done was soon evident. Within a week of his first meeting with Mrs Holford, an appeal for funds had been launched with a letter to *The Times* and other newspapers:

Sir, – Having recently, through the courtesy of the Press, been able to make known the urgent need of convalescent hospitals for those who have lost their limbs in the war, we beg to inform your readers that Roehampton House, near London, has been acquired and will shortly be opened for this purpose, and that Mr Pierpont Morgan has generously offered Dover House (almost adjoining) for the use of officers. These houses together are capable of accommodating about 300 cases.

Her Majesty Queen Mary has graciously consented to the hospitals being named 'Queen Mary's Convalescent Auxiliary Hospitals', and has given a donation of £200.

Her Majesty Queen Alexandra has graciously extended her patronage to the scheme, and, in sending a donation of £100, writes: 'I am delighted to see you are taking up a subject which I have very much at heart – our disabled sailors and soldiers to be kept in chosen convalescent auxiliary hospitals until well enough to earn their own living – officers included'.

The First Lord of the Admiralty and Field Marshal the Secretary of State for War have signified their approval by becoming Presidents.

The following Committee has been formed: The Viscountess Falmouth, Mrs Lewis Harcourt, Lady Lloyd, Lady Hamilton, Lady Henderson, Mrs Gwynne Holford, the Duke of Portland, KG, the Right Hon. Lord St Davids, Admiral Sir James Bruce, KCMG, Surgeon-General Sir Arthur William May, DG, CB, RN, Major General Sir Charles Crutchley, KCVO, Major General Sir Francis Lloyd, KCB, Surgeon-General M W Russell, CCG, AMS, Colonel J Magill, CB, representing the British Red Cross Society and Order of St John.

It is distressing to see the condition of these limbless men, many of them mere lads with all their life before them, and with an outlook on their future more than sad. But hope and confidence return when they are assured that practical steps are being taken for their welfare.

At these convalescent hospitals our brave men will be cared for until they have recovered their strength and nerve; and having learned to use their artificial limbs, they will again be capable of taking up employment in the form best suited to each individual. Working in conjunction with other societies, every effort will be made to fit the men to earn their own living in the future.

To enable this urgent work to proceed without delay, grants have been made by the National Relief Fund and the joint Committee of the British Red Cross Society and Order of St John. But we need a large sum in addition for the equipment, rent and maintenance of

89

the hospitals. It is for these gallant men – sons of our Empire – that we earnestly appeal for funds to carry out the work efficiently. £50 will maintain for a year a bed to be named after the donor, and it is hoped that donations of this amount will be forthcoming from many quarters – including industrial firms – to secure the provision of County beds, beds for Naval, Military and Aircraft units, and also for men from our Overseas Dominions.

Communications and donations should be addressed to C H Kenderdine, Esq., (marked Auxiliary Hospital) at St Stephen's House, Westminster, who will be pleased to answer all inquiries.

Yours obediently,

KATHLEEN FALMOUTH

2 St James's Square, SW

M E GWYNNE HOLFORD

22 Wilton Street, SW., May 19.

Within six weeks grants and donations amounted to £26,218.[90] Preparations went ahead at a great speed, the buildings were cleaned and decorated, lifts, fire escapes and kitchen equipment installed, beds and linen bought and staff engaged. The War Office agreed to pay three shillings a day for each occupied bed and to supply working orderlies or to make an allowance of one shilling a day for their keep. Lloyd interviewed Miss Munn who was appointed matron, and Captain Nicholson was engaged by him as quartermaster. The aim was to provide 200 beds, and by 20 June 1915 the first twenty-five patients were admitted.

The staff at Roehampton were headed by the Commandant (always an army surgeon) and the first to be appointed was Surgeon-General Pearson. Expansion of the Hospital was rapid, with 228 patients in the Hospital by October and 357 by December 1915.[91] Although meetings of the General, Executive and Finance Committees of the Hospital met in London, Lloyd visited the Hospital frequently to see the progress being made. On a visit in early July he met the Commandant and Matron and noted that there were about thirty-nine limbless men in the wards. Later in the month an exhibition of the latest advances in the design and manufacture of artificial limbs was held at Roehampton, combined with a garden party in the spacious grounds. Queen Amelie of Portugal and Princess Louise attended the event. On one occasion it was necessary for Lloyd to visit the Hospital and address the men, appealing to them to see that there were no more cases of drunkenness such as had occurred during the previous few days. Lloyd had always supported the building of a large recreation room to keep the men occupied.

A further appeal for funds was made in October with Sir Francis Lloyd and Charles Kenderdine, the Honorary Treasurer, putting their names to the letter this time:

The nation owes a special debt of gratitude to those gallant men who have lost their limbs in the war. On their behalf we make an earnest appeal for additional funds to extend the work at Queen Mary's Convalescent Hospital, Roehampton, where these sufferers (officers and men) are provided, at the expense of the State, with their artificial appliances and taught how to use them.

The hospitals are officially recognised by the Directors General of the Navy and Army Medical Services, and the Lords Commissioners of the Royal Hospital, Chelsea. Over eight hundred patients are now awaiting admission, among them many men from our Overseas Dominions, and the numbers increase daily. To meet this difficult situation a large outlay has been incurred in the erection and equipment of new wards, which will shortly be opened.

The work at Roehampton can best be judged by the results achieved and by the gratitude of these brave men on realising that, with the aid of the wonderful artificial limbs of recent invention, they will be able to obtain employment and make a fresh start in life. With a view to their future employment and also to provide useful occupation for the men while in hospital, workshops fitted with model motor chassis, electrical appliances, lathes &c., are being organized with competent instructors. A man who has lost his right hand will be taught to write with the left and classes for other industries will be arranged. An employment bureau working in conjunction with existing societies and employers of labour has also been established, and already a number of men have been placed in good situations. From the numerous offers received, it is hoped through this medium to find suitable employment for every man on leaving the hospital.

To maintain and extend this national work, a large additional sum of money is required and we look with confidence to a ready response to our appeal from public and private sources, notwithstanding the urgency of other claims.

Donations sent to the Hon. Treasurer at St Stephen's House, Westminster, will be gratefully acknowledged.

Major General Sir Francis Lloyd,

KCB, DSO, Chairman.

Mr C H Kenderdine, Honorary Treasurer.

The demand for beds continued to increase and the decision was taken in March 1916 to extend the Hospital by the erection of three new wards containing 189 beds.

Lady Lloyd was a member of the General Committee and took an interest in the welfare of both the patients and nurses. She attended a garden party and sale of work in July 1916 when she presented medals to the nurses for good service in the hospital.

Mrs Holford did not like committees and often did not attend meetings of the Executive Committee. She preferred to pursue her own ways of getting things done which sometimes involved employing people without the approval of the Committee. This inevitably led her into conflict with the Chairman. On one occasion she wrote a letter to Sir Francis Lloyd which he considered a direct attack on him and the way he ran the Committee. Lloyd submitted his resignation at the next meeting of the Committee but was prevailed upon to withdraw it on receiving the unanimous support of the Committee. Lady Falmouth described her friend, Mrs Holford, as 'a very impulsive person',[92] and she was often left to smooth over the differences between Mrs Holford and other members of the Committee.

By October 1916 the number of patients who had made use of beds in the Hospital was 4,281, but the waiting list had risen to 3,764. Further expansion was the only solution and by June 1918 there were almost 900 beds, the maximum that could be accommodated on the site, but with a waiting list of 4,321.

Immediately after the war there was some criticism in the Press of the treatment of servicemen who had lost their limbs and were waiting for artificial ones. Lloyd came to the defence of the expert orthopaedic surgeons, engineers and limbmakers, and cited the work done at specialist hospitals including those at Roehampton, where he was still Chairman of the management committee, and the Prince of Wales's Hospital in Cardiff. At Roehampton alone over 16,000 men had passed through the hospital fitted with their artificial limbs.

In 1919, the Committee, which was formally a Trust under a scheme approved by the Charity Commission, entered negotiations with Kenneth Wilson to purchase the freehold of Roehampton House. This was completed by January of the following year. The purchase price was £58,000 and the intention was to raise this by an appeal. However, the British Red Cross indicated that they would be prepared to provide the funds. The final result was a compromise with the Red Cross providing £28,500 and the balance of the purchase price coming from other donors. The Red Cross gave an additional £10,000 to be used in the upkeep of the buildings over the first two years of ownership.

Parallel with these negotiations, the Ministry of Pensions had been discussing with the Committee a new division of responsibilities and funding for the day-to-day running of the Hospital. Control of the Hospital as up to then exercised by the War Office would be transferred to the Ministry of Pensions, who would also now pay the surgeons. The Committee would continue to administer the Hospital on the basis of a capitation grant from the Ministry.

With the end of the war the waiting list for beds for limbless soldiers had quickly reduced, but as the Hospital was a leader in the field of artificial limbs, its facilities were made available to railwaymen who had lost limbs, and other classes were to follow. The accomodation for officer amputees at Dover House was sold to the LCC, and after an interim move to Putney, provision was made for them at Roehampton House. During the war 41,050 men had lost limbs, of whom 26,262 were supplied with their first artificial limbs at Roehampton, throughout which time Lloyd had been Chairman of the hospital.

By 1925, Queen Mary's (Roehampton) Hospital, as it was by then called, had developed from a hospital for sailors and soldiers who had lost limbs during the war, to a national centre for all classes of patient. The Ministry of Pensions could now nominate its own patients, and the small hospital at Shepherds Bush was closed and the patients transferred to Roehampton. This involved a considerable amount of building work at Roehampton, and the Ministry of Pensions agreed to pay for the cost of major rebuilding works. The Governors retained the responsibility for the upkeep of all the buildings and grounds on the estate. In May, Queen Mary paid a visit to the Hospital to open a new extension of brick built wards which gave the Hospital a capacity of 500 beds. The grounds still contained the workshops of many of the limb manufacturers. The Queen was received by General Sir Francis Lloyd, who was still Chairman of the Hospital. In a speech Lloyd pointed out that 90,000 men[94] had been through the Hospital, but there were now only thirty-two limbless men in the place: 'The first principle the Hospital stood for, and must always stand for, was the treatment first of the members of the King's fighting forces, and if ever the emergency arose again, they would always have preference, but arrangements had now been made for accommodation for cases among civilians'.

Visits to the Front

At the end of August 1915, Sir Francis Lloyd left Victoria station on his way to visit Field Marshal Sir John French at his Headquarters in St Omer. This was the first of several visits that Lloyd made to France during the war. After a smooth crossing of the Channel, Lloyd was driven from Boulogne to St Omer in Sir John French's Rolls Royce, a journey which took an hour and a half. On the next day he was taken to see a review of French troops by General (later Marshal) Joffre. Back at St Omer, Lloyd saw tactical operations by the Guards Division, including the 1st Battalion, Welsh Guards, and following an inspection by Lord Cavan, he lunched with him under a haystack![95] Sir Francis was able to visit the Royal Welch Fusiliers, and had intended to go to Ypres, but as it was raining so hard it was decided to return to England.

For some time Sir Francis and Lady Lloyd had been looking for a larger house in London, and in the middle of September they moved to 26 Great Cumberland Place.

At the beginning of October 1915 Sir Francis and Lady Lloyd inspected the 21st (Service) Battalion Middlesex Regiment at a parade on Highbury Fields, prior to the Battalion going into camp for training. Addressing the 1,170 officers and men, Lloyd reminded them that this was but the beginning of what was before them. In France, in Belgium, in Russia, in Turkey, there was going on a struggle for their existence as a nation. 'Let it not be thought for a moment that this war could be lightly won. We had made an effort but a far greater one would be required'.[96] The allied losses in one week in October had been over 30,000.

Sir Francis Lloyd was in his office at Horse Guards on the afternoon of 6 November when he was called to the Home Office, where he met the Lord Chancellor, the Attorney General, the Solicitor General and the Home Secretary. At their instigation Lloyd signed an order to raid the offices of *The Globe* newspaper, and to prevent the sale of the current issue. *The Globe*, London's evening newspaper, was suppressed under the Defence of the Realm Act for publishing false statements 'tending to depress His Majesty's subjects and give comfort to the enemy'. The paper had alleged that disagreements in the Cabinet had led Lord Kitchener to resign and that he had left the War Office. The official explanation was that Kitchener had gone to the Near East to review the military situation at Gallipoli, and that Asquith was acting as Secretary of State for War in his absence. However, the newspaper had repeated the allegation.

The police acting under the authority of Major General Sir Francis Lloyd, as the competent military authority, entered the premises of *The Globe* and seized all copies of the previous and current day's issues of the newspaper, together with the printing plant and type. A large removal van was needed to remove printing machine plates and other important parts of machinery essential to the production of the newspaper. Police officers were left in charge of the office and no indication was given to the editor as to when the authorities might allow the paper to be published again.

After a fortnight's suppression *The Globe* reappeared following an apology from its proprietors in which the newspaper withdrew its allegations that there had been dissension between Kitchener and his colleagues in the Cabinet and that Kitchener had resigned. The proprietors also advised that Charles Palmer, its former editor, would no longer be responsible for the editorial control of the newspaper. As a result of the apology the Home Secretary wrote to Sir Francis Lloyd and instructions were given for the printing plant to be replaced. The whole episode had been reported in other newspapers but there had only been mild criticism of the Government's action, with the exception of one Member of Parliament (Mr Hogge) who had defended *The Globe* in the House of Commons.

Much of Sir Francis Lloyd's time continued to be taken up by the campaign to encourage more men to join the British Army voluntarily. At a meeting held in the Marlborough Theatre at Holloway in north London, Lloyd was reported in the newspapers on the next day as having given a 'most inspiring address'. He spoke for half an hour without a note:

> He said that what was wanted was two things – munitions and men. As regards munitions Lloyd George had mastered that. The vital question was men, men, men. Lord Kitchener had said that he must have the men as he called for them. It looked as if the springs which had promised the men freely and voluntarily were running low. Lord Derby had prepared a scheme which he (Sir Francis) believed to be as good as any scheme could be. It was the last effort for the voluntary system.

Before Christmas Francis, accompanied by Mary, took his niece Gertrude Holbech to see *Tonight's the Night*, at the Gaiety Theatre, which he thought a 'very pretty play'. In the same week Sir Francis was a guest at the annual dinner of the Savage Club. This was his first visit to the Club and he found the evening most amusing and full of incident. Although he was unable to be present, the tradition of giving beef to workers on the estate at Aston took place on 21 December, the birthday of his ancestor who founded the charity. Christmas 1915, was spent in London with visits by Sir Francis and Lady Lloyd to hospitals, rest homes and free buffets. New Year's Day found Lloyd in his office at Horse Guards with 'a great deal to do'.

Links between the city of London and the GOC London District were made even closer with the formation of the Bankers' Battalion, which had been raised by the Lord Mayor, Sir Charles Wakefield. The Lord Mayor and General Sir Francis Lloyd inspected the Battalion at High Beach in Epping Forest, only a dozen miles north-east of the City. About 1,115 men were on parade, and were shortly to go to Aldershot for training, prior to going to the front.

One piece of news which must have given Sir Francis Lloyd much pleasure was his appointment early in 1916, as a member of the Board of Governors of the National Library of Wales. He and Lady Lloyd had been present at the laying of the foundation stone of the new library in Aberystwyth in 1911, and the history of his Welsh ancestors was always of great interest to him. He was not to know that in 1949 many thousands of letters and deeds relating to the Lloyd and Harvey families would be deposited at the Library by his nephew Andrew Lloyd, and subsequently purchased by the Library.[97]

As we have seen, some newspapers, in addition to commenting on Sir Francis Lloyd's abilities as a soldier and administrator, had expressed views on his neatness of dress and interest in fashions. In January 1916, it was Lady Lloyd who came into the spotlight:

> Lady Lloyd wife of the famous Major General has set a new military fashion which is likely to become popular among relatives of the regiments. At the Mansion House last week when Major General Lloyd made a recruiting speech, Lady Lloyd was there wearing gold epaulettes or straps on her shoulders, and gold military clasps fastened her big fur coat. The scheme looked very effective.[98]

The 'Derby scheme' of October-December 1915, overseen by Lord Derby as Director of Recruiting, invited men of military age to 'attest' their willingness to serve. As the scheme failed to meet its targets, the January 1916 Military Service Act provided for conscription of single men aged eighteen to forty-one, though with numerous exemptions (to be administered by a tribunal system) that included war work, hardship due to family or business commitments or ill health, and conscientious objection. After an uneasy interlude in which monthly enlistments under the new regime ran at half those under the voluntary one, a second Military Service Act in May extended compulsion to married men.[99]

6

London's Defences

ZEPPELIN RAIDS

At the beginning of the war Britain's air defences were almost non-existent. In September 1914, Kitchener asked the Admiralty to assume responsibility for air defence and Churchill, First Lord of the Admiralty, quickly drafted a detailed memo setting out the priorities. Fortunately by December the closest to London that the Germans had reached was Dover. However, on Christmas Day a German seaplane was spotted off Sheerness which flew on up the Thames as far as Erith. The sight of a lone Vickers 'Gunbus' aircraft rising to intercept it resulted in the raider turning back towards the coast and unloading its bombs on the village of Cliffe on the Hoo peninsula.

The next threat came from airship raids. In January 1915 two German Zeppelins dropped a series of 50kg bombs on Great Yarmouth and King's Lynn. The first attack on London occurred on 31 May, when at about 11.00pm Zeppelin LZ38 dropped thirty high explosive bombs and ninety incendiaries. Stoke Newington, Dalston, Stepney, Shoreditch, West Ham and Leytonstone suffered the worst damage and casualties. Another air raid in the middle of August caused damage at Leyton (Essex) where bombs had fallen on the Master Bakers Almshouses and one or two streets had been practically blown to pieces. Sir Francis Lloyd visited east London to inspect the damage and then went on to the West Ham Infirmary to see the injured. A more serious raid occurred three weeks later on 8/9 September, when seventeen people were killed, sixty-nine wounded and three reported missing. On this occasion there were many fires, including two very serious ones in the city. In Wood Street and Silver Street, behind Cheapside, and quite close to Guildhall, warehouses were gutted and there were deep holes in the roadway. Liverpool Street was particularly wrecked and damage was done to the Great Eastern railway line. There were more casualties outside London and Lloyd visited the sites to see the destruction.[100] Nor were these the last of the raids. Lloyd later attended the funeral of 14 victims at Deptford.

The Zeppelins reached the West End of London in October when two airships dropped bombs in Wellington Street near the Strand, killing (according to Lloyd) eight people. A bomb exploded just outside the pit entrance to the Strand Theatre, which was crowded for *The Scarlet Pimpernel*, killing one woman. A third bomb fell near the Aldwych Theatre, full for Hall Caine's play *The Prodigal Son*. Had the bombs fallen on the Lyceum, the Strand and the Aldwych Theatres – and each was missed by only a few yards – frightful massacres would have occurred. Later that night there was a further raid on Croydon, Plumpstead and Woolwich, when thirty-one people were killed and eighty-eight wounded.[101] Lloyd thought that the anti-aircraft defences had little effect and he was not alone in thinking that the City's defences were inadequate. No warning was given to the public of air raiders approaching London, and official reports of air raids issued by the Government Press Bureau were meagre and uninforming.

It was not until February 1916 that Asquith's government agreed that the Army should take over the role of mainland defence. Additional anti-aircraft guns were located around the capital, but even then the Royal Naval Air Service continued to deal with enemy aircraft over the North Sea and the Channel, and only those hostile aircraft which reached the mainland of England became the responsibility of the Royal Flying Corps.

The threat to the country from Zeppelin airship raids was increasing and Lloyd received an early warning of the approach of any airship across the Channel or North Sea. At this time the attacks were at night and the destination of a raid did not become known for some hours. However, on receipt of the warning, Francis Lloyd would go down to Horse Guards to await developments. Most of the raids in the early part of 1916 did not reach Central London, but it was often between 2.00am and 4.00am before everyone could be stood down. A typical example occurred on 6 March when a warning of an attack was received, and although the airship ended up over Hull, it was not until 4.00am that the GOC London District retired to his bed.

The heaviest air raid yet on the Home Counties and London, with at Lloyd's estimation thirteen to fifteen airships, took place on 2 September 1916, but poor weather scattered the force and only one airship reached the capital. However, the first Zeppelin to be shot down crashed at Cuffley in Hertfordshire. Later in the month, in another large raid with twelve to fifteen airships, one Zeppelin had flown over Horse Guards but no bombs were dropped. The main damage was done in east London at Victoria Park and Bow where about thirty-five were killed and 125 wounded, but two Zeppelins had been destroyed. This was followed two days later by a raid over wide areas of England with towns as separate as Portsmouth and Sheffield bombed, but London escaped on this occasion. At the beginning of October another raid by ten Zeppelins resulted in one being shot down at Oakmere farm, near Potters Bar, north of London, and in November the Germans lost another two Zeppelins during raids on Hartlepool and Lowestoft.

The balance of air power was now beginning to shift. The British Government had approved the development of aircraft capable of flying at a greater altitude and speed, and the introduction of incendiary and explosive bullets loaded with phosphorous, together with tracer fire, made the airships vulnerable to attack. Meanwhile the London gun defences had been reorganized and by the end of 1916 there were seven ground formations in and immediately around the capital. Searchlights formed the third link in London's anti-aircraft defences and were instructed to work on a specified system cooperating with one another. By the end of November raids by the airships of the German *Fliegerkorps* over mainland England had ceased, although the German Imperial Navy continued to operate airships until 1918, and only one further Zeppelin raid reached London in October 1917. The people of London were, however, only to enjoy a short respite before a new threat from the air began.

Air raids were not the only threat to England, and the War Office considered it necessary to prepare for the possibility of an invasion by the Germans. It was decided to construct a line of trenches around London. Implementation of this strategy had been under the command of Sir Leslie Rundle, Lloyd's old Divisional Commander in South Africa, but progress had been slow, and in the spring of 1916, Sir Francis Lloyd assumed responsibility. He visited many of the sites in Essex, Kent and Surrey and met the Position Commanders, mostly retired Generals. He quickly told them that the defences had not been taken seriously and that he intended to lay out a new line. A new impetus developed which was largely due to Lloyd's ability to win the support of the people carrying out the work, and the formation of the new London Volunteer regiments for home defence, who were under Lloyd's command and did much of the work. In Essex alone over 14,000 troops were involved in digging trenches.

The threat of an invasion was not taken lightly, and on 1 May, Lloyd saw all commanding officers including Lieutenant Colonels in the London District to discuss mobilisation in case of an attack on London. During one of his visits to military establishments around London in early 1916, Lloyd had commented on the importance to the country of the battle that was at that time raging around Verdun:

> In the Great War which is now proceeding, every individual must give up self absolutely and all must unite in one bond to make the war result a victory. Do you realise that a fight is now going on for a passage to Paris? The result will hang in the balance until the Teuton is driven back, as I have great confidence he will be.

But if once our ally's line is pierced the way will be open to the French capital, and if that capital is reached a new complexion will be put on the whole face of the war and on our lives and being. A German success on the French front would not merely mean the loss of Paris, but would endanger London.[102]

He went on to administer a rebuke to those Britons who, he said, had acquired the habit of faultfinding with and criticising the work of their leaders. 'You grumblers', said General Lloyd, 'are putting spokes in the wheels of the war's progress. The people must learn that it is necessary to carry discipline into every corner of private life and home life to turn the great struggle into victory'. Lloyd's comments about Verdun were made only four days after the battle began, when the Germans launched a nine-hour artillery bombardment firing over 1,000,000 shells (including poison gas). The battle was to last for ten months and resulted in more than a quarter of a million deaths, but the Germans failed in their objectives and were eventually forced back.

In between all this activity Sir Francis Lloyd continued his more usual role when he accompanied the King to Warley Barracks in Essex to inspect the Irish Guards on St Patrick's Day, and attended the opening of new YMCA huts in London. In April Lloyd was gazetted a Knight of the Order of St John of Jerusalem.

Sir Roger Casement, the Irish patriot who had sought the help of the Germans in obtaining Home Rule in Ireland, had been arrested in April and charged with treason, sabotage and espionage. He was brought over to London to face trial and held in the Tower of London. Francis Lloyd had overall responsibility for his safety as a prisoner in the Tower, where he was to be kept in close custody under the watch of the Welsh Guards. Casement was found guilty of treason at the Old Bailey on 29 June, and following an unsuccessful appeal, was hanged at Pentonville Prison on 3 August.

News of the Battle at Jutland reached London at the beginning of June 1916. Fourteen British and eleven German ships were sunk with great loss of life. Both sides claimed victory. The British had lost more ships and many more sailors, but the German plan of destroying Admiral Beatty's battlecruiser squadrons had also failed. Lloyd thought that it was anything but a defeat, rather a victory, but as a leading public figure in London he probably had to take this view. Five days later he was just leaving Horse Guards to go to lunch when news came in that Lord Kitchener had been drowned when the ship on which he was going to Russia – the *Hampshire* – struck a mine off the Orkneys. Lloyd George left the Ministry of Munitions and replaced Kitchener as Secretary of State for War.

Field Marshal Sir John French, who had been brought home from

France and given command of all British Home Forces, reviewed 9,900 troops of the Volunteer Training Corps in Hyde Park. The Parade went extremely well, and it was Sir Francis Lloyd who had first realized the working value of the volunteers and had put them to digging trenches. Lloyd was formally appointed C-in-C London Volunteers, as well as GOC London District. The appointment proved an exceedingly popular one, recognizing his organizing powers and the enthusiasm with which he infected all ranks. Lloyd was now over sixty-three years of age and his energy and vitality were remarkable.[103]

Francis Lloyd's brother, Harvey, who was a Lance Corporal in the 88th Battalion of the Canadian Expeditionary Force, came up on leave from Shorncliffe camp at Folkestone to stay with Francis and Mary at Great Cumberland Place. Harvey later received a commission in the Battalion. Following a visit to London by HRH The Crown Prince of Serbia, during which Sir Francis Lloyd was much involved in organizing the ceremonial aspects of the occasion, he was awarded the Grand Cross of the Order of St Saon (Serbia). He subsequently received a note from Buckingham Palace explaining the protocol for when a foreign Order could be worn.

In the women's movement, both the militant Women's Social and Political Union (WSPU), and the more moderate National Union of Women's Suffrage Societies (NUWSS) suspended their campaigns. Emmeline Pankhurst, the WSPU leader, joined Lloyd George in arguing for women to be able to participate on equal terms with men in armaments manufacture. In the City of London thousands of girls were earning their living in offices where they had taken the places of men called up for active service. It was officially stated that the number of women who had replaced men in various forms of civil employment throughout the country was 766,000, and this did not include the thousands of women employed at munitions factories.

On the second anniversary of Great Britain's declaration of war, in August 1916, meetings were held in many towns and cities at which resolutions were passed declaring a 'determination to continue to a victorious end the struggle in the maintenance of those ideals of liberty and justice which are the common and sacred cause of the Allies'. Three meetings were arranged in London and at one, held in the Albert Hall, Sir Francis Lloyd spoke to 4,000 wounded men from the London hospitals. The *Daily Mirror* reported the meeting:

> I never heard Sir Francis Lloyd speak with such fire as he did yesterday at this great demonstration. He surprised me very agreeably. The General is a fighting speaker, as well as a fighting man. He stirred his vast audience to a wonderful pitch of enthusiasm and when he put the resolution the cheers were as

deafening as ever heard even in the Albert Hall.

A week later, Sir Francis and Lady Lloyd were present at the opening by Princess Victoria of a new YMCA hut in Bloomsbury built on a site lent by the Shakespeare Memorial Committee behind the British Museum. The hut had cost £7,000 and included a splendid hall, a lounge, a billiard room, a large refreshment room, cubicle dormitories, silent rooms and a library. In his speech, with the Shakespeare link in mind, Sir Francis had rooted out Shakespeare's opinion of the enemy:

How lik'st then the young German?
At his best he is little worse than a man;
At his worst he is little better than a beast.[104]

Sir Francis Lloyd occasionally received letters from the Grenadier Battalion commanders at the front giving details of the actions in which his old regiment had been involved. One such letter described the Grenadiers' action in the Somme area in September when they took part in the attack towards Fler and the attack on Les Boeufs. The same month also brought news from the front that Mary Lloyd's nephew, Geoffrey Gunnis, a Captain in the Grenadiers, had been seriously wounded and taken to hospital in Rouen. His parents, Frankie and Ivy, travelled to Rouen, but Geoffrey died on 13 October. Sir Francis and Lady Lloyd were asked to break the news to the other two Gunnis sons, Rupert and Nigel, and Lady Lloyd collected Rupert from Eton to stay for a few days at Great Cumberland Place. With no children of their own, Sir Francis and Lady Lloyd were very close to their nephews, and Sir Francis had given Geoffrey one of his Grenadier swords. Geoffrey Gunnis was awarded the MC for his outstanding gallantry.

A notice in the *London Gazette* in October announced that Sir Francis Lloyd had been appointed a Deputy Lieutenant for Shropshire, and a month later he was nominated as a Lieutenant of the City of London. Domestically Sir Francis and Lady Lloyd still found it difficult to keep staff in London, and Martin the butler and a footman left Great Cumberland Place in November. A new valet came, but he too was dismissed a few months later for drunkenness!

A proposal was put forward that the Household Cavalry should also form an Infantry Battalion, and Sir Francis Lloyd visited the King at Windsor to discuss the suggestion. The King was in favour, and steps were immediately taken to find suitable recruits and a Battalion commander. In the latter respect there was some difference of opinion as to whether this should be an infantryman or an officer from the Household Cavalry.

The third Lord Mayor's Banquet of the war was held at Guildhall in

November. The reporter from *The Times* thought that the scene was almost as brilliant as ever. It was a picture of scarlet and gold, fair faces, jewels, rich evening costumes, set in a frame of khaki. In regard to food and drink, the Prime Minister (Asquith) had politely suggested 'a simple dinner in view of war conditions'. This was seen in the unostentatious bill of fare. It consisted of five lines:

Turtle Soup

Fillets of Soles

Removes

Barons of Beef

Sweets[105]

This was possibly slightly economical with the detail as 'Removes' included casserole of pheasant, tongue, and galantine of chicken. It is not recorded what Sir Francis Lloyd thought of the food, but he was impressed by the Prime Minister's 'fine speech', and disappointed by Balfour's, but rated Lord Reading's (Rufus Isaacs – the Lord Chief Justice) the best of all. In the following week the President of the Board of Trade announced that the Government had decided to appoint a Food Controller. Food was not yet scarce, but it was dear. Prices of essential commodities were seventy-five per cent higher than those of July 1914. An order for the regulation of meals came into force limiting luncheons in hotels, restaurants and clubs to two courses and dinners to three courses. Major General Lloyd met with managers of restaurants in London to discuss the maximum prices that officers in uniform should spend on food, and what became known in clubs as the 'Khaki Menu' was agreed:

Lunch	3s 6d
Tea	1s 6d
Dinner	5s 6d
Supper	3s 6d

Asquith announced in the House of Commons on 4 December that the King had approved the reconstruction of the government. However, Asquith's attempts at reconstruction failed and he resigned. The King first sent for Bonar Law, leader of the Unionists, but he intimated that he was unable to form a government. Lloyd George was then asked to form a government, which he agreed to undertake with the co-operation of Bonar Law. The coalition under Asquith was at an end, to be succeeded by another coalition government under Lloyd George. Bonar Law became

Chancellor of the Exchequer, and Sir Edward Carson was brought in as First Lord of the Admiralty. Lord Derby was promoted to Secretary of State for War, and Arthur Balfour succeeded Lord Grey as Secretary of State for Foreign Affairs.

In December 1916, Sir Francis Lloyd paid a second visit to wartime France. He crossed the Channel from Folkestone to Boulogne from where he was driven the eighty-five miles to Amiens. After spending the night at the Hotel de Rhin – his driver was not so lucky and had to sleep in the car – they motored a further twenty miles, in falling snow, to the Headquarters of the Guards Division. The staff were living in a deep dug-out, about thirty feet deep, which had been done by the French. It was lit by electric light and Lloyd thought 'very comfortable'. He described the scene around the HQ:

> Such is the desolation as the whole country is I have never seen. There is nothing but absolute mud, so deep that you cannot walk about – the only way being over duck-boards, of which they have many thousands. No buildings to be seen; trees all cut down by shell; no woods, no houses, no villages, no anything. The site of Guillemont is merely a site, nothing there at all.

On the next day, Major General Fielding, the Divisional Commander, and Lloyd motored over to Lord Cavan's Corps Headquarters. Here he heard about the German Emperor's peace proposal for the Christmas period, but Cavan had ordered no fraternising as he felt sure the Germans would try it on. The Corps headquarters had very comfortable huts, warmed by stoves and lit by electric light. They had been built by Cavan because he was so ill, as were many of the staff. Lloyd next visited the Rest Camp at Maltzhorn, where the two Battalions who had recently come out of the trenches were the 2nd Battalion Scots Guards and 2nd Battalion Irish Guards. He thought that the men looked wearied out, although their spirit was all right. The camp was a miserable place, built on nothing but mud.

Fielding and Sir Francis Lloyd got back into their car and went on down to Headquarters of the 4th Battalion, Grenadiers, where Lloyd met Gilbert Hamilton in a deep dug-out. They left the car there as it was not safe to take it any further.

> We walked on into Combles which is continually under shell fire. There are a few remnants of houses standing and the place was full of heavy guns and others. We went down into the ancient catacombs, where I found an advanced dressing station and a whole lot of men quartered, also Lord Henry Seymour's Brigade Headquarters. He came in with Pereira. After a few minutes we tried to get out to the front trenches. We stayed there some little time and

then walked back, got to the car, motored over the dangerous places and went to Charles Corkran's Headquarters where we had Luncheon, and then home where I found Moss (my servant) packed up.[107]

Although the whole country was a sea of mud and desolation, Lloyd was slightly surprised at the enormous amount of traffic on the roads. It was carefully managed under the continuous shelling. Sir Francis Lloyd returned to Horse Guards a little over a week after he had left London for the front. A few days later he was the chief guest at the annual dinner of the United Wards Club of the City of London. In his speech he made reference to his recent visit to France. In telling members of the conditions under which the British Army was fighting, he recounted a story told to him of a Grenadier who for thirty-six hours had been up to his shoulders in mud: When rescued from the 'Slough of Despond' he said to his Captain, 'Thank you, sir, for the soup that was given me when I was there'.

The morning of Christmas Day was spent in the office at Horse Guards, and in the afternoon Sir Francis and Lady Lloyd visited the Masonic Hospital, where they talked to patients, and the Red Cross Hospital in Finsbury Square, before going on to the Salvation Army Hostel in the Strand and to two YMCA huts. Thick fog developed over the next two days and Joey Gunnis got a nasty cut between the eyes when he was assaulted near the Tube. This led Lloyd to suggest that Assistant Provost Marshals (Military Police) should be accompanied on their patrols in London.

Late in the afternoon of Friday 19 January 1917, the GOC London District was working in his office at Horse Guards when he heard a tremendous explosion. He had received no warning of an air raid but went outside expecting to see smoke rising from bombs dropped near the City. A pall of smoke could be seen to the east which he soon heard was from an explosion in Brunner Mond's chemical factory at Silvertown, where a fire in the melt-pot room had caused about fifty tons of TNT to explode and turned the rest of the factory into a bomb. Whole streets were destroyed in the explosion, over seventy people died, and four hundred were injured. When the full devastation of the explosion soon became known, Lloyd sent 240 men from the Guards Battalion at the Tower to Silvertown to keep order and prevent looting.

At the beginning of the year, a list of promotions in the Army had been published, but Lloyd's name was not included. He went to see Sir John French and expressed to him his disappointment. A few weeks later he received a letter from Lord Derby, the Secretary of State for War, with whom he was on close terms:

Dear Frankie,

> I am pleased to say that I have been able, with the full concurrence of CIGS and the Selection Board, to submit your name to His Majesty for promotion to Lieutenant General, which shall be antedated so as to put you in your same relative position with regard to those who have been recently promoted.
>
> I cannot tell you what pleasure it is to me to be able to congratulate my old friend on his well deserved promotion.

Yours ever,

[signed] Derby

It can only be speculated whether Lloyd's omission from the original list was an oversight, or that his 'enemies' in the War Office had some hand in it. The promotion was gazetted on 29 January, and reported by one newspaper on the next day under the heading 'General Satisfaction':

> The promotion of Sir Francis Lloyd from Major General to Lieutenant General will cause wide satisfaction. 'Frankie' Lloyd as he is known among officers connected with the London Command, is a very popular person. He wears a pretty collection of medal ribbons, and his uniforms are the neatest and nattiest I have ever seen. What is more important, he is a deuced fine soldier. Once, in the long ago, Lord Derby was one of his subalterns.

The *Daily Express* published a more lengthy article[108] about Lloyd and his career, which he considered 'ridiculous and flattering', but much of the article represented a true reflection of his standing in London and the amount of work he got through:

MAN WHO RUNS LONDON

THE MULTIFARIOUS ACTIVITIES OF SIR FRANCIS LLOYD

A 'BOSS' INDEED

During the past year or so the public have frequently read a newspaper paragraph announcing that Sir Francis Lloyd has opened another YMCA hut, or another hostel for officers, or another railway station buffet, or has made a speech on some occasion.

The man in the street has come to think of him as a kind of opener-general to London, who motors about pulling strings here and there and declaring something well and truly opened. If the man in the street spent a day or half a day at the Horse Guards, where Sir Francis Lloyd, who has just been promoted Lieutenant General, has his office, he would realize that the commander of the

London District is one of the hardest working soldiers in the land. He would find the landing and stairs outside his room filled with military and civilian people seeking interviews, and officers of the staff continually going in and out with some order or paper requiring signature.

Outside he would find a military car waiting to whirl the 'competent military authority' of London to some point inside the defences of London requiring his attention. The few remaining hotel proprietors and club committees in London may regard it as a sign of grace that Lieutenant General Sir Francis Lloyd has not commandeered a new headquarters for his large business. If he were a civilian he would by this time probably have seized at least two hotels and a club; his commandeering powers are limited by his sense of what is required 'for securing the public safety and defence of the realm'.

The article continued by describing the wide ranging powers given to the GOC London District: 'There is not a tree, nor a hedge, nor a fence which he may not order to be removed. He may not only take possession of any building in London, but may direct its destruction, if military exigencies require it. He may stop any road, or order the removal of all or any foodstuffs, vehicles, boats, live stock, transport animals, fuel, tools, or implements, from any part of London'. As an exercise in 'hagiography' it could not have been bettered, but at least it gave the public some idea of the problems facing the war-time commander of the London metropolis.

An edited version of the article appeared in another newspaper, but included the story of an American friend visiting the newspaper correspondent in London. On one occasion they were walking along Whitehall when a smart motor car turned into Horse Guards. The sentries at the gate saluted with more than ordinary precision. In a moment the car stopped, and a well-set military officer, replete with scarlet and gold, stepped out and disappeared into the building. 'Some officer that ', commented the American friend. 'He is the man who runs London', replied the correspondent. In concluding the article, the correspondent added that 'Go wherever you may, you will find few more popular men in London and other military circles than General Sir Francis Lloyd. He has always played the game, and expects others to do the same. That is why he has such great numbers of friends and only a few insignificant enemies'.

It was, however, these 'insignificant' enemies who in the spring of 1917 became vociferous in a few newspapers in complaining about some of the orders issued by the GOC London District under the Defence of the Realm Acts (DORA). The sources of the complaints probably came from young officers who felt that an unreasonable kerb had been imposed on their ability to enjoy themselves when in London. 'John Bull', in one newspaper, criticised Lloyd for being too hard on soldiers in London: 'Try to be less of the heavy father and more of the tolerant and kindly chief'. The *Sunday Chronicle*, in an article by Edgar Wallace, criticised the order that officers must always wear uniform, that no supper could be taken after 10.00 pm, that there was to be no dancing, and that Ciro's, a favourite club in the West End, had been put out of bounds. However, the article was written with a degree of 'tongue-in-cheek'.

We have seen that Sir Francis Lloyd had an interest in using the premises of the Automobile Club from an early stage in the war. After much discussion and delay it was decided to use them as a club and hotel where overseas officers could stay. It was given the name, the Royal Overseas Officers Club (the King had earlier become Patron of the Royal Automobile Club) and was opened by the Duke of Connaught in March 1917. Lloyd's brother-in-law, Ronnie Gunnis, became the Club Secretary.

Throughout the war Sir Francis Lloyd paid visits to hospitals in and around London where soldiers wounded in the conflict were sent to recover, and on some of these visits he presented medals awarded for gallantry. One such occasion was in February 1917 when he visited the 3rd London General Hospital at Wandsworth, where he decorated two Newfoundlanders with the Military Medal. Lloyd took the opportunity to comment on the progress of the war:

> We have come more than ever to pull ourselves together to end this struggle, and to end it as quickly as we possibly can. The sacrifices that have been made will continue in an ascending scale, and will have to be greater in the future. The German has proved himself beyond the pale of humanity, and today has gone further than he has ever done before.
>
> We must make it an absolute certainty that never again can the German put himself up against the world of civilization and try to inflict a brutal militarism on peoples all over the globe. I think that if we band ourselves together and cooperate as we are doing, and as things are shaping now, a period must come to the war, and the loss of life and terrible wounds will be put to an end in a glorious triumph over an enemy whose reign has been beneath contempt.[109]

General Smuts arrived in London in March, leading the South African delegation to the Imperial War Conference, and was met at Paddington station by Sir Francis Lloyd. He was able to tell the British Government that the campaign in German East Africa was virtually over. Two events of international consequence to the ending of the war occurred in early 1917. The 'February Revolution' in Russia would bring the Central Powers victory in the east; and America's intervention in April would ultimately see the Germans defeated in the west.

President Woodrow Wilson's decision to reconvene Congress early led to America declaring war against Germany on 6 April 1917, which was as welcome to the British as it was sudden. Two weeks after the announcement a dedicatory service was held at St Paul's Cathedral in the presence of the King and Queen, and Sir Francis Lloyd was in the large congregation. The sermon, preached by the American Bishop of the Philippine Islands, Dr Charles H Brent, included the following declaration:

There was a time when men called war a rough game, to be played by set rules, but our adversaries have proven to us that this was a delusion. War is not a game. War is a wild beast that cannot be tamed by conferences and conventions. And the one thing to do with war is to hunt it to its death, and please God, by this war we shall achieve our purpose.

General Pershing and his American Forces Headquarters Staff arrived at Liverpool in June and travelled to London where they were met by Sir Francis Lloyd.

A month earlier the bands of the Scots, Irish and Welsh Guards, and part of the Grenadiers Band left London for a week's visit to France, and Lloyd joined them. After playing at a concert in Paris, the 250 bandsmen visited the city of Rheims, and the towns of Epernay, Crayonne and Verdun, where they were greeted by large crowds, and the morale boosting exercise was judged a success. On his return to London, Sir Francis Lloyd was summoned to see the King at Buckingham Palace, where they discussed the future of the Brigade of Guards after the war, and it was suggested that the Brigade should include two Battalions of Irish Guards and one Battalion of Welsh Guards. The issue was to be raised again three years later when a proposal was put forward to do away with the separate identities of both Regiments. At a parade in Hyde Park shortly after this meeting, the King presented decorations to many soldiers, including seven VCs.

The food problem was becoming a major issue, not only the high prices, but now scarcities, due in part to the German submarine blockade and the loss of merchant shipping bringing valuable imports of grain to the UK. A new Public Meals Order required hotels, restaurants, clubs and boarding houses to have one meatless day a week and five potato-less days. Everyone in his own house, although under no compulsion, was encouraged voluntarily to adopt the same restrictions. Economy in bread consumption was absolutely essential due to the shortage of imports of wheat. Under an order issued by the London District command, soldiers were not allowed to buy any food outside of their barracks and had to depend exclusively on army rations unless they obtained a special pass.

In April news reached Sir Francis Lloyd of the death of another of his nephews, David Holbech, a 2nd Lieutenant in the King's Royal Rifle Corps, and a son of his sister Ada. He was killed in action when shot by a sniper while on duty in the front line trenches.[110]

The Gotha Bombers

In the summer of 1917, the Germans launched a major air campaign against the British mainland. Until then, airships and a lone aircraft had been used in the attacks, but now there was a change of tack, and a squadron of purpose-built heavy bombers, called Gothas, with wingspans of seventy-five feet and a fuselage with a width of forty-one feet were developed. The original target of the first attack in May was London, but thick cloud could be seen over the capital as the squadron flew up the Thames, and the attack was switched to Folkestone where severe damage was done, with ninety-seven people killed and 195 injured. Further attacks in daylight took place on other Kent and Essex coastal towns and in the Thames estuary, but it was not until 13 June that the Gothas reached London.

At nine o'clock on the Wednesday morning of the raid, twenty-two Gothas left their two airfields in Belgium with the objective of attacking London. Two aircraft shortly returned to their bases with engine trouble, and on reaching the English coast three left the main group to attack Margate and Shoeburyness as a diversionary tactic. A fourth Gotha temporarily left the group to reconnoitre the Thames estuary before rejoining the remaining sixteen aircraft as they headed for London. By 10.30 am the Gothas were flying along the north bank of the Thames, unchallenged by any British aircraft. On the morning of the air raid Sir Francis Lloyd had gone down to Liverpool Street Station, and soon after his arrival he was forewarned of the approaching aeroplanes. He immediately returned to Horse Guards and was met by the information that aircraft action had been ordered.

The first bombs were dropped by the Gothas at Barking and East Ham, killing four people. By now the anti-aircraft defences of London had opened up, but with little effect on the Gothas flying at 12,000 feet. At eleven o'clock three Home Defence Squadrons were scrambled and thirty-five aircraft took to the air, but although the enemy aircraft were engaged it was to little effect. A prime target was Liverpool Street Station, which was reached at 11.40 am and in two minutes was bombarded by seventy-two bombs. The attackers then split into two flights, with one group targeting railways north of the river, and the other going to attack the docks south of the river. The latter group then re-crossed the river to join the rest of the formation and unloaded the remainder of their bombs on Poplar, where the worst incident of the raid occurred. The Upper North Street School in East India Dock Road had a roll of 600, and eighteen young children were killed and many injured when bombs destroyed the building. Later in the afternoon, Lloyd went back to Liverpool Street and saw the havoc that the bombs had caused.

The Gothas also attacked other towns in Essex and Kent during the raid, and the total casualties were 162 killed and 432 injured. Shock at the attack was soon replaced by outrage with demands for an early warning system to be introduced, and local anti-German feeling resulted in property owned by people with German names being attacked. The War Cabinet met the day after the raid and set up a committee, under General Jan Smuts, to plan a long-term strategy for improving the defences of London against air attack, but rejected calls for an early warning system and reprisals. On 20 June Sir Francis Lloyd attended the funeral of sixteen of the young children killed at Poplar:

> We went down to Poplar to the Town Hall, where a procession formed and we went to the Parish Church of Poplar. The sixteen coffins [two children were buried in private graves] of the little school children (victims of the air raid) were arranged in the Chancel of the Church just in front of us. The Bishop of London preached, and the whole thing was exceedingly affecting. There was an enormous crowd. I followed the Procession to the [East London] Cemetery, which was a considerable distance, and then returned to the Horse Guards, getting there at four o'clock. It was a most affecting sight.[111]

The next attack on London came on a Saturday morning three weeks later, when most of the bombs fell in the City and East End, with the Central Telegraph Office in St Martin's-le-Grand badly damaged. On this occasion fifty-seven people were killed and 141 injured. Sir Francis Lloyd visited the City to see for himself the damage caused by the attack. The business of the House of Commons was preoccupied with the air raids and it was felt that the raids were a blow to national pride. The House went into secret session to consider the weaknesses of the defences of London. The Government changed its mind before the end of July, agreeing to a primitive early warning system of mortars firing 'sound bombs' and policemen blowing their whistles as they walked around the streets during an impending raid with a placard hung from their neck telling people to 'take cover'. Winston Churchill also thought that there should be 'a perfectly clear guidance by the Government and the authorities that when an air raid takes place it is the duty of every person to seek such accommodation in the lower parts of those buildings as is convenient'.[112]

At the end of the month the Government established the London Air Defence Area (LADA) under the command of Brigadier General Edward Ashmore, who set to work coordinating the work of the observation and listening posts, anti-aircraft batteries and Home Defence squadrons. He set up an operations room in Horse Guards equipped with a giant map table lit from below and divided into numbered squares from which the position of hostile aircraft could be quickly identified.

There was now a brief interlude before the next series of air raids reached London, during which Lloyd continued to visit the defences around the capital. He and Field Marshal Lord French, the C-in-C of Home Land Forces, were still concerned about the real threat as they saw it of an invasion, and General Lloyd referred to this in a speech at an Old English Fair in Brunswick Park, Camberwell:

> The theory is that the enemy, realising at length the futility of their plan to starve out this country by indiscriminate destruction of shipping, and realising also that there is no real prospect of achieving decisive military success, will be driven to make a desperate dash to land troops on our shores.

Some sections of the Press criticised Lloyd for expressing these views in public, presumably they thought to the alarm of the population.

September saw a resumption of the air raids on London. The Germans had been using the previous two months to practice night time bombing and were now ready to implement their new tactics. A fine clear night was forecast for 4 September and eleven Gothas left their base at ten o'clock with London their target. Bombs fell on Barking, West Ham and Stratford, to the east of London, and most damage was done in central London along the Embankment, where Cleopatra's Needle was struck by shrapnel, and in the Strand. Lloyd wrote that the attack had caused little damage, but this was only relative to some of the earlier attacks, and a further five raids at the end of the month, with the benefit to the raiders of a Harvest Moon, was beginning to shatter the nerves of the tired residents of the metropolis. The Germans had also developed a new incendiary bomb as part of their plan to engulf London in firestorms. In the last of these attacks, on 1 October, it appeared that the objective of the raiders was Victoria railway station. The station escaped but considerable damage was done to houses in Grosvenor Road (Place), close to Buckingham Palace. One bomb dropped in the Serpentine in Hyde Park, killing fish, and the Royal Academy in Piccadilly was slightly damaged by a bomb.[113]

Sir Francis Lloyd wrote to the Bishop of London and asked him to issue an order that when an aircraft warning was given, all the churches in London would be opened for the admission of those who wished to take shelter in the crypt: 'I am sure that it will be a boon, especially in the east of London', he added. The Bishop replied, welcoming the suggestion.

At a meeting at Poplar Town Hall attended by between 600 to 700 people, Lloyd spoke about the measures to be taken to protect London against air raids:

> Referring to the recent aeroplane raids by night, Sir Francis said that we suffered nothing from them in comparison with the daylight raid of one Saturday morning.
>
> In the air defence of London they had the assistance of one of the ablest engineers, who for many months past had exercised his brain in trying the best that could be done with the materials at his disposal to defeat the invaders. The engineer he had referred to directed the barrage which went up – it was not quite clear how high, but as high as the enemy aeroplanes could go.
>
> 'I was in my office for the whole of the last raids,' Sir Francis Lloyd added, 'and when the enemy attacks came on, up went the barrage, and they were prevented from coming into the interior of London in force. They did not all get turned'. We were going to have more men, more machines, and more ammunition. People should remember when air raids were on that the terrible barrage put up was their very best friend.
>
> Urging the necessity of shelter, Sir Francis said: 'Do not do what I am afraid I did – go and look out to see what is going on. Something has been said about the dangers of the Tubes. My advice is to go down into the Tubes. We are doing our very best to increase our powers of defence by more guns and more lights, which are very essential in attacking aeroplanes. We have no experience yet of the enemy coming on dark nights.'[114]

The effectiveness of the early warning system was put into doubt in the middle of October when two bombs were dropped by a lone German Zeppelin – one in Piccadilly, near the Circus, and the other at Camberwell Green. The correspondent of *The Times* heard no warning and questioned whether one had been given. The crater in Piccadilly Circus was ten feet in diameter and nine feet deep, and the windows of surrounding shops and buildings broken. Nine people were killed and about fifteen others were injured. At Camberwell ten people were killed, including five women and two children. It was said to be one of the largest bombs that had yet been used in the attacks on London, and many houses were demolished and about one thousand people left homeless.

Sir Francis Lloyd attended an investiture at Buckingham Palace when the King decorated nine soldiers with the VC, and Lloyd was gazetted a Grand Officer of the Crown of Belgium. A month later he received the Order of the White Eagle of Russia from the Military Attaché at the Russian Embassy.

The success of the free buffets at the principal railway stations was not without problems. No financial assistance was provided by the Government, the running of the buffets having to rely on voluntary contributions. The cost was not inconsiderable, particularly at Victoria where the number of customers had risen to 42,000 a week. In October, Lloyd wrote to the newspapers indicating that the free buffet at Victoria might have to close, and appealed for substantial donations. Subscriptions quickly reached £3,000, but the *Evening News* took up the appeal and within three weeks was able to hand over a cheque for £15,309. At the end of October donations had reached a total of £26,320, far more than had either been hoped for or needed.

With heavy losses on the Western Front in 1916, the British Army became concerned by its reduced number of fighting soldiers. After talks with the government it was decided to use women to replace men doing certain administrative jobs in Britain and France. In January 1917, the government announced the establishment of a new voluntary service, the Women's Auxiliary Army Corps (WAAC). The plan was for these women to serve as clerks, telephonists, waitresses, cooks and as instructors in the use of gas masks. They would serve both at home and in France.

By November there were 9,600 women employed and the venture was growing rapidly. General Lloyd attended the opening of a new recruiting hut for the WAAC in Trafalgar Square where he reported that the WAAC in the London District had been an enormous success: 'wherever the women cooks were employed, there was cleanliness where there had been dirt, good cooking where there had been indifferent, and economy where there had been waste'.[115] Again one section of the Press was critical of his speech, commenting that he 'should not have allowed a momentary enthusiasm to get the better of his discretion. On the acceptability of the WAAC for efficient mess and canteen service there can be no difference of opinion'. By the time of the Armistice over 57,000 women had served in the WAAC.

The VADs (Voluntary Aid Detachments) was also one of the first bodies to provide an outlet for the patriotism and devotion of women as Red Cross nurses for the military hospitals at home and abroad. Sir Francis Lloyd gave his full support to the VADs and distributed London District Badges to many of the nurses when he visited the military hospitals in the metropolis. Significantly, Parliament recognized the services of women to the state in March 1917, by approving by 341 votes to 62, womens' suffrage, which was to be included in a scheme of electoral reform to come into operation at the end of the war.

Lloyd was at Guildhall in November for the annual Lord Mayor's banquet. However Prime Minister Lloyd George was absent on a visit to Italy, and Bonar Law represented him at the dinner. The depressing close of Bonar Law's speech was characteristic of this leading spokesman of the 'Die-Hards':

> I cannot hold out any hope of an early end of this war. I see no prospect of it. There is only one way to peace – the way over the hard and rugged road through which you have to pass to victory. That is the only way to peace. It is a question now of nerve and staying power. I have faith in the character of our people; I have faith in the justice of our cause.

In Sir Francis Lloyd's view all the speeches were good except for Lord Curzon (Leader of the House of Lords) who he thought was very pompous – F E Smith (Attorney General who later became Lord Birkenhead) was amusing. The food was well down (on the previous year) which must have pleased him.

One exception from Bonar Law's prediction occurred towards the end of November with the news of a great victory on the Western Front. The victory was the success of the Third Army under General Sir Julian Byng in breaking through the Hindenburg Line to a length of ten miles and a depth of four or five near Cambrai. The bells of the churches in London rang out in popular rejoicing for the first time since the outbreak of war. Two days later Lloyd accompanied Field Marshal Lord French on an inspection of Volunteer Regiments south of London at Shoreham. A blinding snow storm came on and continued throughout the day. Hopes of a change in the progress of the war were dashed three weeks later with the news that most of the ground gained near Cambrai had been lost, with thousands killed or wounded and thousands more taken prisoner.

The prominence of Sir Francis Lloyd as a public figure in London was acknowledged by the War Office when they authorized the drawing of a caricature of him. This was probably the drawing by L H Sacré which appeared in some newspapers and was also included in *Sidelights*, a series of caricature portraits by Sacré published by Constable in 1918. Lloyd notes in his diary that he had seen the caricature but made no comment on the likeness.

In December 1917, Sir Francis and Lady Lloyd opened their house in Great Cumberland Place for a Yuletide sale in aid of the St Nicholas Home for Children suffering from raid shock. The charity was connected with the

Chailey Heritage Cripple Schools in Sussex. After a five week hiatus in air raids due to bad weather, twenty-five Gothas attacked England on 6 December, but few of the planes unloaded their payload on London and little damage was done.

Lloyd paid a short visit to his house at Aston in mid-December, and on his return attended a dinner at Grays Inn where Lloyd George made 'the finest speech I have heard and F. E. Smith spoke with great force'. However, even if the politicians were making fine speeches, the scarcity of food was increasing, with tea, sugar, butter, margarine and bacon all difficult to get. On an average fourteen ships bringing food and raw materials were being sunk each week by enemy submarines.[116]

On 18 December another air raid took place in intense cold weather one evening while Parliament was sitting. On the advice of the military authorities the sitting was suspended, much to the annoyance of some Members who raised an angry shout of 'No! No!' and it was nearly two hours before the sitting was resumed. Fifteen Gothas and one of the new Giant R-planes took part in the raid which, in terms of the financial cost of bomb damage, was the most successful of the entire campaign. Incendiaries fell in the gardens of Buckingham Palace and a 300kg projectile, the heaviest bomb dropped during the campaign so far, exploded in Lyall Street, near Eaton Square. The raid resulted in ten people killed, seventy injured and severe damage to buildings. The raiders, however, also suffered severe losses with one Gotha shot down by a British fighter, two burning out after crash-landing and catching fire, two others suffering major damage after forced landings in open fields, and another two crashing while trying to land on their home airfields.

Sir Francis Lloyd's term as GOC London District was due to end in September 1917, but in May of that year it had been extended until the end of the year. It was announced before Christmas that a further extension until the end of March 1918 had been agreed. Lloyd met Lord Derby, Secretary of State for War, at the Carlton on New Year's Eve:

> I thanked him for giving me an extension of three months. He told me that I should stay there as long as he was there, which is a good augury for my being kept on till the end of the war.

There had also been discussion for some months on the London District Command Staff moving out of Horse Guards to provide more room for the War Office. Lloyd had looked at offices in Carlton House Terrace, and on 21 December he moved the Command to No.s 11, 12, 13, & 23 Carlton House Terrace, which was to be called in future the Horse Guards Annex. A fresh body called GHQ Great Britain was created there, between him and the War Office, chiefly in order to settle the problem of unemployment in high places. Meanwhile the Headquarters of the Eastern Command, another autonomous department, were situated in Pall Mall, almost opposite the Guards Club. Among all these the feeling ran high that the regulations enforced by the GOC London District should not be considered to bind themselves: and this unreasonable but very natural antipathy was a constant obstacle in the way of Sir Francis and his staff.[117]

In the New Year, the Press reported the extension to Lloyd's term of office, with one newspaper commenting:

> There is considerable satisfaction at the news that General Sir Francis Lloyd's period in command of the London District is to be extended to March 31st. General Lloyd has had a very difficult task to perform during the war, and he has shown the greatest tact and intelligence in carrying it out.
>
> A less sympathetic man in the peculiar position of military chief of the capital in war time might have come frequently into collision with the civil authorities and the public, but Sir Francis has all along shown full appreciation of the claims of the public, and where he has had to interfere or to restrict, he has done so with as much consideration as possible.
>
> The good order that has been kept in the Metropolis through the long period of recruiting and movement of troops is very largely due to the sensible handling of the problems which have confronted him.
>
> So far as the public authorities are concerned, there would, I think, be satisfaction if Sir Francis could be continued in his post not only for three months, but to the end of the war. The relations which have been established with him are on such a basis of complete understanding that it would be a pity to disturb them until the urgent necessities of the time are past.

On Christmas Eve, Lloyd had received a letter from the War Office informing him that the Household Battalion (the infantry battalion made up from the Household Cavalry Regiments) was to be done away with, and that officers and NCOs were to be relegated to their original Corps and the men to the Brigade of Guards. In the New Year Sir Francis Lloyd, together with Generals Johnston and Ruthven, went down to Windsor to inspect the Battalion and to tell them of the decision:

> I inspected the Household Battalion at 11 o'clock and after they had marched past in slow and quick time, told them that they were disbanded.
>
> I read the conditions of transfer and then spoke to them, saying how sorry I was etc. I finally read the King's message – which ran as follows:

117

'Colonel Portal, Officers, Non-Commissioned Officers and Men of the Household Battalion –

It is with feelings of sympathy and regret that I communicate this farewell Order.

Military policy, however, demands the absorption of the Household Battalion into other Units of my Army.

Though the career of the Battalion has been short, the gallant conduct of all ranks on the field of battle has earned for it an honoured name among Infantry Regiments.

As your Colonel-in-Chief, I have followed with pride and admiration your doings at the front.

I know what you have suffered and Superior Commanders have testified to the splendid services rendered by Officers and men.

You can rest assured that as an Infantry Battalion formed from the First and Second Life Guards and the Royal Horse Guards, you have added yet another chapter to the grand traditions of my Household Cavalry.

GEORGE R.I.

Three cheers for the King, and our being photographed completed the business. I was back to London a little before one o'clock.[118]

The first air raid of 1918 had been planned by the Germans for the time of the next full moon but had to be delayed by three days due to fog. However, on 28 January thirteen Gothas and one Giant R-plane took off from their base in Belgium. Mist began to develop and six returned to base. The remaining aircraft reached London at about nine o'clock and unloaded their bombs over a wide area in one of the most prolonged attacks on the capital. Lloyd recorded that forty-seven people were killed and 169 injured. A large number of the killed and injured had taken refuge in the printing-works of Odhams, in Long Acre, where a bomb had exploded right in the heart of the works, bringing down the roof, ceilings, and machinery on the unfortunate people in the basement. One Gotha had been shot down and another four sustained serious damage in crash landing on their return to their home airfield. On top of the losses at the end of the previous year, this led to a temporary suspension of attacks on England until the German squadron could be reorganized.

A few days after the raid Lloyd managed to escape from all the carnage for a few hours when he visited the Coliseum to see George Robey give a matinee in aid of the Waterloo free buffet – £4,000 was raised. More air raids by R-planes followed in February, with three in succession in the third week of the month, and people taking refuge whenever possible on the platforms at the Tube stations. Five bombs fell around St Pancras Station, severely damaging the Midland Grand Hotel, and twenty-one people were killed.

Further changes to the deployment of forces at the front were contemplated. As these concerned the Foot Guards and Household Cavalry, Lloyd was sent to see the King to discuss the proposals, which were contained in a secret memorandum:

1. It has been proposed to dismount the three Regiments of Household Cavalry in France, and to convert them into three Guards Machine Gun Battalions, with an establishment of 46 Officers and 887 Other Ranks per Battalion, and to make up the deficit in these three Battalions by drafts from the Guards Machine Gun Centre, and re-inforcements in the future to be furnished from the same sources.

   The three Reserve Regiments of Household Cavalry will become the three Regiments of Household Cavalry and be put on the old peace establishment (27 Officers and 406 Other Ranks). Half the men in these Regiments will be 'B' men.

   The Headquarters of the three Regiments in France will be by degree brought home and become the Headquarters of these three Regiments at home and take their names.

   Any surplus men of category 'A' of the Reserve Regiments of Household Cavalry will be transferred to the Guards Machine Gun Corps.

2. It is further proposed to constitute a new 'Corps' entitled Machine Gun Guards (His Majesty approves of the whole of the above, except that the name is to be 'VI' or Machine Gun Regiment of Foot Guards', to be called 'Machine Gun Guards' for short). This Corps to be an additional Regiment to the existing five Regiments of Foot Guards. The Corps would have its own Regimental Headquarters with Record Office, and will consist of:

   a) Four Battalions in the Field

   b) One reserve Battalion at home.

The approximate strength of the Regiment would be 250 Officers and 4,500 Other Ranks.

The steps necessary to give effect to this proposal would be similar to those which were adopted on the formation of the Welsh Guards.[119]

Later on the same day Lloyd attended a conference with General

Ruthven and all commanding officers of the Household Cavalry both abroad and at home. The Secretary of State for War (Lord Derby) who was in the Chair explained the proposals contained in the memorandum. Lloyd was very adverse to the three Battalions made from the Household Cavalry at the front continuing to represent them, as he feared that it would lead to difficulties in the future. He was, however, overruled, and it was decided that they should remain under their existing names.

Compulsory rationing of certain foods was finally introduced at the beginning of March. This applied to London and the Home Counties, covering an estimated population of 10,000,000. Each household was provided with two cards: a 'meat card' for butcher's meat and bacon; and a 'food card' for butter or margarine. The weekly allowances for each person were 15 oz of beef, mutton, lamb or pork; 5 oz of bacon; and 4 oz of butter or margarine. The allowances were only obtainable from the butcher or grocer with whom each person was registered. Each meat card had detachable coupons, and the food card had numbered squares that were cancelled when each weekly allowance was purchased. The rationing system seemed to work and queues practically disappeared.

Coal was the next commodity on which action was required in order to conserve supplies, and in the same month that food rationing was introduced in London, a 'Curfew Order' was announced:

No lights shall be used for the purpose of illuminating shop windows.

No food is to be cooked or hot meals served in any hotel, club, inn, restaurant or boarding-house between 9.30 at night and 5 in the morning.

All lights in the dining-rooms of these places must be put out at 10 at night.

No performances in theatres, music-halls, cinemas or other places of amusement shall be continued after 10.30 at night.

The object of the order was the saving of coal, and a warning was issued that unless large stocks of coal were accumulated by economy during the spring and summer, there would be insufficient supplies to last through the winter.

More air raids followed in the first half of March and in a raid at the end of the first week three Giant R-planes reached London and released a 1,000kg bomb. This monster was probably aimed at Paddington Station but instead struck Warrington Crescent in Maida Vale, demolishing a row of five-storied houses and damaging another 140 houses in the neighbourhood. However, in the third week of March strategic bombing raids on England were suspended, and all available German aircraft were redeployed as part of the new German offensive on the Western Front.

The bombardment for the offensive, codenamed 'Michael', began at 4.40 am on 21 March 1918, and continued through seven successive phases until zero hour at 9.40 am. To a British machine-gunner 'It seemed as though the bowels of the earth had erupted, while beyond the ridge there was one long and continuous yellow flash'.[120] *The Times* described it as 'The greatest and most critical battle of the war'. Germany having concluded a peace with the Bolsheviks, now in control of Russia, was relieved of the task of waging war on the Eastern front, and could concentrate on the Western. Hundreds of thousands of men were rushed from their training camps and around London to the front to provide reinforcements.

The Germans initially achieved major successes, retaking many of the Allied gains over the previous three years. Paris was shelled from a distance of about seventy-five miles. Matters looked very serious, but Field Marshal Lord French told Lloyd that the line should be held although undoubtedly the Allies had lost a lot of ground. Lord Derby reported that the Guards Division had been deeply involved in the fighting but the Germans had 'never dented their line at all'.

At the end of March, Lloyd's term as GOC London District was again extended by a further three months. On 1 April, he was summoned to Buckingham Palace to see the King's Private Secretary, Lord Stamfordham, when he was told in no uncertain terms of the displeasure of the King who had heard that Lord Drogheda held a dance on Easter Eve, at a time when British soldiers were fighting a desperate battle on the Western Front. Stamfordham put the complaint in writing to Lloyd on the next day:

> Dear Lloyd,
>
> The King says certainly you may say that he heard but could not believe that a dance had taken place on Easter Eve and during one of the biggest and fiercest battles that the world has ever seen; His Majesty does not know if the report be true: but he is certain had anyone experienced what he did on Thursday, Friday & Saturday among our splendid troops they would have not been dancing on Saturday night – you are at liberty to say that the King does not understand people dancing when our troops are fighting & dying for us who are at home.
>
> Yours very truly
>
> Stamfordham

A meeting was quickly arranged between Sir Francis Lloyd and Lord Drogheda, at which the offender claimed that the 'dance' was in fact a large dinner party of twenty people, and some men came in to dance afterwards, but he did not deny that there was a band. Lloyd next called a meeting of the five Lieutenant Colonels commanding Regiments of the Foot Guards and Officers commanding the Regiments of the Household Cavalry, and read them the 'King's' letter. Dances were definitely off-limits.

The administrative burden of 'running' London had increased enormously as the war progressed and Lloyd had made some proposals to the War Office for additional support. He received a favourable response in April when he was told that a Brigadier-General was to be put in charge of administration and that there would also be an Assistant Adjutant General and Assistant Quarter Master General.

News from the front was not good, with the Germans pressing at the Messines Ridge where the fighting was desperate. The Military Service Act was further amended to provide that: 'every man between the age of eighteen years and less than fifty-one shall be deemed to have been duly enlisted in His Majesty's Regular Forces for general service with the Colours'. It completed the structure of compulsory service which had begun in January 1916, with the calling up of married men of middle age with families. April also brought news that Lord Derby was to leave the War Office and to go to Paris as Ambassador. He was succeeded by Lord Milner, who lost no time in asking to see Lloyd. Less than a month later it was announced that Field Marshal Lord French was going to Ireland as Lord Lieutenant.

A regiment of American troops, 2,700 strong, marched through London to be reviewed by the King at Buckingham Palace. The King, accompanied by the Duke of Connaught, stood on the pavement outside the railings of Buckingham Palace to take the salute. Each man was given a facsimile copy of a letter from the King, written in his own hand:

WINDSOR CASTLE

Soldiers of the United States, the people of the British Isles welcome you on your way to take your stand beside the Armies of many Nations now fighting in the Old World the great battle for human freedom.

The Allies will gain new heart & spirit in your company.

I wish that I could shake the hand of each one of you & bid you God speed on your mission.

George R.I.

April 1918.

The hiatus in air raids was broken on Whit Sunday, 19 May, when late in the evening 'one of the most determined and almost the biggest raid that we have ever had' took place. Lloyd went down to Horse Guards and was told that a great many machines, thirty or forty, had crossed into England, some of which succeeded in getting to London. Bombs were dropped all over the capital – one in King Street, St James's, one in Park Crescent, and in many other places in London. Lloyd's diary shows thirty-seven deaths and about 161 injured, with the Old Kent Road and Lewisham taking the brunt of the attack. He thought that seven of the German planes had been shot down. The barrage had been very heavy with about 11,000 rounds fired. The 'All Clear' went at two o'clock. Lloyd subsequently added a note to his diary entry: 'the last raid of the war on London'.[121] A further series of raids on London had been planned, but the Gotha squadrons were diverted to support the fresh German offensive on the Western Front which started in Champagne on 27 May.

Sir Francis Lloyd paid a visit to Harrods, where he distributed London District Badges to voluntary workers in connection with the Belgravia War Hospital Supply Depot. There were a great many girls at Harrods in a large room, all working at bandages after they had done their day's work. Badges were given to voluntary workers in recognition of regular and devoted service in the interests of soldiers, and workers at the free buffets and YMCA huts were among many who received the award.

With American troops in London training before going to the front, Lloyd met with the Commissioner of the Metropolitan Police to see if parks could be made available for baseball. The King and Queen, with Sir Francis Lloyd in attendance, visited Stamford Bridge to watch a baseball game, but Lloyd confessed that he never understood the sport. Sir Francis and Lady Lloyd attended a concert at the Palace Theatre given by all the 'best artistes in London', as a welcome to the Americans – Lloyd thought the concert excellent – and the 'Washington Inn' was opened in St James's Square as a club for American Officers.

The Union Jack Club in the Waterloo Road was a popular home for British servicemen, but its location in an area which became renowned for prostitution often created difficulties which Lloyd did not consider his responsibility, but which he was blamed for doing nothing about.

General Sir William Robertson had succeeded Field Marshal Lord French as GOC Home Forces, and at their first meeting he questioned Lloyd a great deal on the London defences. The number of recruits in training at various camps around London had risen enormously, and on a visit to the Guards Depot at Caterham in June 1918, Lloyd toured camps containing 11,000 men.

In the middle of the month, Sir Francis Lloyd received a letter from the Military Secretary at GHQ Home Forces, enclosing an extract of a letter from Sir William Robertson to the War Office:

With regard to other Officers the position of Lieutenant General Sir Francis Lloyd, whose command of the London District has recently

123

been extended for a further period of three months, is most unsatisfactory, both from his point of view and from mine. The Command of the London District is an important appointment, from a training point of view as well as on account of work connected with the defence of London, and no Commander can be expected to do justice either to himself or to his Command if he continues liable to be displaced in the course of a few weeks. I therefore recommend that at the end of the recent three months extension granted to Lieutenant General Sir Francis Lloyd, a Commander may be appointed to the London District on the same conditions as all other Commanders.[122]

It subsequently transpired that Robertson's letter was in reply to one from the Army Council asking for the names of GOCs who could be replaced by officers returning from France. Robertson told Lloyd that the initiative had not come from him and he had no wish to get rid of him.

The GOC Home Forces always took a keen interest in the training of troops and on occasion he gave very short notice to Lloyd of his wish to visit barracks in central London. Lloyd had quickly to rearrange his schedule one day when told in the morning that Robertson wished to go round Wellington, Chelsea, Knightsbridge and Regent's Park Barracks that afternoon. The visit appeared to go well and Robertson was pleased with what he saw, Lloyd thought, principally because everybody seemed to know their business. He was especially interested in the School of Instruction at Chelsea and the recruits there.

A Coronation Day service was held at Westminster Abbey in aid of the Welsh Prisoner of War Fund. Queen Mother Alexandra, Lloyd George, the Lord Chancellor, and the Prime Minister of Australia were present, and Sir Francis Lloyd thought the service magnificent.

Ambulance Trains bringing back wounded soldiers from the front arrived regularly at Waterloo Station, and Lloyd was always keen to ensure that the soldiers were speedily transferred to the hospitals where they were to recover. He was often at Waterloo when the trains arrived, and on one occasion it was arranged for the King and Queen, together with Princess Mary, to be present. After talking to the wounded soldiers, Lloyd took the Royal party to the free buffet where he introduced them to the volunteer staff. The importance of women workers in the war effort was later recognized by a procession of between 2,000 to 3,000 of them to Buckingham Palace, where they were reviewed by the King.

THE BEGINNING OF THE END

The King and Queen's Silver Wedding Anniversary was celebrated with a service at St Paul's Cathedral on 6 July, followed by a reception at

Guildhall, where they were presented with wedding presents on behalf of the city – the only personal gifts they agreed to accept. Lloyd, as GOC London District, played a major part in arranging the ceremonial aspects of the celebration, with troops lining the streets.

In the middle of July, food rationing was extended to the whole country, and now included sugar and lard. Tea and cheese were not rationed but authority was given to local food committees to ration them in their areas should supplies fall short. There was no rationing of potatoes or other vegetables, the King having set the example in directing that the flower beds surrounding the Queen Victoria Memorial at Buckingham Palace should be planted with potatoes, cabbages, parsnips and carrots.

Sir Francis Lloyd's nephew, Ian Gunnis, son of Joey and Ina Gunnis, had been reported missing at the front in July 1917. A year later Ina came to see Francis Lloyd to ask him if there was still a chance that her son might be alive. Lloyd had to tell her that this was extremely unlikely as no report had been received of him being a prisoner of war. Ina's distress was compounded by the fact that she was no longer living with Joey, and any chance of her and Joey 'making it up' was also remote. Laurence Holbech, another nephew, became a temporary ADC to Sir Francis Lloyd whilst in hospital at Millbank. Laurence had been gassed in the trenches whilst commanding a company of the 3rd Battalion Grenadier Guards. When in London, Laurence often stayed with Francis and Mary at Great Cumberland Place.

On 13 August Joey Davies, Military Secretary at the War Office, told Sir Francis Lloyd that it was practically decided that his term as GOC London District would end on 1 October, and a week later he received a copy of a letter from the War Office to the GOC Home Land Forces confirming this. He was to be succeeded by Major General Geoffrey Fielding.

Lloyd had for many years been a member of the Carlton, the Club of 'High Tories', and he was on the executive committee. Shortly after receiving the letter confirming the date for the end of his Command of the London District, he discussed with an MP member of the Carlton the possibility of his name being put forward as a prospective candidate for Parliament. On his next meeting with the Lord Mayor he also told him that he would like to go into the House of Commons. He received support for the idea, and the Lord Mayor undertook to speak to the Conservative Party organizer about a London constituency. Lloyd also spoke to Lionel Curtis on the subject and he recommended that he speak to Lloyd George's Parliamentary Secretary. This was probably in relation to his support for the Coalition Government and not the Liberal Party.

The newspapers were now full of the news of his retirement and he received many requests for interviews. Most of the comments about the term of his command were positive and included descriptions of him as 'to all intents and purposes as the Military Governor of London', 'the best dressed man since Disraeli', and 'the velvet glove covering the grip of steel'; the last no doubt alluding to his reputation as a strict disciplinarian.

Industrial unrest was growing in the country, with even the threat of a strike by the Metropolitan Police. The National Union of Police and Prison Officers had never been recognized by the government, but this did not stop them from submitting a claim for better pay, war bonuses, and improvements to the pension scheme. When the authorities failed to respond to the claim, the union called its members out on strike. On 30 August, most of the Metropolitan Police's 12,000 officers came out and marched through the streets. The Acting Chief Commissioner advised Lloyd that he might need his help, and all troops in the London District were confined to barracks. Troops were then deployed at the entrances to all Government offices, with the Scots Guards at Scotland Yard, and the Grenadiers at the Foreign Office, both fully armed and wearing the tin hats of active service.[123] By some accounts the first the Prime Minister knew of the strike was when a detachment of Guards replaced police officers at the front of Number Ten.[124] Lloyd George entered into negotiations with the union and succeeded in buying them off, and the strike was over within two days. Sir Edward Henry, the Chief Commissioner of the Metropolitan Police, subsequently resigned.

Visits to hospitals around London continued, and a report on the City of London Military Hospital at Homerton was severely critical of the food and the way it was prepared and served to patients. Often after making a criticism, Lloyd returned to the hospital a month later to see if matters had improved. If he thought that the senior management were at fault, he called either for their dismissal or for them to be moved to another position.

One of the District Orders published in the last month of his Command was the cancellation of the ban on dancing in clubs. This received much comment both favourable and adverse. The *National News* treated the announcement with a degree of sarcasm:

'Gentlemen you may dance in public places and at clubs. The Order which was intended to protect you from the perils and traps that surrounded you in the past has been cancelled. Henceforth you must look after yourselves; for the attempt which was made to save you, has only aggravated the evil it sought to remove.'

Baldly and brutally stated this is the meaning of the announcement by General Sir Francis Lloyd.

More industrial unrest continued with the threat of a strike by firemen in London. The Chief Commissioner of the Metropolitan Police was again uncertain about the attitude of the police in this event, and asked Lloyd to be prepared to provide military support should it be needed.

With his time as GOC London District rapidly coming to an end, Sir Francis and Lady Lloyd received an invitation from the King to stay at Windsor Castle. They motored down to Windsor on 12 September, instead of going by train in case Lloyd might be wanted in a hurry to return to London because of the threats of strikes by the public services. On arrival at the Castle they found everything most comfortably arranged – 'sleeping apartments with sitting rooms and every possible luxury and comfort'.

> Before dinner the King sent for me and after telling me that he was greatly pleased with all I had done during the last five years in London, His Majesty gave me the Grand Cross of the Victorian Order in recognition of my services to him. He also talked a good deal about things in general.
>
> We then went into dinner. I sat on the right of the Queen, and Mary on the right of the King. Lady Airlie was on the other side. The others there were: Colonel Hankey, Commanding 2nd Life Guards, dining; Princess Mary; Princess Helena Victoria; Madame D'Hautpoul; Lady Bertha Dawkins; Lord Ranksborough; Lord Cromer; Colonel Wigram; and Sir Edward Wallington.
>
> After dinner the King talked for half an hour or more on the Brigade of Guards and many other subjects. His Majesty thanked me very much for all I had done. The whole party at Windsor was most agreeable.[125]

Sir Francis and Lady Lloyd returned to London on the next day and a week later they went to an investiture at Buckingham Palace, where they saw Francis's sister, Selina, receive the Royal Red Cross Medal, and his nephew, Laurence Holbech, decorated with the Military Cross. In the evening they all went to the Playhouse Theatre where they saw Hawtrey, Gladys Cooper and Ellis Jeffreys in *The Naughty Wife*.

The time was now approaching for Lloyd to make farewell visits to the Regiments of the Household Division, stationed in the London District. He first visited the Blues and Life Guards at Regents Park Barracks where he did not inspect them, but addressed them and said goodbye. Similar visits took place at Chelsea Barracks with his old Regiment the Grenadiers, the Welsh Guards at Ranelagh, and the Irish Guards at Warley. During a visit to Windsor he spoke to men of the Coldstream Guards and 2nd Life Guards, and his final farewell was to the Scots Guards (Reserve Battalion) at Wellington Barracks.

While all these visits were taking place, the Great Western Railway had gone on strike and others seemed likely to follow. Again Lloyd confined all troops to barracks and a few days later sent a company of Scots Guards to Stratford where trouble had been reported.

The War Office requested a portrait of Sir Francis Lloyd and he sat for a pencil drawing (life size of head and shoulders) by Percival Anderson. A photograph of the portrait subsequently appeared in *The Tatler*. A courtesy farewell visit was made to the CIGS, Sir Henry Wilson, and Lloyd dined with his old friend Field Marshal Lord French. By 29 September, Lloyd had developed a chill on the liver and was exhausted by all the meetings and visits. The result was that he was unable to attend a dinner given in his honour by the London District Staff at the Café Royal, and he returned to his house in Great Cumberland Place: 'Thoroughly broken down by overwork'. However, he sent a message to all Officers and Men of the Brigade of Guards:

> I cannot go into retirement after forty-four years service, most of which has been spent with the Brigade, without expressing my sorrow at the parting, but after five years of Command of the London District I do feel that I have had the best that can be given.
>
> That best has been earned for me by yourselves, and I am deeply grateful for all that I have received at your hands. For the education that you have given me in my early days; for the trust that has enabled me to carry out all my duties; and for the unfailing help and loyalty that I have always received.

It was a month before Lloyd had recovered, and he and Lady Lloyd spent three weeks at the Grand Hotel in Eastbourne as part of the recuperation. While there an article appeared in *The Graphic* written by Lloyd in which he put down some thoughts on his career and changes to the Army over the past forty-four years:

> I recall many remarkable changes in the dress, equipment, training, terms of service, and general conditions of the soldier during my forty-four years as a Guardsman. In those early days I had under me men wearing Crimean medals, but now a man with seven years' service is called 'an old soldier'. Smoking out of doors was forbidden, the bearskin had to be worn on Sundays, even off parade, the pioneers wore beards and white aprons, and the weapons carried were the Schneider rifle and the old pointed bayonet.
>
> Army rations and cookery of the seventies would be looked upon as a punishment today. Drill and sentry duty were supposed to provide all requisite physical exercise, gymnastics being unknown. Little attention was paid to the education of the private, who was content to be 'no scholar', spending his leisure and scanty pay in the

convivial comradeship of the canteen and barrack-room.

Undoubtedly a more generous scale of wound pensions has relieved him of the fear of ending his days a pauper as a reward for patriotism.

I received my baptism of fire at Suakin, as a signalling officer to the Guards' Brigade. During those operations khaki was worn, although we had left home in red coats, blue trousers and white helmets.

The Allies' counter-attacks after the German offensives of March and May, had started on the Matz on 11 June and on the Marne on 18 July, and continued with a succession of operations over the next three months. What broke the Germans was the combination of American numbers, which rose from 284,000 at the end of March to 1,872,000 by the beginning of November, with Anglo-French combat effectiveness that both halted the March-May offensives and broke through every position after July.[126] Four days after Lloyd retired as GOC London District on 1 October 1918, the Germans requested a ceasefire and a settlement based on President Woodrow Wilson's peace programme. It was to take a further five weeks of negotiations before the guns along the Western front at last fell silent.

7

London in the 1920s

On 11 November 1918 the Great War came to an end with the signing of the Armistice. Sir Francis Lloyd heard the news between 10.30 am and 11.00 am that morning as he walked down Bond Street. In the House of Commons the Prime Minister, Lloyd George, read the terms of the Armistice. He then added:

> Thus, Mr Speaker, at eleven o'clock this morning came to an end the cruellest and most terrible war that has ever scourged mankind. I hope we may say that thus, this fateful morning, came to an end all wars.

Later in the day crowds gathered in central London and the celebrations continued long into the night. Lloyd believed there to be, 'All sorts of orgies going on'.[127] Within three days of peace the Prime Minister announced that Parliament was to be prorogued and a General Election held on 14 December. Lloyd attended a thanksgiving service in the Guards Chapel at Wellington Barracks in the presence of the King and Queen, with Princess Mary and the Duke of Connaught.

The election campaign began and although Lloyd had not found a constituency party to nominate him, he spoke at several meetings in the London area, in support of the Conservative Coalition candidate. Sir Alfred Warren received his endorsement at Poplar, and 1,500 to 2,000 people heard him support Sir William Davison, the Coalition candidate, at a meeting at Kensington Town Hall.

With Christmas approaching, Sir Francis and Lady Lloyd held a sale of work at Great Cumberland Place in aid of the Chailey Heritage Craft Schools for Crippled Children, which made £235, and they attended an investiture at Buckingham Palace when Lord Gort received the VC and DSO with two bars.

Two days before polling was due to take place, Sir Francis Lloyd heard that Colonel Lucas, MP for Kennington had died. He went to see Sir John Boreston at Party Headquarters in Great Smith Street, in the hope that he might be nominated for the seat but was told that it had been agreed not to put up a Coalition candidate. In any event time was too short for Lloyd to mount a campaign.

The General Election of 1918 was the first to be held after the Representation of the People Act had been passed earlier in the year, which gave women over thirty the right to vote. Polling was held on 14 December, although the count did not begin until 28 December. The reason for the fourteen day gap was to allow soldiers and sailors still serving overseas to vote. Being a serving soldier, Lloyd was able to vote by post at Oswestry. He supported Willie Bridgeman, the Coalition candidate. On the day of the count Lloyd went to the Carlton to hear the election results as they came in. The election was won by a coalition of the Conservatives under Andrew Bonar Law, most of the Liberals under David Lloyd George, and a few independent and former Labour MPs, and produced a government which retained Lloyd George as Prime Minister. The anti-coalition Liberals under the former Prime Minister, Asquith, won few seats, which according to Lloyd 'was a great delight' to the members of the Carlton. He added that 'Everybody was very delighted about the election – the wonderful sweep in favour of the Coalition Government, far more than was expected. Only one woman was returned – a Sinn Feiner'.[128]

A month after his retirement Sir Francis Lloyd had met Lieutenant Colonel Murray-Threipland, who asked him if he would write the history of the Welsh Guards. Although he had never served in the Regiment he had, as we have seen, been very involved in its formation and, as GOC London District, had closely watched its performance at home and at the front. Lloyd agreed to take on the task provided he was given the assistance of a typist.

General Sir Francis Lloyd was still Colonel of the Royal Welch Fusiliers and he approached the King with a request for a goat from the Royal herd to be given to the 2nd Battalion. The Keeper of the Privy Purse was able to respond that the King had agreed with much pleasure to provide one from the herd in Windsor Park. President Woodrow Wilson had arrived from America on Boxing Day and the streets of London had been lined for him, but the arrangements were no longer the responsibility of Francis Lloyd.

LCC: THE MEMBER FOR EAST FULHAM

Although Lloyd's hopes to enter Parliament had not been realized, his interest in entering the political arena had not diminished, and he discussed with Sir Shirley Benn the possibility of standing as a candidate for the London County Council in the elections to be held in March 1919. At the end of January, Sir Henry Norris, the Mayor of Fulham, invited Lloyd to stand as one of the Municipal Reform Party candidates for East Fulham (there were two seats). Before he was adopted and could start campaigning, London was more or less paralysed by a Tube strike, which also included the District Electric Railway. The strike continued for five days and it took another couple of days before the trains were running again, during which the electrical engineers threatened to plunge all London into darkness. Two days later Lloyd was adopted as a candidate at a meeting at Fulham Town Hall. The second Municipal Reform candidate running with Lloyd was Mrs Hudson Lyall. In an interview with the *Daily Express* on the day after his adoption, Lloyd gave some indication of the major issues on which he intended to campaign:

SIR FRANCIS LLOYD

FOR THE LCC

LONDON'S LATE GOC TO

FIGHT FULHAM

Lieutenant General Sir Francis Lloyd, who has just retired from the London Command, was last evening adopted Municipal Reform candidate to contest East Fulham at the forthcoming London County Council election.

In an interview with a *Daily Express* representative, Sir Francis said: 'I originally intended contesting a Parliamentary seat, but I relinquished the London Command too late. I have been approached to stand for the London County Council, which I am going to do.

'Housing is the first question which will have my attention. I consider it scandalous that such slums should exist in a great country such as ours. Thousands of houses should be erected with the least possible delay, and personally I favour an extension of the garden suburb plan wherever possible.

'Improved travelling facilities and the best possible system of education, so that children should be made fit for citizenship, are other matters to which I am deeply interested. Child welfare is even more important, as it is necessary to make good the wastage of the war. To develop a healthy manhood and womanhood is a matter for which I shall press.

'During five years command of the London District, apart from my ordinary military duties, there were many things that came my way, such as securing meals for soldiers, providing hostels for officers and men, and helping great philanthropic societies for sailors and soldiers. This gave me a good insight into various matters, and I therefore suggest that I have some qualification for representing Fulham on the London County Council.

'I know the needs of the demobilised soldier, and the best way, I think, to help him is to make him as comfortable as possible on his return. After what the majority of them have endured, let there not be a lack of entertainments. A new system for the development of municipal restaurants would have my support.'

There are two candidates for East Fulham, Sir Francis Lloyd and Mrs Hudson Lyall, who has done valuable work in connection with the Ministry of Food.

The next three weeks were taken up in treading the streets of Fulham canvassing with Mrs Lyall, of whom Lloyd had a high opinion, and speaking in the evening at election meetings. A list of the candidates was published and showed four people contesting East Fulham: Sir Francis Lloyd and Mrs Hudson Lyall for the Municipal Reform Party, and Robert Dunstan, a doctor, and Louis Albert Hill, a pacifist, for Labour. A meeting of all four candidates developed into a heckling match, from which Lloyd concluded that the meeting was a front for the Socialists. Posters appeared seeking support for each Party and one for Lloyd and Lyall referred to the alleged link between Socialism and Bolshevism:

London County Council Election
EAST FULHAM
Don't fail to VOTE for
LT. GENERAL SIR
FRANCIS LLOYD
GCVO, KCB, DSO
AND MRS
HUDSON LYALL
Municipal Reform Candidates
AGAINST
Socialism,
OTHERWISE
Bolshevism.
THURSDAY, 6 MARCH.
MEETINGS - 8 P.M.
Friday, Feb. 28th – Bethel Lecture Hall,
North End Road
Tuesday , March 4th – Christchurch Hall,
Studdridge Street.
CENTRAL COMMITTEE ROOMS,
404, NORTH END ROAD.

Lloyd and Lyall were the successful candidates by some margin:

Lloyd	2747
Lyall	2673
Dunstan	1264
Hill	1218

In the new Council the Municipal Reformers held sixty-eight seats out of the total 124 seats, and with the Aldermanic bench their overall majority was twenty-six. The Progressives won forty seats, with the Labour Party fifteen, and one Independent. The turnout at the Poll was, however, the lowest on record, with public apathy leading to only eighteen percent of the electorate voting.

Sir Francis Lloyd took his seat on the LCC on 18 March, and on the same day went to Westminster Guildhall to receive a silver Treasury Inkstand presented to him by the Mayors of the London Boroughs in appreciation of his services rendered to London during the war as GOC London District. The meeting of the full Council on 1 April was a long sitting, with much discussion on the housing problem, and a great deal of verbal 'fighting'. Lloyd thought that the Independent Labour Party made themselves very objectionable. He was appointed to the Public Health Committee and considered that its work was extremely well done.

Sittings of the main Council were at times dull and at others interesting, but always long, with agendas covering a wide variety of subjects from tramways, steamboats on the Thames, and unemployment, to teachers' salaries, allotments and housing. Lloyd's maiden speech was on housing, an issue that he was to return to on several occasions. The LCC decided to purchase 143 acres of the Dover House estate at Roehampton for housing, and Lloyd was concerned that East Fulham should not lose out in the provision of council housing. At a party meeting he complained at not being kept informed about housing – a subject which he came with a mandate from Fulham to do something about, and if nothing was done he would have to resign. He also spoke on unemployment and in particular the demobilized sailors and soldiers for whom no work had been found. Over 1,000,000 ex-servicemen were out of work across the country, 170,000 of whom were in London.

Sir Francis and Lady Lloyd spent Easter with the Van Bergens at Attingham Park near Shrewsbury. This provided an opportunity for them to visit Francis's sister Eva at Wrexham, and to see his brother Rossendale and his family at Selattyn. Rossendale's son, Andrew, talked to his uncle about joining the Army either as a Grenadier or in the Royal Welch Fusiliers. With regards the latter Lloyd as Colonel of the Regiment presented medals at a parade at Wrexham.

On his return to London, Sir Francis was visited by Murray-Threipland who came to talk about the writing of the history of the Welsh Guards. He wanted it done in a great hurry and proposed to take it away from Lloyd and to ask Dudley Ward to do it. This was agreed but Lloyd suggested that the work he had already done should be published. Murray-Threipland was dubious but agreed to speak to the publishers.

Invitations to military functions were still received by Lloyd, and at a dinner for Cadet Officers he spoke about the possible uses in the future of auxiliary forces. He was also critical of the League of Nations, which he thought 'absolutely worthless'. He added that 'it was all nonsense to talk about the Lion lying down with the Lamb when dealing with a nation that had torn up solemn treaties in the past. His advice was to prepare, in spite of all promises of universal peace, for any eventualities that might arise'.[129] In 1919, the King's Birthday parade was held in Hyde Park, when for the first time the Colour was not trooped on Horse Guards Parade. General Pershing, the Commander of the American Forces in London during the war, received the Freedom of the City of London at Guildhall, and at the Lunch afterwards at Mansion House, Winston Churchill, now Secretary of State for War, was among the speakers.

Another caricature of Sir Francis Lloyd appeared in an edition of *The World*, this time by the well known illustrator and cartoonist, Bert Thomas, whose posters had appeared on walls throughout the capital during the war.[130] The picture of Lloyd was one in a series of politicians and military figures drawn by Thomas in the weekly journal during 1919. A short article accompanied the drawing:

The World Celebrity of the Week

No.19 – Lieutenant General Sir Francis Lloyd

GCVO, KCB, DSO

'Frankie' is – or must we say, was? – a gallant soldier. Fought with distinction in the Sudan. Won the DSO at Khartoum. Got more honours in South Africa, where he was with the Eighth Division under Rundle, and badly wounded.

But more than just a mere soldier. He is an institution. The glass of military fashion and the mould of khaki form. Where else shall we look for such perfectly tailored tunics, such faultless breeches, such inimitable boots, such nuttily glossy Sam Brownes? And such a perfect figure to set them off? So perfect that the envious have even hinted he wears ____. But hush. Doesn't look anything like his sixty-five years, either. And a complexion so perfect that once more the envious ____. But once more, hush.

A Guardsman, of course – once commanded the First Brigade – and also guardian of the Guards. If in earlier days he ever transgressed the Puritan canons of Guards' fashion, has made up for it since. In matters of uniform, Ensigns of the Guards have known no stricter disciplinarian. A good talker, too, as well as speaker. Much in request at dinner parties and public meetings. Fluent on all occasions, and never inaudible. Quite the contrary.

135

> Brave in peace as in war – shuns publicity no more than he did bullets. As GOC London District in the Great War, lived perforce in the limelight. And it became him well. Has he really left the stage for good? No *Jeune premier* will be more missed.

JEHU JUNIOR

Sir Francis and Lady Lloyd left London at the beginning of August to spend three months at Aston Hall. They drove down to Aston, the journey taking them just over eight hours, arriving at 10.00pm. They found Horbury with his wife and the other servants and dogs waiting for them. Everything was in good order inside the house thanks to the Horburys. The outside was fair, although of course much overgrown. German prisoners of war were working in the garden. Only a few days after their arrival, Sir Francis Lloyd attended a 'victory' march in Shrewsbury when 7,000 men from all the Shropshire regiments marched past, and on the next day Sir Francis and Lady Lloyd celebrated thirty-eight years of marriage.

At this time, Aston was still considered the family home, although in the preceding six years they had been unable to spend much time there. Their other large house at Rolls Park, Chigwell, was let but they now needed to consider the long term future of both houses. Lloyd discussed the matter with his solicitor, Ronald Peake, when he came to stay at Aston for a few days. The idea was put forward that the lease on 26 Great Cumberland Place should be purchased, and then the house sold, presumably at a profit. Peake produced a summary of the annual costs of No.26:

Rent	£260
Taxes and general rates	£179
Electricity	£61
Water	£25
Gas	£237
Coal	£21
Total	£783

The proceeds would be used to modernise Rolls Park, which would become the Lloyds 'London' home, being less than twelve miles from the city. A visit was made to Rolls Park, where they spent a couple of hours going over the house and grounds, but nothing was decided yet. Lloyd returned to Aston where he and Mary spent the rest of the summer. However, at the end of September 'we woke up to find a Railway strike, no trains, no papers, no letters'.[131] This caused few difficulties for Lloyd, although a shortage of petrol was threatened, and he continued to visit his tenants with his agent, and to supervise the work being carried out in the garden and park at Aston Hall. The strike ended after about ten days and longer visits were resumed. He presided at the Regimental Dinner of the Royal Welch Fusiliers at Chester in the middle of October and on the next day he represented the King at a memorial service in Wrexham Parish Church for those of the Regiment killed in the Great War.

During a brief visit to London he met Clifton, the estate agent who had been appointed to find a buyer for 26 Great Cumberland Place. An offer initially for £7,000 had been made by a Mr Young, but they finally settled on £7,500. Shortly before the end of October, Sir Francis and Lady Lloyd returned to London and quickly paid another visit to Rolls Park. They went all over the house and gardens and carefully thought out the reconstruction and decoration that was required. Heat and lighting were the most burning questions.

FOOD COMMISSIONER

In November 1919, Lloyd was surprised to receive a letter from General Romer, on Lord Haig's Staff at GHQ the Forces in Great Britain, offering him the Food Commissionership for London and the Home Counties, which previously had been two separate Divisions but had now been amalgamated. He discussed the offer with Peck, Secretary to the Food Controller and told him that he was prepared to accept provided he was responsible directly to the Minister (Roberts). A formal letter of appointment was sent to Lloyd, which indicated that the position was a temporary one which could be terminated by either side at one month's notice. His duties were to start on 15 December. The *Daily Express* gave its opinion on the 'food' problem, which Lloyd was appointed to solve:

> The enemy of disorganization which has continued to threaten London's food by congesting docks, railway sidings, warehouses and wharves and preventing the free flow of food from the producers to the consumers. The straightening out of the tangle which has kept food scarce and dear twelve months after the armistice calls for the firm handling which a soldier of Sir Francis Lloyd's experience is especially qualified to give.

The anniversary of the Armistice was commemorated for the first time with two minutes silence at 11.00am on the 11th November.

Criticism was expressed of Lloyd's appointment as Food Commissioner in the House of Commons by one Member, who questioned his suitability for the job:

> Mr Gilbert asked the Minister of Food why he has recently

appointed a food controller for the County of London; if he will state to whom the appointment has been given, what is the salary he is to receive, and if the person appointed has had any previous experience of this kind of work; if he has in the Food Ministry more than one official who has this experience; and why a complete stranger to the Department has been appointed to an entirely new appointment?

Mr Roberts: I presume that the hon. Member refers to the appointment of Lieutenant General Sir Francis Lloyd, GCVO, KCB, to the position of Divisional Food Commissioner for the new administrative area formed by the recent combination of the London and Home Counties Divisions. The salary attached to the appointment is at the rate of £1,200 per annum. The combination of the two divisions was made for administrative reasons, and although Sir Francis Lloyd has no previous experience of the work of the Ministry of Food, I came to the conclusion, after consideration of all the circumstances, that he was the most suitable of the persons available for the appointment.[132]

Other comments were more positive, pointing out that there were 321 Food Control Committees serving a population of 9,274,000 and it was the new Commissioner's principal purpose to secure unity and economy of administration and improved distribution of food. One newspaper published a photograph of Lloyd in his civvies seated in his office, to which they gave the title 'The Man who Rations London'. Lloyd had made arrangements to visit Ceylon for a holiday and had even booked his passage before he was approached for the job as Food Commissioner, and all the arrangements had to be cancelled. Instead all that he and Lady Lloyd managed was a week at the Hotel Bedford in Brighton before he started work.

The offices of the London and Home Counties Division were in Portman Square, where Lloyd had 110 staff. After the Christmas holidays he went round every room and wished the staff 'A Happy New Year'. He had two Deputies: Greenwood and Jackson, and heads for each food department, ranging from the Milk Department to the Margarine Department. Sitting above the Division was the Ministry of Food with yet further tiers of civil servants. It was not long before Lloyd was finding it difficult to handle Greenwood, and arguing with his superiors at the Ministry.

During the next six months he visited endless numbers of Food Offices in towns and villages in London and the Home Counties, to check their efficiency, often travelling over 150 miles each day. Within two months of his appointment he recommended that the Food Committees should be consolidated into groups of ten, with paid officials, and the existing committees scrapped. The Divisional office was later moved to Grosvenor House. Food distribution continued to be a problem, with overwhelming supplies of mutton and a shortage of potatoes and butter.

There was the threat of a strike by gas workers in June which came to nothing, but in October the miners came out. Lloyd made arrangements to sleep in London during the strike. It became a question of whether the transport and railway workers would join the miners, which would lead to even more difficulties in food distribution. Somewhat controversially, Lloyd set up Volunteer Labour Bureaux where people could register to help in the event of a general strike. The Government had opposed the claim of the miners for a two shillings per shift increase, but offered an independent inquiry. Ten days after the start of the strike both sides were anxious to find a settlement, but the situation had been complicated by the National Union of Railwaymen taking the decision to strike. Fortunately at the insistence of the General Secretary of the NUR their strike was postponed, and in the intervening period Lloyd George continued negotiations with the miners and reached a successful conclusion.

Further moves of the Divisional Food office were made to Park Street in July 1920, and to George Street, Hanover Square later in the year, following a reorganization of the Division, and at the end of the year many of the District Food offices were closed. By the beginning of the New Year, Sir Francis Lloyd was already contemplating resigning as Commissioner. The Ministry of Food was interfering more with the work of the Division and Lloyd's role was being reduced. As a result he handed in his resignation in March and told Coller at the Ministry that he considered that the way he had been treated was very bad and that had he known what he was in for he never would have accepted the position, as he was not given the full power in his own Division that he had been promised.

His successor, Brigadier General H A Jones, was given the title Divisional Officer with a more limited role. The Wholesale Food Markets Committee of which Lloyd had been a member also ceased to exist, and in April 1921 the Government announced that the Ministry of Food, the Ministry of Munitions and the Ministry of Shipping would all cease to exist with their functions transferred to other Ministries. The Ministry of Food lingered on for a few months while its stocks of bacon, wheat, frozen meat, sugar and butter were sold in the open market at current prices.

Lloyd had been a Commissioner for fifteen months, during which he had been able to slim down part of the bureaucracy, but why he took on the role in the first place must be questioned. It is doubtful if he did so because of a sense of public duty, as he was still invited to attend many functions associated with his military career, albeit as a retired General, and the management of Roehampton Hospital occupied much of his time. There may have been financial considerations that led him to accept the post, as he was always seeking to balance his income and expenditure. In 1919 he had paid £923 in super tax and Lady Lloyd had paid £600. In any event the period must be considered one of the less successful ones in his public life.

During all these problems the restoration of Rolls Park at Chigwell was continuing. An architect, Murray, was employed to draw up plans for the necessary work to be done before Sir Francis and Lady Lloyd could move in. Regular meetings took place with Murray and Osborne, the builder who was to carry out the work.

In December 1919, Lloyd's brother Harvey and his wife Kathleen had returned from Canada, and it was decided that they would live at Aston Hall during the winter and for practical purposes act as 'Steward' on the estate, looking after the interests of Sir Francis, and ensuring that the house and gardens were maintained. Lloyd purchased another motor vehicle, this time a one ton Buick truck, for £375, which he used to transport some of the smaller items of furniture and pictures from Aston Hall and Great Cumberland Place to Rolls Park. Lloyd heard at about this time that Major General Geoffrey Fielding had resigned as GOC London District after only fifteen months in the post, and was to be replaced by General 'Ma' Jeffreys.

While still a Food Commissioner, Sir Francis Lloyd was appointed a Special Commissioner of the Duke of York's School, which had moved to Dover. His main role was to sit on the Committee that selected boys for the school based on their father's merits and services, but he also visited the school, where he inspected a parade of the boys, and considered the 'whole thing as good as it could possibly be'.[133]

Lloyd's enthusiasm for his work as a Member of the LCC was either beginning to wane or he found attending full Council meetings less interesting, for he frequently sought a 'pair' to allow his absence. However, his attendance was required at the all-night sitting in March 1920, when the Council rose at 7.10 am after twenty-six divisions on tramway fares called by the opposition. Earlier he had attended a full meeting of the Council at which there was 'a great storm' on whether the LCC should re-employ conscientious objectors who had previously worked for the Council, now that the war had ended. The debate was fierce and at times abusive and Lloyd spoke for the motion that they should not be re-employed. The motion was carried. After a year as a Member, he and Mrs Hudson Lyall, as the two members for East Fulham, arranged a meeting with their constituents to report progress on housing and other problems of London Government. In hindsight they thought that this was a mistake, but the meeting went well without any opposition party members attending.

Housing and other Problems
of
London Government

A
MEETING
Will be held at the
Town Hall, Fulham
on
Wednesday, April 14th,
At 8pm, when
Lt.-Gen Sir FRANCIS LLOYD
GCVO, KCB, DSO, LCC
AND
Mrs HUDSON LYALL, LCC
Will give an account of the work of the
London County Council during the past year.
Chairman:
Sir CYRIL COBB, KBE, MVO, MP, LCC

About thirty members of the Main Drainage Committee, including Lloyd, were taken down the river on a steamer from Charing Cross Pier, through the 'Pool of London', to Barking to see the main sewage treatment works and outfall. He found this far more interesting than sitting in County Hall listening to debates. He still spoke on housing matters at County Hall and on one occasion voted with the Labour and Progressive Parties during a debate on slums in Tabard Street when he felt that something had to be done. Shortly before the Christmas recess in 1921 the Council debated film censorship when Lloyd was reported as saying:

My idea is that there should be strong censorship of films. I do not care how it is carried out, whether by trade or a public body. But there should be no attempt to make age restrictions for the spectators. Parents are the best judges.

A motion was passed which provided that no young person under sixteen should be admitted to see 'public' films (passed by the British Board of Film Censors as suitable for Adults only) unless with a parent or bona fide guardian.

The LCC elections in March 1922 did not include Francis Lloyd's or Mrs Hudson Lyall's seats, but the results showed an increase in the number of seats held by the Municipal Reform Party at the expense of the Labour and Progressive parties. In July Francis Lloyd attended the last meeting of the LCC at Spring Gardens before the Council moved across the River to its new headquarters on the South Bank.

THE WELSH GUARDS SAVED

Towards the end of May 1920, Sir Francis Lloyd heard that the War Office was considering abolishing the Irish and Welsh Guards as separate regiments, as part of proposals for the reorganization of the post-war army. Before the proposals became public, Lloyd and Lieutenant Colonel Murray-Threipland, the commanding officer of the Welsh Guards went to 10 Downing Street on 31 May, where they saw Mr Davies, Private Secretary to Lloyd George, and moved him very strongly to urge the Prime Minister to prevent the Welsh Guards being abolished.[134]

The proposals had been under consideration for some time, during which the Colonels and Lieutenant Colonels of the Brigade of Guards had been involved in the discussions. The War Office proposal was to brigade the Irish Guards and the Welsh Guards with certain other regiments of the Guards, thus abolishing their separate organizations. They stated that in no sense was it intended that the regiments should lose their distinctive titles, but it was thought that the Irish Guards might be attached to the Scots Guards, as the Irish Guards Battalion, and that the Scots Guards would revert to their old title the 'Third Regiment of Foot Guards'. They would then have three battalions. The Irish Guards would keep their own regimental adjutant, but would lose their independent regimental lieutenant colonel and headquarters. The Welsh Guards would fare even worse and be reduced to a Welsh Guards company of the Grenadier Guards, regimental headquarters and lieutenant colonel being abolished.

The War Office insisted that the proposals were solely directed by considerations of economy. They argued that the Irish and Welsh Guards, with only one battalion each, were practically as expensive to keep up in regard to headquarters and depots as the Grenadiers and Coldstream Guards with their three battalions each, or the Scots, with their two battalions – hence the proposal to merge the Irish Guards with the Scots to make them up to three battalions. There were obviously questions of sentiment involved, but with the taxpayers (through the medium of their representatives in Parliament) clamouring for economy, the War Office did not feel entitled to give more than its due and proper weight to the sentiment involved.

The proposals were supported by a majority of the Colonels and Lieutenant Colonels of the Brigade of Guards, but Field Marshal Lord French, Colonel of the Irish Guards, and Lieutenant Colonel Murray-Threipland of the Welsh Guards strongly disagreed. The proposals were shortly to be submitted to the King in a 'Majority' Report, but a 'Minority' Report signed by French and Murray-Threipland would also go to him.

Details of the proposals and their justification were in the public domain by 5 June when all the major newspapers published long articles mostly arguing against them. The Military Correspondent of *The Times* described them as essentially in the nature of a false economy and that it would be well that protest should be made at the outset:

> The Guards have a good case and can fight it. It is to be feared that if once the principle is admitted, all sorts of revolutionary changes might be made with the old county regiments of England. Tradition cannot be ignored, and national spirit lives in the outward and visible signs of military pomp. In Lord French the Irish Guards have a firm friend; the Welsh Guards are looking hopefully to support from their Colonel, the Prince of Wales, and, above all, the King may still prefer to have a completely representative body of Household troops.[135]

Responses to the proposals were soon to appear in the newspapers. The Welsh MPs referred to the indignation of those who felt that the move on the part of Mr Churchill (the Secretary of State for War) and his experts was a new slight to Wales. Major General Sir Ivor Philipps expressed the view that to disband the Welsh Guards or to submerge the regiment would be a great national misfortune. Three days after the initial newspaper reports, Sir Francis Lloyd wrote a letter to *The Times*, *The Morning Post*, *The Daily Telegraph*, and *Daily Express*, protesting against the abolition of the Welsh Guards. All the newspapers with the exception of *The Morning Post*, published his letter:

TO THE EDITOR OF THE TIMES

> Sir, – With reference to your announcement in *The Times* on June 5 and General Thomas's letter of yesterday, I seek your indulgence, as the officer who was charged with raising the Welsh Guards under the command of the King and the direct orders of Lord Kitchener.
>
> The Welsh Guards were raised at the instigation of the Welsh nation – by no means a sudden thought or an impulse of the moment, but in response to a feeling that had been growing for many years, that the King should have among his Guards a regiment of Welsh nationality. Of all the nations that make up the British Empire, there is none that is more loyal than the Principality, and in having given a gracious response to their deep-seated wish, the King brought into being a factor which had been the desire of the Cymru almost since the days of Henry VII. Now, Sir, to destroy this is not only a crime, but a blunder of the worst description. The nation is undoubtedly desirous of economy, but economy at the price of such sentiment is not to be thought of. If it is necessary to cut down the Brigade of Guards, there are other and wiser methods which I need not detail here. The reasons for doing it on the grounds of recruiting are

absolutely unsound, and rest on fictitious figures.

There is every reason for maintaining this great regiment in its entirety. A great regiment it is, for we do not base our reasons for its retention on show or parade ceremonial, but on the fact that it has proved itself worthy to stand beside the greatest and best fighting troops that carry the King's uniform. It earned a worthy baptism of fire at the Battle of Loos and in some of the greatest battles that the world has ever known, and it has maintained the best traditions of our nation.

Let it never be forgotten that the lifeblood of some of our best, both gentle and simple, has watered the fields of France and Flanders, as has that of the other component parts of the British Empire, but with this difference, that the other regiments are to remain, and these great names are to be lost with the dissolution of the Welsh Guards.

Sir, the counsellors of the King cannot give such purblind advice, and I cannot believe that his Most Gracious Majesty, who loves the Welsh nation, will listen to such counsels.

I am, Sir, yours obediently,

FRANCIS LLOYD, Lieutenant General.

P.S. – The policy of adding the Irish Guards as the 3rd Battalion of the Scots Guards, the whole under the name of the 3rd Regiment of Foot Guards, and thereby losing the identity of both, is an equally great outrage on the susceptibilities of two great national regiments.

Carlton Club, SW1, June 8.

The War Office began to retreat and Winston Churchill made a statement in the House of Commons:

There has never been any intention of abolishing the Irish Guards. With regard to the Welsh Guards the position of recruiting has raised a question of the regiment continuing, but I have certainly expressed no opinion one way or the other. I have allowed the discussion to proceed between the various parties, but the Army Council and the Secretary of State have reserved their judgment.

The intervention of Lloyd George in support of the Welsh Guards and the influence of Sir Francis Lloyd were probably crucial in the survival of the regiment, but it was a close run thing. It was also perhaps fortunate that as Francis Lloyd had retired he was able to speak in public on the matter. Within a few days *The Daily Telegraph* was reporting that they had learned officially that the proposed rearrangement of the Brigade of Guards had definitely been dropped, and the Correspondent of the *Western Mail* reported that:

> The proposal to abolish the Welsh and Irish Guards may be regarded as dead. This is the view in Ministerial circles to night, and I understand that the proposal has been killed by representations made by Mr Lloyd George to Mr Winston Churchill, the War Minister.

RETIREMENT

Lieutenant General Sir Francis Lloyd formally retired from the Army on 12 August 1920, his sixty-seventh birthday, when he was relegated to the retired list after forty-six years service, and was put on retired pay. One newspaper included a final valedictory note on his career:

> Only those who were behind the scenes can realize in the faintest degree what it meant to have a man of his force, administrative ability, enthusiasm, and unswerving energy at the head of affairs during those critical years. In no small measure we owe to him the success of the recruiting campaigns, and the organisation of the defence of London.

Sir Francis Lloyd was known to his close family and friends as 'Frankie', but at a meeting of the Grenadier Old Comrades Association in 1920, one 'old comrade' called him 'Bunker', which Lloyd admitted was a very old nickname for him, without explaining its derivation. In July, Lloyd had been appointed Honorary Colonel of the 13th (County of London) Princess Louise's Kensington Battalion of the London Regiment, which was part of the Territorial Force. As the unit was based in London, he was able to take a close interest in the Battalion and regularly visit their headquarters to inspect training and also to attend social functions held for recruiting purposes.

Lloyd's interest in motor cars continued with the purchase of another car, this time a Metalurgique for which he paid £550. Although it was already eight years old, the car remained in his ownership for the rest of his life.

Francis Lloyd's links with the Scouting movement had started in Shropshire during the time that he commanded the Welsh Territorial Division. Throughout his career in the Army, Lloyd was invited to inspect troops of Scouts at annual camps, and this continued into his retirement when on one occasion he went to Dulwich Common. 2,000 Scouts from the Camberwell Division marched past him - at the time he thought that this must have been the largest single rally of Scouts in the world!

The second anniversary of the Armistice was commemorated by the

145

unveiling by the King of the Cenotaph in Whitehall and the burial of the 'unknown soldier' in Westminster Abbey. On the following day Lloyd was present at the unveiling of the memorial in the front of the Royal Exchange, to troops from London who lost their lives in the Great War. From the end of the war until his illness at the end of 1925, Sir Francis Lloyd was invited to unveil countless war memorials, not only in the metropolis of London, where he had become such a well-known figure during the war, but over the length and breadth of England and Wales. The memorials varied from commemorative windows in churches to 'crosses' in churchyards, cenotaphs and other substantial monuments in town centres.

At the opening of Parliament in February 1921, Lloyd noted that it was the first time since the beginning of the war that the Brigade of Guards appeared in red tunics. In the new parliament, Churchill was no longer Secretary of State for War, and had been succeeded by Sir Laming Worthington-Evans, who Lloyd met at a recruiting meeting for the Territorial Force at Guildhall. Lloyd spoke at the meeting and emphasised again the need in his view to maintain the Territorial and Volunteer Forces in peacetime, to be ready for any eventuality. Bonar Law resigned as leader of the Unionists in March due to illness and was succeeded by Austen Chamberlain.

At intervals over many years Francis Lloyd took French lessons at the Berlitz School in London. Apart from visits to France before the war, Lloyd took several holidays in North Africa, the first of which was in 1921, when he spent two months in Algeria and Tunisia, and where no doubt his ability to speak fluent French was of use. Francis and Mary also spent some of their leisure time at the Ranelagh Club at Barnes on the banks of the Thames. Lloyd became a member of the management committee of the Club, and *The Sketch* published a montage of caricatures of the leading members under the title *Personalities at a Popular Rendevous*, including one of Lloyd.

In July 1921, the King presented new Colours to the Grenadier, Coldstream and Scots Guards at Horse Guards Parade. Lloyd attended the ceremony at which over 3,300 men were on parade, and thought that it 'was all very well done'. The first State Ball at Buckingham Palace since 1914 was held during the visit of the King and Queen of the Belgians. About 2,000 people attended, including Sir Francis and Lady Lloyd, but they left after supper. Lloyd continued to attend the quarterly meetings in London of the Duke of York's School, together with the occasional visit to the school at Dover. In June 1922 he accompanied HRH the Duke of Connaught to the school when the Duke unveiled the War Memorial.

Francis Lloyd's association with the Territorial Army continued with his appointment as Colonel Commandant of the Essex Cadet Force. In his first Order of the Day as Commandant he emphasised the high value of cadet training 'both to the individual trained and to the State, good citizen of which the cadets are thus helped to become'. Lloyd added that he intended 'to personally direct, inspect and advise in the cadet affairs which pertain to my appointment'. However, his time in this role was an increasingly frustrating one, as he felt that he was used just as a figure-head and not involved in any of the decision making. In addition, some people went over his head on certain issues without telling him, and this led him to resign in July 1925, after three years in the post.

As Colonel of the Royal Welch Fusiliers, Lloyd paid annual visits to the camps of several battalions of the Regiment and this meant travelling to both Wrexham in north Wales and Pembroke in the south, and more rarely to Aberystwyth in the west, which was familiar to him from his time as Commander of the Welsh Territorial Division.

By October 1922, there was tremendous excitement in the country about the political situation. The Coalition led by Lloyd George had become embroiled in corruption and at a famous meeting at the Carlton, Bonar Law persuaded the Conservative backbenchers to end the Coalition and fight the next election as an independent party. Austen Chamberlain resigned as party leader, Lloyd George resigned as Prime Minister, and Bonar Law was returned on 23 October in both jobs. Parliament was immediately dissolved and a General Election called.

At Chigwell, Sir Francis Lloyd and his other landowner friends put posters on their gates in support of Sir Richard Beale Colvin, the Conservative candidate. Polling day was on 15 November, and on the next day Lloyd went up to London, where he visited the Carlton to hear the election results as they came in. The result was an overall majority for the Conservatives who won 344 out of the 616 seats, but Lloyd noted that the Labour Party had substantially increased their number of seats to 150, at the expense of the Liberals who were split between Asquith and Lloyd George.

Away from politics Sir Francis Lloyd received a letter from the Privy Council Office informing him that he had been reappointed as a Member of the Court of Governors of the National Library of Wales for another five years from December 1922. After Christmas, Francis Lloyd took his sister Maudie with him on his second tour of Tunisia and Algeria, which lasted for two months and during which they travelled 1,550 miles.

Lloyd was now attending regular meetings at Chigwell School in his role as Chairman of the Governors. A sub-committee was set up to seek tenders for repairs to the roof and the tender from Foster of Loughton was accepted. In the following year Lloyd with Savill and Dent agreed to purchase Sandon Lodge for £3,000. The intention was to convert the house for use as a sanatorium which was urgently needed by the School.

Parliament was dissolved in November 1923, only a year after the previous election, when the Conservative Prime Minister, Stanley Baldwin,[136] announced that his Government would be seeking a mandate to introduce tariff protection in order to tackle growing levels of unemployment. The mood of the country, according to Lloyd, was that Baldwin would be re-elected: 'Everyone admires his courage and straightforwardness, but fears that no Party will have a working majority'.[137]

At Chigwell the local Conservative Party swung into action and Lloyd attended a meeting in the Parish Room at which the organization for canvassing was settled. Sir Leonard Lyle had been adopted as the Conservative candidate for the Epping Division, in the place of Brigadier General Sir Richard Beale Colvin who had retired. Lyle was a resident in the constituency but had to overcome the disadvantage of being comparatively unknown personally to a large number of the electors. His opponent, Granville Sharp, the Liberal Party candidate, had the advantage of having fought the constituency in the previous November, when he lowered the Conservative majority very considerably. On Polling Day on 6 December there was dense fog locally in the evening which Francis Lloyd thought must have prevented many from voting. However, Lyle was successful, polling 14,528 votes to the 12,954 for Granville Sharp. Overall the Conservatives won the most seats (258), but Labour led by Ramsay MacDonald (191) and Asquith's reunited Liberal Party (158) gained enough to produce a hung Parliament. The first ever Labour government was formed in January 1924, but being in a minority dependent on the support of the Liberals, it only lasted for ten months. Lloyd met his friend John Buchan, a strong Conservative, 'but he was not so afraid of the Labour Government as we are'.[138]

Sir Francis left London, with his sister Maudie, on their now annual visit to Tunisia and Algeria, not returning until the middle of April.

In June 1924, Francis Lloyd met Howard Wall, Chairman of the local Conservative Party at Chigwell. Sir Leonard Lyle had indicated that he would not seek re-election at the next General Election, and with Ramsay MacDonald's minority Labour Government only surviving with the support of the Liberals, Wall wanted to have a new candidate ready should an election be called in the autumn. He had not found any suitable candidate and Sir Francis Lloyd suggested that they should ask Winston. Wall reported back in early September that Winston Churchill would in all probability be adopted as a candidate for Essex, but it was not quite settled. Confirmation was soon received but the reaction in the constituency was mixed, with 'some people very doubtful about him, but on the whole, as far as I can find out, people are pleased'.[139]

Ever since its formation, Sir Francis Lloyd had supported the British Legion. In the summer of 1924 he was asked if he would give a short talk on the 'wireless' to commemorate the tenth anniversary of the start of the Great War. Lloyd spent some time preparing a speech which was then typed by his secretary Kitty Mitchell, and on 4 August Lloyd made his way to the studios of the British Broadcasting Company at 2 Savoy Hill in London: 'I read a speech on what occurred ten years ago on 4th August 1914 and also on the British Legion. It was broadcast all over the Empire'. He received many letters of thanks and congratulations on his broadcast, which was valuable publicity for the British Legion.

Notwithstanding his financial difficulties, Francis Lloyd continued to enjoy his lifestyle at Rolls Park, commenting one evening that we had 'a very good bottle of Chambertin for dinner which we discussed with much feeling. Pepys could not have liked it better'.

At the beginning of October Sir Francis Lloyd saw his local doctor in Loughton, Dr Butler Harris, when it was thought that he might be suffering from cancer of the prostate, and he also saw his physician in London, Sir George Hastings. Medical opinion was divided on the seriousness of the condition, but he was recommended to see Dr Finzi at his rooms in Harley Street, who was known to treat the condition with x-rays. Lloyd underwent the course of treatment and the outcome was that the size of any tumour had been reduced.

Sir Francis returned to Rolls Park at Chigwell. Winston Churchill had been adopted as the Constitutionalist candidate for the Epping Division, and had already started his campaign in anticipation that Parliament would be dissolved within the next couple of months and an election called. Sir Francis and Lady Lloyd not only acted as host to Churchill when he stayed at Rolls Park during the campaign but followed his progress daily as he toured the constituency speaking at meetings.

Churchill opened his campaign on 3 October at Waltham Abbey where he said that he believed that an election would come in the next few months or even within the next few weeks, and that a political crisis was arising very quickly. A week later Winston and Clementine Churchill visited Rolls Park in the afternoon to meet many of the ladies and gentlemen of Chigwell for tea. Churchill informally addressed the tea party in the Drawing Room and made a most excellent short speech.[140] He had already told his agent James Hawkey that he would be staying with Sir Francis Lloyd, 'the old general', as he referred to him privately. That evening dinner was taken early when Lord Wodehouse, and James Hawkey joined the party, and afterwards they all went to Woodford Hall where Churchill spoke for sixty-two minutes – 'very eloquent and full of common sense' – Lloyd wrote in his diary, adding:

He attacked the Government most incisively, at the same time exceedingly moderate and never personal. His final stroke was that Socialism was the definite issue before the Country, and that the duty of the Country was to provide a solid, stable Government capable of carrying out its principles for a definite period of years.

The Churchills stayed at Rolls Park that night, and the next morning Francis Lloyd took Winston to the King's Head where he introduced him to Arnold, the landlord. Churchill went on to a meeting at Wanstead, but Francis Lloyd had to attend the dedication of the Memorial Chapel at Chigwell School.

Lord Lambourne was there, like a bear with a sore head, and would scarcely speak to Lloyd. Lambourne hated Churchill and Francis thought that he did not like him entertaining him at Rolls. That evening Churchill, accompanied by Francis Lloyd, first spoke at a meeting at Lopping Hall, Loughton, after which he went on to Chingford. That night the Churchills went back to Chartwell.

The campaign continued and the Churchills next stayed at Rolls Park on the following Wednesday after more meetings at Wanstead, Woodford and Buckhurst Hill. 'We all went home to supper arriving shortly before 11.00pm', Francis Lloyd noted in his diary. On the next day about twenty farmers came to Rolls Park and talked to Winston in the Drawing Room. They brought forward their grievances and wishes, while he told them shortly his opinions. More meetings took place in the evening before they all returned to Rolls Park.

Sir Francis Lloyd next heard Churchill speak at a meeting in the Queen's Hall in London, where there was an audience of 2,500. Lloyd drove Clementine Churchill up to London, where they had lunch at Pagani's before going on to the meeting. They were back in Loughton and later Aldersbrook that evening for more electioneering.

The next day was Nomination Day when three candidates were declared: Winston Churchill, Constitutionalist; Granville Sharp, Liberal; and McPhie, Labour or Communist. The Conservatives were all delighted when they heard that the Communist (Socialist) was standing as they hoped that it would spoil the vote. That evening Winston 'being in a communicative mood, we stayed up till about twelve o'clock talking'.[141] The campaign continued until Polling Day on 29 October. The count took place in the Church Room in St John's Road at Epping, and the declaration for the Epping Division was made at 2.00pm on the following day:

Winston Churchill (Constitutionalist):19,843

G Granville Sharp (Liberal): 10,080

J R McPhie (Socialist): 3,768

MAJORITY   9,763

When all the constituencies had declared, the Conservatives (including Constitutionalists) had won 419 seats and obtained a large parliamentary majority. Winston Churchill was appointed Chancellor of the Exchequer in Stanley Baldwin's government.

At the end of November, Mrs Churchill wrote a letter to Sir Francis Lloyd, the original of which has survived:

My Dear Sir Francis

How nice of you to want photographs of Winston & me.

We have not any left, but we soon shall have some more & then we will send them.

This has been a wonderful month beginning with our Epping Campaign in which you and Lady Lloyd helped so much, both by your influence & speeches & by your great personal kindness to us, & sending in Winston's appointment which I hope & trust may be for the good of the Country.

Yours very sincerely,

Clementine S Churchill

In the middle of November 1924, Sir Francis Lloyd went up to North Wales to unveil the War Memorial in Wrexham to the 9,657 officers and men of the Royal Welch Fusiliers who lost their lives in the war. This was of particular significance to Lloyd as he was not only Colonel of the Regiment, but his ancestors came from Denbighshire and he was of course born in the Welsh Marches. The monument is a very imposing one, by the noted Welsh sculptor Sir William Goscombe John, and the two bronze figures represent an eighteenth century fusilier passing the Colours to his twentieth century counterpart. The overall height of the memorial is about twenty feet and the figures are about ten feet.

The unveiling and dedication of the memorial took place in the presence of a very large gathering. The *North Wales Guardian* considered that the ceremony was in every way worthy of the occasion, and was immensely impressive and inspiring: 'It was of course almost exclusively military in character, but the human touch was present throughout, and all who took part were deeply moved'. In his address Sir Francis Lloyd said that it was good that memorials were erected up and down the land to tell future generations what had been done, and it was the pride of the town and of Wales that they had one of the best there to remind them of what those men died for.

The memorial was originally erected on the corner of Grosvenor Road and Regent Street, but was moved in the mid 1960s to its present site on land at the junction of Park Avenue and Chester Street.

The success of the Conservatives at the General Election and that of

151

Winston Churchill in the Epping Division was celebrated at two functions in London in December. The Essex District Unionist Association held a lunch at the Connaught Rooms at which one of their MPs, Winston Churchill, was present and Lloyd managed to have a few words with him before he left. Two weeks later a more grand event was held at the Abercorn Rooms in Liverpool Street when the West Essex Committee gave a Dinner for 500 guests and at which Winston Churchill made a speech. Lloyd thought that the Churchills were more popular than ever. West Essex had been a very wise choice and it had also done Churchill a very good turn. The Churchills visited the constituency whenever they could but Winston's position as Chancellor of the Exchequer kept him busy in London. In May 1925, Francis Lloyd was invited to lunch with Churchill at 11 Downing Street. Although he thought Churchill looked tired, 'Winston was full of his recent Budget (he took sixpence off income tax) and what he was going to do'.

Eight months after Lloyd had visited Wrexham he unveiled a much smaller war memorial in the village of Hempstead in north Essex. It was here that the ancestors of his grandmother, Louisa Harvey, came to live in the middle of the seventeenth century when they purchased the manor of Wincelow Hall. Although the family soon moved further south in the county to live at Rolls Park at Chigwell, they still retained the manor at Hempstead, where by tradition the coffins of seven generations of Harveys lie in the vault of the parish church of St Andrew.

The war memorial to the men of Hempstead is a simple Celtic cross in Cornish granite, ten feet high, bearing the names of fourteen men from the village who made the great sacrifice in the 1914-1918 war. The memorial is in the centre of the village. At the unveiling of the memorial on 4 July 1925 a procession led by the Salvation Army Band, and including Boy Scouts from Saffron Walden, the Sampfords and Hempstead, ex-Servicemen, and children from the local school made its way to the Bluebell Inn, where on the opposite side of the road the memorial had been erected. In the presence of a large company of villagers and friends, Sir Francis Lloyd inspected the Boy Scouts and ex-Servicemen. After the unveiling, two Scout buglers sounded the Last Post and Lloyd gave a 'stirring address'.[142] Patriotic selections were played by the band and sung by the school children, and the proceedings ended with the Reveille and the National Anthem.

'To Protect the Weak'

The economic recession and unemployment became of increasing concern to the Government, and some of the more right-wing newspapers and organizations saw the threat of communism lurking behind events.

Early in 1925 Sir Francis Lloyd met Major Caryl Fiennes, who was canvassing interest in forming a society for people who would be prepared to work on the railways, Tubes, buses and at power stations in the event of a revolution or general strike. The name of the proposed organization changed several times during its gestation, but an early one was The Public Supply (Defence) Association. This was a politically sensitive proposal and most politicians seemed disinterested.

Francis Lloyd was out of the country in March and April on his annual visit to North Africa but by July, Fiennes had formed an Executive Committee including some well-known names: Lord Hardinge, a former Viceroy of India, Admiral of the Fleet Earl Jellicoe, Sir James Rennell Rudd, the Earl of Scarbrough and Lieutenant General Sir Francis Lloyd. In August Lloyd was appointed Vice Chairman of the Executive Committee, and the Association called itself the Organisation for the Maintenance of Supplies (OMS).

In the event of a General Strike the volunteers would have to be organized on a local basis and it was therefore decided to set up local committees. Members of the Executive Committee visited most of the Metropolitan boroughs around London and by the autumn the movement had been established in twenty-two of the boroughs. Later, Lloyd was even to go to Oswestry to address a meeting of a local committee set up in the Welsh Marches.

The organization was now ready to seek the support of the Press and on 25 September issued a statement about its aims and objectives which was widely reported. The statement explained that the organization was strictly non-political and non-party in character, and the object it had in view was to register and classify those citizens of all classes and either sex who were prepared to provide voluntary assistance in maintaining the supply of food, water and fuel, and the efficient running of public services indispensable to the normal life of the community. It was emphasized that the organization 'has no aggressive or provocative aims. It is not formed with any idea of opposing the legitimate efforts of Trade Unions to better the status and conditions of employment of their members, and it is in complete sympathy with any constitutional action to bring about a more equitable adjustment of social and economic conditions'.

Registered members were to be placed in various categories:

1. Voluntary workers on railways, Tubes, power stations, gas and water works, and in the handling of foodstuffs

2. Drivers for motor vehicles, etc.

3. Volunteers for postal and telegraph and telephone services.

4. Volunteers unfit for manual or technical service, but ready to give

153

clerical, hospital and general help.

All the persons enrolled in Class 1 were to be available for service as special constables.

Francis Lloyd thought that on the whole the Press was favourable. However, in a 'leader', the *Daily Express* had some reservations:

> Is it the duty of a voluntary organisation to undertake so vital a task as the safeguarding of the indispensable services of the community? Surely not. It is plainly the duty of the Government. If the Government feels itself unable to cope with the difficulty, then having abrogated its function, it should be replaced by another Government.
>
> The simple truth is that the OMS is but the latest manifestation of the fear of Communism. That fear is being played upon a little too violently at the present time.

The *Daily Mail* in a 'leader' under the title 'To Protect the Weak' had some sympathy for the objectives of the OMS but with similar concerns:

> The appeal to the able-bodied men and women of the country should be sure of an immediate and stirring response.
>
> What the Communists propose is to starve the country into submission to their tyranny by methods which Moscow has taught them.
>
> But we are bound to say that *the obvious and plain duty of the Government was to do itself what he* [Lord Hardinge and the OMS] *is doing*. It ought long ago to have issued a call for volunteers to meet the emergency and defend the liberties of the nation. Unfortunately the Government has shirked its plain duty.

Some people also questioned its role and wrote to newspapers. Lloyd responded to a letter in *The Times* and tried to explain how the OMS fitted in with the public authorities such as the police:

> The letter … appears to suggest that OMS desires to encroach on the province of the Special Constabulary Reserve in the duty of maintaining law and order should an emergency unhappily arise.
>
> There is no such intention and no possibility of such overlapping. It is surely plain that in so far as the preservation of law and order is a matter of the suppression or prevention of rioting, such duty can only be undertaken under the authority of the responsible Government.
>
> The function which the OMS has set before itself in this particular goes no further than the registration of men who are willing to offer

their services for such duty, but should those services be called for they would pass at once under the control of the proper police authorities. It will, therefore, come to precisely the same thing whether a citizen prefers to enrol himself at once in the official Special Constabulary Reserve or to register with his local Committee of the OMS and so pass on.[143]

Sir Francis Lloyd was to die before the organization was put to the test. He consulted Dr Finzi at the end of October 1925, and the prognosis was not good. The prostate was enlarged again and further treatment was recommended. Lloyd was undecided whether to proceed with the treatment but both Dr Butler Harris and Sir George Hastings recommended that he should. Sessions of electrical treatment took place at the end of November but left Lloyd in great pain, and the end was only two months away. One of his last public meetings locally had been early in November when on Remembrance Sunday he went to Waltham Abbey Church:

I stayed in bed and got up my speech – I do not think I have ever taken so much trouble about one. I got to Waltham Abbey at three o'clock where I found an enormous congregation of about or over one thousand people. I spoke from the pulpit as I could not see or be seen unless I did so.

I spoke for about twenty minutes and I have reason to believe it was a success.[144]

Did he realize that this would be his last opportunity to use his powers of oratory and to remind people of what so many soldiers had lost their lives for? But he need not have worried, his popularity had still not faltered.

8

A Hard-working Soldier

Sir Francis Lloyd died at Rolls Park, Chigwell, on 26 February 1926 at the age of seventy-two, having been ill for two months. He was a distinguished soldier, a great gentleman and a lovable squire of the Welsh border. With all he carried great popularity. His few enemies were insignificant compared to his many devoted and influential friends.

Many newspapers, national and local, reported his death, and an obituary in *The Times* assessed his character and appearance:

> To those who saw him infrequently, on parade, in his office, at an investiture, or casually in the town, Sir Francis Lloyd presented a striking and memorable appearance. His stern and searching eye, his black and heavy moustache, contrasted somewhat with his exquisitely clothed figure, the tunic in which breathing, let alone muscular movement, seemed impossible, and the row upon row of medal ribbons. With his quaint love of finery he was nevertheless a strong man, scrupulous in behaviour, a wise administrator, a painstaking commander, not intolerant, but of high principle, not stern but just.[145]

Sir Francis had ideas of discipline and decorum which were at that time considered old-fashioned. This caused some friction, but his sense of justice was firm enough to control his naturally quick temper – a trait that he had possibly inherited from his great-grandfather, Admiral Sir Eliab Harvey who commanded the *Temeraire* at Trafalgar.

In the days of strenuous endeavour during the war, Sir Francis was one of the busiest men in the country, but he was a proved man of push and go, and was always capable of keeping abreast of his great task. While in command of the Welsh Division he came into intimate contact with Wales and its people, who loved, honoured and respected him. There was no part of the Principality he did not visit in the course of his duties.[146]

His skill as a leader of men was revealed in many directions, but seldom more strikingly than on the occasion of the collective training of the Welsh Division at Aberystwyth in 1910, when the Territorials acquitted themselves well in the manoeuvres against the Regulars.

It was in his private life, on the visits to his Welsh border home that one saw Sir Francis at his best. Here loyalty to the town of Oswestry found interesting expression. It was his habit, when at Aston in November to 'walk' with the Mayor of Oswestry to church on Civic Sunday. One year the Chief Magistrate, who happened to be a Methodist, invited the corporation and friends to accompany him to his own place of worship instead of the Parish Church. On his way to the Guildhall to take his place in the procession, where he was a notable figure in his full military dress, the Major General met a neighbouring squire: 'Hello, Franky', said the latter, 'where are you off to in your fine feathers?' 'To walk with the Mayor', replied Sir Francis. 'But', explained the other in disgusted surprise, 'I am told the Mayor is going to the Methodist Chapel'. 'I don't care,' retorted Sir Francis. 'If he is going to ... I am going to follow him'.[147]

At Chigwell, Sir Francis was remembered for his personal charm and interest in the village. He unveiled the two War Memorials, the screen in the chancel of St Mary's Church, and the cross adjacent to the churchyard.

On the day before Sir Francis Lloyd's funeral his coffin was taken from Rolls Park to the Guards' Chapel at Wellington Barracks in London. The coffin, borne in an open Army lorry, was escorted by detachments of the Essex Field Artillery, the Essex Territorials, and the Chigwell Grammar School Cadet Corps to Chigwell Church where the procession halted for a two minutes silence, after which the Last Post was sounded, before continuing its journey to London.[148]

At the service held in the Chapel on the following day the King was represented by Colonel J V Campbell VC, the Prince of Wales by Major the Hon Piers Legh, and the Duke of Connaught by Lieutenant Colonel Douglas Gordon. Supporters of the pall were General the Earl of Cavan, General Sir Henry Mackinnon, Major General Sir Harold Ruggles-Brise, Lieutenant General the Hon Sir Frederick Stopford, Colonel B N Sergison-Brooke, Major General Sir George Jeffreys, Colonel Sir Henry Streatfeild, Lord Treowen, Lord Blythswood, Lieutenant Colonel W Garton, and Colonel Maxwell Earle.

After the service the coffin was taken to Knightsbridge Barracks and then transported to Aston Hall for burial. It remained in the private chapel at Aston overnight, with the committal service at noon on the following day. The Chapel was too small to accommodate even one-third of those attending the service, which was conducted by the Archbishop of Wales. The coffin was draped in a Union Jack, on which lay General Lloyd's plumed hat, sword, medals and decorations, and was carried by eight tall warrant officers and sergeants of the Royal Welch Fusiliers.[149]

Although the chapel is now derelict, the grave and monument to Sir Francis Lloyd may be seen today in the churchyard adjoining the chapel.

Reminiscences

A mourner at the service in the Guards Chapel:

> It was strange to see how many men in the congregation were deeply moved at the beautiful military funeral service to Sir Francis Lloyd in the Guards' Chapel. Men do not easily show emotion, but 'Frankie' was beloved. He was the very devil of a martinet, yet every officer ever under him in the Guards and all who served closely with him in other services were simply devoted to him. It was amazing how he could overcome the impression caused by his corseted figure and the two gold bangles he always wore and by his habit of only drinking a crème de menthe or kummel at lunch. Yet these were forgotten by everybody who knew him. No man was ever so loyal to his subordinates. Time after time he took the blame on himself for things they had done, sometimes against his own orders, solely lest they should suffer. He was fearless, just, tremendously conscientious, and a very good speaker. It is a great pity both for the Conservative party and the Club that he was never made chairman of the Carlton Club. Last time this triennial appointment became vacant, it rested between him and Lord Younger, who received the preference for political reasons. Sir Francis bore his very long and painful illness with singular fortitude, though he himself never doubted its fatal termination.[150]

One of the mourners in the Chapel at Aston Hall recalled that:

> In the early part of November 1914 I happened to be at a certain regimental headquarters in Westminster. News of the exploits around Ypres, of the first battalion of a famous London Territorial unit had just come through – the military censorship had not then been tightened – and the consequence was that recruiting for the second battalion was brisk. The first contingent of reinforcements to the first line battalion were drawn up in the spacious drill hall, awaiting the arrival and inspection of Sir Francis Lloyd, General Officer Commanding, London District. The reinforcements were representative of many social grades: West End 'nuts', commercial travellers, mechanics, City clerks, and world-wanderers from British Colombia, the Argentine and the Back o' Beyond generally. They were sound in wind and limb and athletes all. The ponderous doors of the hall swung open; the sentry at the entrance saluted and in stepped a red-tabbed 'brass-hat', picturesque in appearance, lively in manner – General Lloyd. Behind Sir Francis – a good many yards – were one or two staff-majors and 'buckshee' subalterns. Swiftly

through the ranks went the General, after responding to the salutes of the Commanding Officer and others. As he went along the lines, looking into each man's eyes – a parade characteristic he shared with Ian Hamilton – his keen dark face wore a look of soldiery satisfaction. He returned to the front rank of the contingent and then the following sotto voce dialogue took place (as near as I can remember the words):

'D____d good men, Colonel.'
'They are, sir.'
'Arms and ammunition good?'
'Yes, sir.'
'Rations been good?'
'Yes, sir.'
'When are the men going?'
'Tonight.'

Then addressing the reinforcements the General said again in words as far as I can recall:

'Well gentleman I have very little I need say to you except that I feel sure you will do well. As far as I can judge there won't be much cavalry work for a long time. You know what your first battalion did. You do the same – give them the 'bayonet'! Good bye and best of luck.'

The doors swung open again. The little Welshman strode out. The whole business had taken about ten minutes.

Sir Francis Lloyd came from a large family: he was the eldest of the five sons and five daughters of Richard and Frances Lloyd. His relationship between all his brothers and sisters appears to have been a close one, not only in their younger years but continuing into their adult life. He was possibly slightly critical of Rossendale, who succeeded him as owner of Aston Hall and Rolls Park, who Francis thought remained at Selattyn looking after his parishioners, and did little else, whereas Francis was forever active as a soldier.

Francis married in 1881, but it was four years before he left England for active service in the Sudan and it was not until 1900 that he was severely wounded in the Boer War at the age of forty-seven years. No children were born of the marriage, although it is clear that they enjoyed the company of their young nephews and nieces. Visits were often made to Selattyn to see Rossendale and Katie's three children, and Mary Lloyd's brother, Francis Gunnis, and his wife Ivy lived in London with their three sons Geoffrey, Rupert and Nigel, who often visited their uncle and aunt. Laurence Holbech, a son of Francis Lloyd's sister, Ada, was commissioned in the

Grenadiers and was a frequent visitor to Great Cumberland Place. He was given one of Lloyd's swords and had a distinguished career in the Grenadiers.

The letters from Francis Lloyd to his wife, Mary, during the two Sudan campaigns and the Boer War, show clearly the love they both shared for each other. In the years between the Boer War and the Great War, Francis and Mary Lloyd enjoyed a social lifestyle that included regular visits to the theatre in London and holidays in Europe. During the 1914-1918 war Lady Lloyd, as she had become by then, became actively involved in charitable work including organizing a unit of the VADs, and supporting voluntary work looking after amputees at Queen Mary's Convalescent Auxiliary Hospital at Roehampton where her husband was Chairman of the Trustees. At Rolls Park in the 1920s she was hostess to the Churchills, and this continued after the death of Sir Francis.

As a soldier Lloyd saw active service in three campaigns, during which his leadership was 'Mentioned in Despatches' and recognized in the award of the DSO. He commented in his diaries that he had served under fire in each of the three battalions of the Grenadiers, something of which he was proud. During his time as commander of the Guards Brigade at Aldershot for four years from 1904, his reputation as a strict disciplinarian may have been forged. The allegation, made later, that he was too hard on his troops has never been substantiated, and may have only been suggested by a rival faction at the time of his appointment as GOC London District. The welfare of his soldiers was always his first concern and he always acted fairly in matters of discipline.

At the outbreak of the Great War in 1914, Lloyd was not given a field command. This he regretted, and he felt that given the opportunity he would have brought invaluable experience to the task. Whether the powers in the War Office considered that there were other more qualified commanders or that Lloyd's health would not stand up to the conditions of the Western Front can only be conjectured. However, as matters turned out, the expansion of the role of the GOC London District between 1914 and 1918 showed that he was the right man for that command.

Lloyd's diaries provide little insight into his views on the conduct of the Great War by the politicians or the commanders-in-chief. When Field Marshal Sir John French returned from France at the end of 1915, and became C-in-C Home Forces, Francis Lloyd continued a close working relationship with him that had started many years earlier. In many of the speeches that Lloyd made at the unveiling of War Memorials after the war, he emphasized the need for people to be unselfish and to build a new country; otherwise the sacrifice of the fallen would have been in vain. An economic depression was already on the horizon and industrial unrest was simmering, but Lloyd's plea for the nation to work together was to go unheeded.

The reputation of Sir Francis Lloyd as a hard-working soldier was reflected throughout his time as GOC London District when the volume of work he dealt with was enormous. His ability to arrive at a rapid decision and to assimilate very quickly the points of any issue enabled him to accomplish what many bureaucrats would have considered impossible. He was criticized sometimes for the many orders which appeared under his name, few people realising that as a soldier he was merely carrying out those which he received from higher authority.

It was Lieutenant General Sir Francis Lloyd's untiring energy throughout his life that earned him the respect and love of his fellow soldiers. To this may be added his talent for oratory which made him a popular commander, always in demand to make a speech, whether the occasion was unveiling a war memorial in a rural village, or addressing a St David's Day gathering with an audience of thousands. It is a pity that his wish to enter Parliament was never fulfilled, where he could have displayed his gift to the nation.

9

Aston Hall, Shropshire

Aston Hall was one of the most ancient county seats in Shropshire, situated some two and a half miles south-east of Oswestry, and had been the home of the Lloyd family since the sixteenth century when they accumulated land in Aston, Hisland and Maesbury. The Hall was rebuilt at several different times, with the Palladian front and principal rooms of today being constructed for the Rev J R Lloyd, between 1789 and 1793, to the designs of the celebrated architect James Wyatt.

Grey sandstone from the nearby Sweeney Mountain quarry was used, and a fine, quiet ashlar-faced house of comfortable clean proportions was the result. It appears that plans for the new house were first discussed with Wyatt when he was carrying out some work nearby at Wynnstay in 1785. Wyatt's bill amounted to £149 12s 6d for designs of the house, offices and various rooms (including dining, drawing and breakfast rooms, library and the great staircase).

Two storeys high, with the roof hidden behind a parapet, the former entrance (west) front is of seven bays. At the angles there are arched niches and blank ovals with garlands hanging over them. The centre had a one-storeyed porch with Doric pilasters, but this was removed in 1975, leaving a recessed portico consisting of two giant fluted Ionic columns between fluted Ionic pilasters. The south front has three widely spaced bays. In 1975 the north and east fronts were both reformed, with a new entrance, after the Victorian service buildings had been demolished.

The narrow west entrance hall is flanked by three-bay rooms with restrained Neo-classical stucco friezes and marble chimney pieces with inlaid coloured fluting. Beyond the hall the spacious stone staircase rises in a single flight and returns in two. Wyatt's top lighting of a circular opening with a lantern overhead has been replaced by a large round-headed window at the half-landing, a less flattering form of illumination. At the time of the sale of the mansion in 1968, there were twenty-three bedrooms, subsequently much reduced after the demolition of the Victorian wings.

The private chapel to the south of the Hall was built in 1742, to replace a chapel of 1594, but is now unfortunately derelict. The chapel is of red brick with lavish stone dressings and a three-stage west tower with angle pilasters. The four-bay body also has broad angle pilasters. Some alterations were made to the chapel in 1887, by Sir Francis Lloyd's father, as part of a memorial to his wife. In the graveyard can be found some of the oldest yew trees in England, and two magnificent cedar trees stand between the chapel and the Hall.

The Hall and chapel stand in a fine park with a large lake, landscaped in 1780 by William Emes. The gateway at the entrance to the park was built in 1836 to designs by Edward Haycock. Constructed from Grinshill ashlar, two giant Doric columns carry a deep straight entablature.[151] The delicate wrought-iron gates were installed in 1910 (see below).

From 1754 to 1803 the owners of Aston Hall were clergymen. The Rev J R Lloyd was the Rector of Whittington and Selattyn as well as being the owner of the family estates. He was Mayor of Oswestry in 1795 and received two gold medals from the Society of Arts and Science, and the London Agricultural Society, for planting 60,000 trees. The estate originally extended over 10,000 acres from Weston to Whittington. The picturesque remains of Whittington Castle remain in the ownership of Sir Francis Lloyd's great niece.

When Richard Lloyd died in November 1898, his son Francis inherited Aston Hall and the estates in Shropshire. The estate then consisted of most of Aston, extending into Maesbury, Hisland, Wootton, Middleton and most of the Babbins Wood area of Whittington. Little over a year later Francis was on his way to South Africa in command of the 2nd Battalion of the Grenadier Guards and was not to return for two years. He had had little time to decide on any changes to the mansion or the running of the estate, and his wife Mary was left to look after the Hall. In many letters to Francis Lloyd while he was on active service in the Orange Free State and the Transvaal, Mary wrote of the improvements that she was making to the Hall, both internally and in the garden. These improvements must have cost a considerable sum at a time when there was an agricultural depression and income from the estate had probably reduced. It is clear from correspondence in April and May 1902 that the Aston Hall account was heavily in debt. Mary was encouraged to discuss the situation with Savill, Lloyd's London based land agent and to consider two alternatives: either to 'shut up' the Hall or to let it, and Francis Lloyd seems to have favoured the first alternative as the best means to reduce expenses. Under either alternative he and his wife would live in London 'till we can pull things round, especially should I get the Regiment'.[152] After two months of correspondence it was decided on Savill's advice not to let the Aston Hall and that Mary would continue to live there, but presumably other economies were found to help reduce the debt.

As we have seen, electric light was installed in 1908, together with a new heating system, and in 1910 Lloyd made a further small but noticeable improvement to Aston Hall when he substituted the plain iron gate at the main entrance to the park from the Holyhead road with a handsome double gate over thirteen feet high. It was hand made from wrought-iron, with a flower designed by Mary Lloyd based on the Tudor Rose, in several forms in bud and full bloom, for the decorative work. The gate was made by the village blacksmiths of Meifod and took almost a year to produce. According to Francis Lloyd it cost £186.[153]

The size of the house and the staff needed to maintain it and allow the Lloyds to entertain house guests can be judged from the entry for the 1911 Census:[154]

Major General Lloyd (aged 57)

Mrs Lloyd (wife)

Miss Forbes (Mary) (79) Aunt of Mrs Lloyd

Alfred King (60) butler

Minnie Gibson (24) cook

Rose Cox (30) lady's maid

Tom Jones (24) valet

Rose Davis (39) head housemaid

Frederick Wright (26) footman (learning)

Margaret Papple (26) housemaid

Ethel Vernon (24) kitchenmaid

Mary Inwood (18) housemaid

Henry Greatorex (17) hall boy

Laura Wilson (20) scullery maid

Henry Andrews (25) footman

Eliza Wotherspoon (38) lady's maid to Miss Forbes

The thirteen servants exclude the gardeners, who may have lived in separate accommodation. Even so there seem to be an extraordinarily high number of them. However, the Lloyds were forever inviting friends and relations to luncheon and dinner, and there would often be up to twelve people staying overnight. This was particularly true of the three years when Francis was Major General commanding the Welsh Territorial Division with its headquarters at Shrewsbury.

The opposite was the case during the five years that Sir Francis Lloyd was GOC London District, which included the First World War, when visits to Aston Hall were very rare. It was decided in 1914 to employ a caretaker at the Hall and Francis found a retired Pioneer Sergeant, Tallis, from the 1st Battalion of the Grenadiers to fulfil the role.[155] In January 1916, Lloyd paid a brief visit to Aston Hall to see some of the damage done by recent gales. Many trees in the park had been blown down, but he looked all round and inspected the house and felt that generally things were in good order. He selected some pictures from the Aston Hall collection to take back to London.

A few months later Lloyd had a long talk with his solicitor, Ronald Peake, about cutting down the cost of maintaining the Aston estate. It was decided that the blacksmith should be kept on, but that the carpenter, bricklayer and brickmaker's labourer should be dismissed. The three estate labourers were to be kept on so long as they were cutting firewood for the military camps. A fairly competent gardener was to be found to replace Steward, and the vegetables in the ground were to be gathered and sent to London, after which only rough vegetables were to be planted.[156]

Sir Francis Lloyd left the running of the estate to his local agent, Williams, and on the occasions when he was in Shropshire on military matters they met to discuss Aston Hall. In October 1916, when Lloyd saw Williams in Shrewsbury for a few minutes on his way back to London by train, the question of a new tenant for Wootton Farm was discussed and Williams suggested Richard Evans.

In the spring of 1917 Sir Francis Lloyd met Peake in London to discuss felling Babbins Wood, which he thought ought to bring in about £3,000 that could be used to make some necessary repairs to the house and pay for the taxation on the estate. It was nearly the end of the year before he was able to visit Aston again. This time he drove down with Joey Gunnis:

I went all over the house and found it in admirable order, Mrs Horbury having taken immense trouble. I went round the garden. Went down to Babbins Wood, which is nearly down. I asked Mr Williams to see that two or three trees were left to mark what the timber was. Went down to Decoy Wood and walked through it – it had grown immensely. Visited some tenants. After lunch went into the park to look at trees. Looked at Lake – three swans, Canadian Geese all there and a good many duck. A satisfactory day.[157]

In 1918 Sir Francis Lloyd talked to his solicitor about selling part of the Aston estate. His income was not enough to maintain the house and estate unless he sold some land, and the decision was taken to sell 2,000 acres. An advertisement appeared in the *Oswestry Advertizer* in October giving details of the land and buildings to be sold including:

Several valuable Shropshire Stock and Dairy Farms, Small Holdings, Accommodation Lands, Fully Licensed Houses, Cottage Holdings, Business Premises and Woodlands, all situate within four miles of the important market town of Oswestry.

The sale by auction raised £82,900, roughly £10,000 over the reserves, and Lloyd went to see Fane at Child's Bank to discuss the reinvestment of the proceeds.

While staying at Attingham Park near Shrewsbury during Easter 1919, Sir Francis and Lady Lloyd spent an afternoon at Aston Hall where they found things in good order 'considering everything'. Lloyd drove round Babbins Wood and Wootton and settled some questions about land and cottages, and went to see one of his old tenants, Mrs Griffiths, who was 95 years old. At Hisland matters were much less satisfactory, with Lewis, the tenant, a dirty and untidy man, who Lloyd decided must go. The next visit to Aston was in the summer when three months were spent at the Hall. Improvements were made to the house and Lloyd spent much time superintending the German prisoners who were working in the garden and lopping trees in the park. He also toured the estate, visiting Whittington Castle and Hisland where he looked at farm buildings, and walked over to Foxall. It was decided to ask his brother Harvey Lloyd to stay at Aston Hall during the winter to look after the interests of Sir Francis and Lady Lloyd while they were in London, and act as steward on the estate. Lloyd's work in London as a Food Commissioner and his move to Rolls Park at Chigwell meant that a year was to pass before he was able to address again the issue of what to do with Aston Hall and the estate. In September 1920 he had a long talk with Peake, who had recently visited Aston and was very clear on a number of issues concerning the estate:

That the farms were in a very bad state.

That Hisland and Whitehall must at once be tackled but Hisland first.

That nothing should be done at present to Aston Farm or Foxhall – in fact that it was inadvisable to do anything till the tenants were changed.

That the work was to be done by Lloyd.

That Lloyd should instruct his brother (Harvey) to carry on.

That Harvey was showing great keenness and doing very well.[158]

Six weeks later Lloyd went down to Aston where he was met by Harvey and his wife Kathleen, and thought that the house was in as good order as could be considering the lack of labour and previous neglect.

His brother drove him up to Wrexham where he talked to various people in the town who knew his sister Eva. There had been concern for sometime that Eva was not looking after herself properly, and was frittering away money, leaving herself in debt, and then asking her brother to sort things out. It was decided that Rossendale's wife Katie should go over from Selattyn to Wrexham to see Eva and at least ensure that she was properly clothed.

One his return from Wrexham, Francis inspected the garden at Aston Hall. He walked over to the new plantation and found that all the spruce had died, but the black poplar was doing well. Later he walked round the large lake in the park.

It was February 1921 before Sir Francis Lloyd next visited Aston, and this time he drove down in the Buick truck. He spent three days looking over the house and selecting items to take back to Rolls Park, and visited his tenants in the farms at Aston, Whitehall, Hisland and Foxhall. As agreed with Peake, Hisland was being modernized but Frank Lloyd, the local auctioneer, advised that all the other farms should be sold. A month later Lloyd took the truck down to Aston again and brought more items back to Rolls Park, including the transom of the *Temeraire*, which had originally been at Chigwell in the time of Admiral Sir Eliab Harvey, who had commanded the ship at Trafalgar, and was Sir Francis Lloyd's great grandfather. The transom remains with descendants of the family today.

Lloyd had a further meeting with Peake in April about the land at Aston and it was decided that the enormous expense of practically rebuilding the farm at Aston was more than he could afford and the only thing to do was to sell. Frank Lloyd organized the sale by auction and divided the land and cottages into seventeen lots, with 630 acres of some of the outlying portions of the estate, including three stock and dairy farms and ten small and cottage holdings offered for sale. At the sale on 9 June all but two of the lots were sold, but these accounted for almost half the acreage. Foxhall which covered 233 acres was unsold. Aston Farm, which was not sold at the auction, found a buyer two weeks later. The smaller farms and cottages were in the main bought by the existing tenants. Overall the sale produced £13,289, with a further £2,000 for Aston, which was about ten percent above the total of the reserve prices.[159]

Peake wanted to shut down Aston Hall as far as possible, transfer to Rolls Park as much as Francis and Mary wanted of the pictures and furniture, and to sell the rest – and Lloyd did not disagree. Further reductions to the workforce at Aston took place when it was decided to do away with a gamekeeper, two estate men and two gardeners. The possibility of Mr and Mrs McAlpine taking Aston, preferably unfurnished, was raised but did not come to fruition. At the end of the year, for the first time in over a century, the few remaining tenants did not receive the customary gift of beef from the Lloyd charity.

Although he had the estate at Rolls Park at Chigwell, some eleven miles north-east of London, it was not until 1920 that Sir Francis and Lady Lloyd went to live there, having spent many thousands of pounds in restoring the mansion. He now had two large houses and estates to maintain and in 1922 it was decided to let Aston Hall. To Lloyd this was a terrible wrench but it had to be done. His income could not support two large houses, certainly if he was to continue living in the lifestyle to which he had become accustomed. As far as Aston Hall was concerned, as long as there was a stick of furniture in the house, he had to pay rates and taxes. He estimated that Aston Hall was costing him £1,000 a year without living there!

Why Sir Francis decided to live at Rolls Park, and not to return to Aston Hall, his ancestral home and the place he grew up in, is not clear, but he no longer had a house in central London and was still active in many spheres in the capital which he could reach from Rolls Park without much difficulty. However, it was plain that the cost of maintaining both mansions in the continuing depression was prohibitive.

Lloyd started the process of having the furniture, pictures and family heirlooms valued. It was not his intention to sell all of them but he needed the approval of his brothers and Andrew Lloyd, Rossendale's son and ultimate heir to the family estates, if any of the heirlooms were to be sold. Rossendale subsequently objected and it took an action in the High Court before the sale could go ahead. A decision was taken to use a firm of Birmingham auctioneers, Ludlow, Briscoe & Hughes for the sale of the contents of the house. It was also decided, after several changes of mind, not to sell the pictures separately at Christie's but to include them in the sale at Aston. The library at Aston was not included in the sale, but was privately sold to Sotheran's for about £500, after Francis Lloyd had decided which books he wished to take to Rolls Park.

Some of the family portraits that had come from Rolls Park when that house was let in the second half of the nineteenth century were returned to Chigwell, as was some of the armour that had decorated a room at Aston Hall. However, this still left over 2,700 lots of furniture, pictures, porcelain and clocks that were put up for sale.

Among the most notable of the portraits for sale were those of Lady Louisa Harvey and two of her children, by Sir Thomas Lawrence,[160] a fine pastel drawing of Mrs Wilbraham (Admiral Sir Eliab Harvey's sister, Maria) by Daniel Gardiner, and one of Mrs Louisa Lloyd, Sir Francis Lloyd's grandmother, by Sir George Hayter.[161] [162] The prints and engravings, some 900 in number, comprised rare examples of Bunbury, Hogarth, Bartolozzi, Alkin and many others. A fine collection of seventeenth and eighteenth century furniture included examples of the work of Adam, Chippendale, Sheraton and Hepplewhite.[163]

Shortly before the sale at Aston Hall, Francis had lunch with his niece

Ivy Pigott Brown, who agreed to buy the portraits of Louisa Lloyd by Sir George Hayter, and Mrs Wilbraham by Daniel Gardiner. At the last minute, Lloyd decided to withdraw five of the most important pictures from the sale.

The sale took place at Aston Hall over nine days in July 1923. Reports of the sale suggest that the prices realized were mixed but most of the family portraits found considerable interest, although contrary to some newspapers, the portrait of Lady Louisa Harvey and two of her children by Lawrence did not receive a bid.[164] As previously agreed, Ivy Pigott-Brown bought two of the portraits: Mrs Louisa Lloyd by Hayter, and Maria Wilbraham by Daniel Gardiner, together with an Italian ebony cabinet which had been at Aston Hall for upwards of 300 years.

The sale realized a little over £10,000, of which £4,333 came from the sale of heirlooms, and the proceeds had to go into the Aston Trust. After expenses and commissions Francis Lloyd was left with a little over £5,000 with which to pay off his debts at Child's Bank, which amounted to £7,000. The Trustees of the Aston Trust later agreed to release to Sir Francis Lloyd £3,500 which allowed him to clear most of his debt at Child's Bank and to pay substantial amounts of super tax and back income tax. He met Fane from Child's Bank who described his financial situation as: 'Difficult as your situation has been, it is not half as bad as others'. Harvey Lloyd and Kathleen, who had been living in the main house at Aston Hall as caretaker and steward of the estate, moved into a flat which had been converted from one of the outbuildings, and the house was now empty and fit to be let or occupied.

Francis was eager to place a memorial to his mother and father in the chapel at Aston Hall and he visited Aston in the summer of 1925 to look for a suitable position in the chapel for the memorial. He found the house in a better condition than he expected, although it was still empty and unlet. He took the opportunity to go over to Whittington to look at the Castle which remained in the ownership of the Lloyd family.

On the death of Sir Francis Lloyd in 1926, ownership of Aston Hall passed to his brother the Rev Rossendale Lloyd and on his death in 1940 to his son Andrew Lloyd. Rossendale lived at Aston Hall with his wife Katie and their two daughters Gwenever and Lorna from 1927, when he retired as rector of Selattyn, until 1940. It is not clear whether they resided in the main house or in the flat previously occupied by Harvey Lloyd and his wife while they were acting as stewards for the Aston estate. By this time Andrew Lloyd was working in London, but as the two daughters were still living with their parents for part of the time it seems likely that the main house was in use. This would have meant that Rossendale had to furnish the house, or at least part of it, as the sale of the contents in 1923 had deliberately left it empty to avoid paying rates. After the Second World War, Andrew Lloyd decided that he could not afford to maintain two large mansions and, as we shall see, Rolls Park at Chigwell was demolished in 1953.

Aston Hall remained in Andrew Lloyd's ownership, and during the Second World War had been let as an annex to the orthopaedic hospital at Gobowen, a couple of miles north-east of Oswestry. In 1954 the house was empty, the hospital having relinquished it, and a new lease was taken for the expanding preparatory department of Adcote School, a girl's boarding school between Nescliffe and Baschurch. Aston Hall accommodated fifty girls, all boarding, together with six mistresses and two matrons.[165] The school had departed by 1968, when the house was put up for sale at a public auction and was purchased, together with some 232 acres of land formerly part of the Aston Hall estate, by F Tudor Griffiths (Transport) Ltd.

In January 1970 the new owner made a planning application to demolish the Hall, a listed building, and to build a new house on the site. Oswestry Civic Society, the Georgian Society, the CPRE and the Society for the Protection of Ancient Buildings, were among many people and organizations who opposed the application, which was duly refused by Oswestry Borough Council. The owner subsequently appealed to the Ministry for the Environment but this was also refused in August 1971, although the Secretary of State indicated that the owner could apply for consent to remove the Victorian wings, provided provision was made to avoid damage to the main eighteenth century building.

The inspector's conclusions had been that Aston Hall had special architectural interest in its main eighteenth century block. Its Victorian additions were detrimental to its essential character and their removal with appropriate making good of the north wall would result in 'an appreciable architectural improvement'.[166] The Hall remained empty for over five years, but after the approved alterations to the house had been made, occupation as a private house resumed. The house and park have been restored to a very high standard and remain in private occupation today. The owner has also re-acquired some of the outlying farms that originally formed part of the estate.

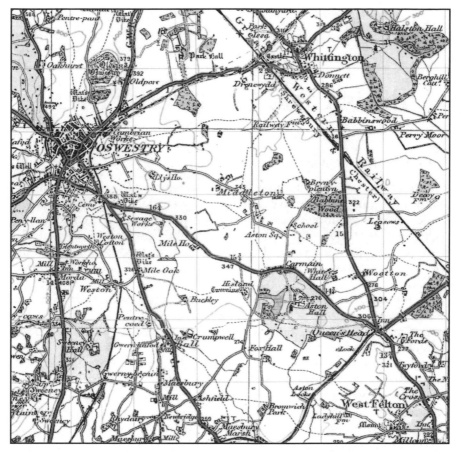

1921 Map of Oswestry. © Cassini Publishing Ltd.

10

Rolls Park, Chigwell, Essex

A LLOYD AT CHIGWELL

Eliab Harvey had been the first Harvey to come to live at Rolls Park in about 1648, and another five generations were to make it their family home. Various additions were made to the house in the seventeenth and eighteenth centuries. The exterior was quite unexceptional, and did nothing to prepare the visitor for the grandeur of the interior. The house has been described as one of the most richly decorated in Georgian England.

Admiral Sir Eliab Harvey (1758-1830) was the last Harvey to live at Rolls Park. His two sons predeceased him, leaving his six daughters to inherit the Harvey estates in Essex and other counties. Sir Eliab's eldest daughter Louisa had married William Lloyd of Aston Hall in 1804, and she inherited the Rolls Park mansion and adjoining estate. After the death of her mother in 1841, the house was mainly occupied by tenants.

In the early years of the twentieth century the house was leased to Vivian Hugh Smith, later Lord Bicester, who took up residence with his wife, Lady Sybil, daughter of the 6th Earl of Antrim. As we have seen a decision was taken in the autumn of 1919 to sell the Lloyds' London house at 26 Great Cumberland Place, and for Sir Francis and Lady Lloyd to move to Rolls Park. Chigwell could be reached by car in about forty minutes from London and the journey by train from Liverpool Street to Chigwell or Chigwell Lane stations took a similar time, although arrangements had to be made for visitors by train to be met at the station by motor car or pony and trap for the last mile to Rolls Park.

The lease of the house to Vivian Smith was terminated and on a visit to Rolls in November, Sir Francis and Lady Lloyd found Sybil Smith packing up in preparation for their move, although it was the beginning of January before they left Rolls. Sir Francis Lloyd took possession of Rolls Park on 15 January 1920, and Tapper the gardener moved in as caretaker while the repairs and modernisation works were carried out.

Sir Francis and Lady Lloyd left Great Cumberland Place in February, but as the work at Rolls was not yet finished, they took a short lease on 12A Curzon Street. Horbury, who had been employed by Sir Francis for many years, moved to Rolls Park from Aston Hall to supervise the arrival of furniture, which was being delivered by Maple's, and Sir Francis paid a visit, with Murray the architect and Osborne the builder, in the middle of March to review progress. After the meeting they all went to the King's Head where, according to Lloyd, they had a 'very expensive lunch'.[167] The installation of electricity and a new hot water system were two of the major items for modernisation of Rolls Park. Cooper the electrician and Gascoigne the hot water man met Sir Francis, with Osborne the builder, in April to discuss what was needed to be done. Lloyd received a letter from Ronald Peake, his solicitor, advising that Vivian Smith had settled the dilapidations account for Rolls, and that he would be receiving a cheque for £1,700 which could go towards the cost of the modernisation.

On the Whit Monday Bank Holiday, Sir Francis and Lady Lloyd drove down to Rolls Park and were surprised by the 'thousands of holiday makers in every conceivable vehicle, on bicycles, in donkey carts, in wagons, on omnibuses and in every way except on horseback, who were on the roads to Epping Forest'.[168] Progress was being made at Rolls, with the grand staircase, which had been carved by Thomas Kinward in the seventeenth century, 'coming out beautifully' according to Lloyd. The substantial stock of wine which had been accumulated at Great Cumberland Place arrived, and it took Horbury and Joey Gunnis, who was visiting Rolls Park, all afternoon to bin it in the cellar. Sir Francis had employed Kitty Mitchell, who originally came from Forest Gate, and who had previously worked for him, as his secretary, and she helped to sort out the library at Rolls. This chiefly involved placing Sir Francis's new bookplate showing his coat of arms with supporters, which had recently been approved by the Garter King of Arms following his award of the GCVO, in any books that did not have it already. Tapper was working in the garden which included an orchard of fruit trees and soft fruit, and it was estimated that they would need 2cwt of sugar for bottling in the autumn.

The short lease of 12A Curzon Street was due to expire on 31 July, and with Rolls Park still not ready, Sir Francis and Lady Lloyd went to Loughton Hall, a mile from Rolls Park, where they saw Mr and Mrs Maitland, and it was agreed that they would live at the Hall for a month while getting into Rolls. (The Maitlands were living at one of their other houses at Loughton). The remaining servants, with the exception of Shackleshaft, the butler, came to Rolls Park on 11 September and a week later Sir Francis and Lady Lloyd took up residence: 'We had an excellent dinner and drank to the Admiral and Lady Louisa Harvey'.[169] It was estimated that so far the cost of repairs and alterations at Rolls Park had been £8,000 (approximately £500,000 at today's prices). Lloyd estimated that it cost £12 12s a week roughly to heat, fire and light Rolls, using gas for cooking, and in all £20, including servants' wages.

Christmas Day 1920 was spent at Chigwell when Frankie and Ivy Gunnis and their two sons Rupert and Nigel came to lunch. A near neighbour who the Lloyds knew was Lord Lambourne at Bishops Hall, and he was one of several local landowners invited to Rolls Park. Sir Francis would often walk into Chigwell village and look in at St Mary's Church, where a marvellous collection of hatchments included some belonging to his ancestors in the Harvey family.

Ronald Peake came to stay at Rolls for a few days, and he and Sir Francis went over to Gravel Lane to look at a property which formed part of the estate. Next they visited Wilkins Farm in Pudding Lane which they considered only fit to be pulled down, unless someone wanted to buy it with the thirty-five acres that made up the farm. They were more impressed by Home Farm where they met Mr and Mrs Padfield: 'I was impressed by his ability and she seemed a nice woman. He seemed a really good go-ahead farmer'.[170] On another occasion he saw Padfield getting in his hay in a new and approved way – 'far ahead of the Shropshire farmers'. At a meeting of the West Essex Lodge of Fremasons at the King's Head, where Lloyd was the guest of Brigadier General Sir Richard Beale Colvin, a former tenant named Ball drove him home after the meeting. In addition there were two other former tenants at the meeting, which Sir Francis described as a really nice evening. He was quickly establishing himself as a well-known figure in Chigwell and the surrounding area.

In February 1921, Lloyd received a visit from Captain Farrow, the District Inspector of Main Roads at Epping, who came to see him about lopping the elms near the high road at the back of the garden wall. Later that year the rural surroundings of Rolls Park saw the first omnibus drive along the High Road on its way to and from Abridge and the Elephant and Castle in London. One of the pictures that Francis Lloyd brought back to Rolls from Aston Hall was the portrait of Admiral Sir Eliab Harvey, and this was hung in the Dining Room among the collection of portraits of Dr William Harvey, discoverer of the circulation of the blood, and his six brothers.

Domestically Sir Francis and Lady Lloyd still found it difficult to employ and keep satisfactory staff at Rolls Park. In the New Year the kitchen maid and her assistant were sacked for waste and incompetence, flagrant breakage and idleness, but one wonders if Lloyd's short temper and reputation as a strict disciplinarian had something to do with it. A new butler, Wright, arrived and Lloyd paid him £95 a year all included. Although Rolls Park was only eleven miles from the city, the Lloyds decided to take an apartment at 12A Curzon Street from January to the beginning of May, and they followed this practice for the next three years. They may have found Rolls Park too cold in the winter, even despite the improvements made by Sir Francis. One of Lloyd's ancestors in the Harvey family had described the house as 'the coldest in England'.

Lord Lambourne wrote to Sir Francis in June 1922 and invited him to become a governor of Chigwell School and to take over from him as chairman of the governors. Many of Lloyd's Harvey ancestors had also been governors of the school. Later in the month Sir Francis attended quarter sessions at Chelmsford where he was sworn in as a Justice of the Peace for Essex.

A distinguished visitor to Rolls Park in the 1920s was Winston Churchill. His first visit to the house was in 1924 when, as we have seen, he stood as an Independent Constitutionalist, with full Conservative support, for the Epping Division, at the General Election in October. Churchill's friendship with the Lloyd family continued after the death of Sir Francis, and Lady Lloyd occasionally provided dinner parties for him at Rolls Park during his constituency visits.

At Rolls Park there was a constant need to maintain and repair the fabric of the mansion and outbuildings. The brewhouse needed a new roof, and the roof of the old stable needed repair. An internal wall between the dining room and a corridor was threatening to fall down as a result of Osborne, the builder, removing a support when the gas was put in. Underpinning was urgently needed. Estimates were obtained for the repair of these and other items which came to £340, or in today's money about £30,000, which only served to prove that Lloyd could not maintain two large mansions, and that the decision to let or sell Aston Hall had been the right one.

Lady Lloyd continued to live at Rolls Park for several years after her husband's death. With no children of their own to inherit Rolls Park, the manor of Barringtons and the mansion passed to Sir Francis's brother, the Rev Rossendale Lloyd, rector of Selattyn in Shropshire. He soon after sold the manorial rights, but not the freehold of the estate, to Mr Lawrence Lydale Savill, a member of a well known Chigwell family. The estate in Chigwell consisted of about 420 acres.[171] With the Rev Rossendale Lloyd living in Shropshire, Rolls became empty. It was, however, let for a few years to A C M Spearman.

An inventory of the contents of Rolls Park taken in 1932 indicates that there were at least fifteen bedrooms.

LIFE AT ROLLS PARK IN THE 1920-30S

In 1978 a former servant at Rolls Park, Mrs Hems, was interviewed about her time there when Lady Lloyd was still living in the house after the death of Sir Francis. A transcript of the recording of the interview was subsequently published in the December 1978 Newsletter of the Chigwell Local History Society.[172] It gives a fascinating insight into life in a bygone age:

> It was in April 1929 when I went to Rolls Park. I'd always lived in London and I thought how lovely it seemed. I sat in the servants' hall and the cook – Miss Carrie Roberts – gave me tea. I heard the birds singing. I was about seventeen then and a housemaid. I thought Rolls Park was a wonderful house. It had an atmosphere as though all the people who lived there had led happy lives and had left something of themselves.
>
> We were a happy band of workers there. There was Mr Humphrey, the butler, Miss Roberts, the cook, and Miss Woodward who was Lady Lloyd's personal maid. We also had a kitchen maid. They used to come from Barnardo's homes, stay for a time and then be replaced by another girl. We had a chauffeur who used to do odd jobs in the house as well.
>
> We used to get up at half-past six in the morning. It was hard in the winter because although we had central heating there were great fires which were iron and brass so that I had blackleading to do and brass to clean. My hands were always chapped and grimed with dirt, although I always wore gloves.
>
> Each morning I went round the house and undid all the big wooden shutters which folded right back. There was such a clatter because they had big iron bars on them but nobody complained. I had the Dining Room, the Morning Room, the Library, the Music Room and the big hall to do before I had my breakfast, and of course, we didn't have vacuum cleaners. I polished the floor with a mixture I made up myself by breaking up pieces of beeswax and shaking them in a jar of turpentine until they dissolved. The floor absorbed it quickly and it took a lot of rubbing off but it looked lovely when it was finished.
>
> I had a little dog – Lady Lloyd's Pekinese. I used to take it out for a walk and then we'd have our breakfast. Then I would go upstairs to the bedrooms. Although they were not being used they had to be freshened and dusted every day and an awful lot of brass to clean.
>
> I thoroughly enjoyed it all. I was left to do it as I liked and the ornaments and pictures were so beautiful that it was a joy to handle them. Nearly all of them had a history and were mementoes of Sir Francis Lloyd's military service. I remember a silver cigarette case, all open work and pieces of stained glass from Ypres Cathedral from the war when it was bombed. There was a big alabaster statue on a

base in a glass case and the case was bound with lead from the first Zeppelin shot down in England. There were also flags of the different regiments in which Sir Francis had served.

Sir Francis died before I went to Rolls Park. Lady Lloyd kept all his uniform beside her bed – the busby[173] and everyday uniform in a case in her bedroom and down in the front hall a big brass screen; because he was in the Grenadier Guards, there was his Dress uniform, all his medals, swords, everything down to his boots. In the front hall were the Grenadier Guards drums – two big drums. Upstairs on the big landing was everything Sir Francis used for his exercises – a bar suspended on two ropes and he used to swing up there. It was all out of the ordinary.

Lady Lloyd had a beautiful bedroom that looked over the park – how she sat there on her own I do not know but she was miles away from the rest of us.

At 10 o'clock [pm] I used to have to go and fetch a dog from the bailiff's cottage – it was a black retriever – I used to have to take him for a walk round the grounds and then he'd go in his basket by the side of Lady Lloyd's bed and he'd stop there for the night and she would also have the Peke on her bed.

Of course, there was the Chinese bedroom and the Japanese bedroom which were furnished in that style – beautiful – and the haunted bedroom which, fortunately, was never used. I never saw any sign of a ghost and I never heard of anyone who did but I wouldn't go down there if I could help it. I didn't know of any legend about it. There was supposed to be a ghost that rode along the top of the wall in a carriage, which always mystified me. I believe people had seen that but I never did and I didn't think anybody did while I was there.

There was a famous Grinling Gibbons staircase and in the park a large cork tree stood. It was very quiet, there wasn't much entertaining. Occasionally at weekends, Lady Lloyd would have friends to stay – mostly elderly ladies like herself and quite a few famous people used to stay now and again. We used to have Mr Winston Churchill. He used to come especially at election time because this was his constituency and he used to come down for meetings round about, he and his wife, a very sweet woman by the way. He was a bit overpowering, but I suppose a man in his position would be.

We used to play cards in the evenings – Miss Roberts, the chauffeur and I. Sometimes, Lady Lloyd would go away to friends and relations and then we were free to do as we liked as long as the place was clean and safe. There was a big bustle before she came back.

She let the house for three months once and went down to Eridge to stay with a brother. She left us to keep an eye on the place. One day they let us have the car and we went to Bradwell-on-Sea in Essex, but it was a small car; the cook was a very big woman and there was about five of us in it. Every time we went round a bend we all had to lean in the opposite direction from the cook to keep the car balanced.

Normally, I was busy doing housework all the morning. Miss Roberts was in the kitchen preparing meals and the kitchen maid was doing her cleaning. She did have a hard time. She had to scrub the stone paving stones and being so old they were all trodden up and down.

We had very good food – not the same as Lady Lloyd – she had a very small appetite and had light meals, but she was fond of bananas cooked in rum. We had plenty of good meat dinners with vegetables that were grown on the estate. Breakfast we always had eggs, bacon, fish, fishcakes, toast and marmalade and, of course tea. At tea time we had bread, jam, eggs and cakes and supper consisted of such things as Shepherds pie and soup. We were very well fed and we always had sausages from Epping on Sundays.

Lady Lloyd's meals were always served on pewter plates. Miss Roberts was instructed never to put them in the oven. One day the meal was ready but she could not find the butler so she put the plate of food in the oven. The dish melted. Next day when Lady Lloyd went to the kitchen, Miss Roberts said 'I'm very sorry m'lady, I've melted the dish.' 'What have I told you?' she said. 'Well, I've been honest with you m'lady. Look on top of your pantry – you'll find many bits of pewter.'

I found Lady Lloyd very kind and she was the only one who worried about my pale cheeks. I remember she said 'I do not like the colour of your face. I've been to see Mr Hutchin (the chemist whose shop still stands today). He has recommended these Dr Williams pink pills for pale people.' I had to take these pills and they made no difference. She bought me one thing after another until in the end she said 'I do not think there is anything more I can buy now except a box of rouge.' (Of course, she didn't buy it and I wouldn't have used it in any case).

The days were long from half-past six in the morning till ten o'clock at night but we were very happy. I think it was the happiest time of my life. Rolls Park was a beautiful house with the forest and the woods all round and a lovely garden. If one wanted to go for a walk we could take the dogs out in the woods – it was really lovely.

I still go out there to have a peep as I became attached to the place.

THE DECLINE OF ROLLS PARK 1939-1953

Sir Francis Lloyd spent many thousands of pounds on restoring and maintaining Rolls Park during the time that he owned it and lived there. As we have seen he also had the upkeep of another large house at Aston in Shropshire. The story of the last three decades of the fight to save Rolls was recounted in correspondence between Sir Francis Lloyd's nephew, Andrew Lloyd, who inherited Rolls in 1940, and *Country Life* magazine.

In a letter to *Country Life*, published in the edition of 28 November 1974, Andrew Lloyd explained that:

Rolls Park, Essex, came into my family on the death in 1830 of Admiral Sir Eliab Harvey whose eldest child, Louisa had already married William Lloyd of Aston in 1804. Thereafter during the 19th century, and well into the 20th, the old house was always let, and rather badly too, because even in those days tenants could not properly afford its upkeep.

Sir Francis Lloyd decided that he would leave Shropshire and go to live at Rolls. He sank many thousands of pounds into the house and eventually took up residence there for the few years that were left to him. When Sir Francis died, my father, a humble country parson, inherited. He secured a let, but very soon he was in trouble over the huge maintenance costs, and despite all the money that had so recently been sunk into the house. There is no doubt in my mind that the Essex country house, unlike its Shropshire or Cotswold counterpart, does suffer certain structural weaknesses.

Then in 1939 came the Second World War. Rolls was immediately taken over by the army. It was while I was waiting a posting overseas that my father died, and I, for my sins, not only became the owner of Rolls, but of Aston too.

During the war, sections of different regiments of troops were to be stationed at Rolls, and it would be difficult indeed for me to describe the damage that they did. They hacked off chunks of the delectable Tudor back staircase until it was barely safe, and they had even started work on the Grinling Gibbons front staircase. Fortunately old Gibbons was just a bit too tough for them, and so in the main his work was preserved. One of the officers in charge whom I met when on leave was sufficiently shocked to suggest that an extensive 'boarding up' should be carried out and though rather

179

late in the day, much was saved in this manner.

While the army was active inside the house, other agents of even greater destruction were more active outside it. Rolls lay some thirteen miles north east of London and right on the Luftwaffe's shortest way in. The result was that the immediate area was plastered with ack-ack gun sites containing guns of the largest calibre, and as the barrage went up each night, the poor old house was shaken to its very foundations. Ack-ack guns attract bombs, and though Rolls never had a direct hit, there were many near misses. It is true that the bombs mostly fell on soft ground, but their impact was considerable nevertheless, to say nothing of the V1s and V2s.

One of the V1s circled the house many times until it cleared the old garden wall literally by inches. That wall saved us from the full force of the blast, but the explosion was enough to bring down enormous chunks of masonry and roof. Fortunately the only casualty was a heifer.

I was handed back my shambles soon after the war ended – plus a cheque for £8,000 by way of compensation. I was told at the time that even £50,000 would have gone but a short way towards the work of restoration, and in those days £50,000 was a lot of money.

One day a young man came and visited me. I think he was representing some body interested in the preservation of country houses. He went into great detail as to what I should be doing, and when I ventured to ask him how he thought I could pay for such a monumental work of restoration, when I already had another, even larger mansion on my hands also suffering war damage, he was strangely silent. For once he could make no suggestions.

Meantime, and I am talking about the early 1950s now, an industrial area showed signs of growing up around Rolls,[174] and pilfering became widespread. I think it was this fact that made me finally throw in my hand in 1953 and allow the house to be demolished.

Today all that remain of the original buildings are the stables and a cottage, although a new house has been built on the site of the orangery. However, the grand staircase, which Lloyd attributed to Grinling Gibbons, but may in fact have been by Thomas Kinward, joiner to King Charles II, was moved to Hinchingbrooke House Cambridgeshire in 1953. The original staircase at this house, destroyed by fire in 1830, was also by Kinward.

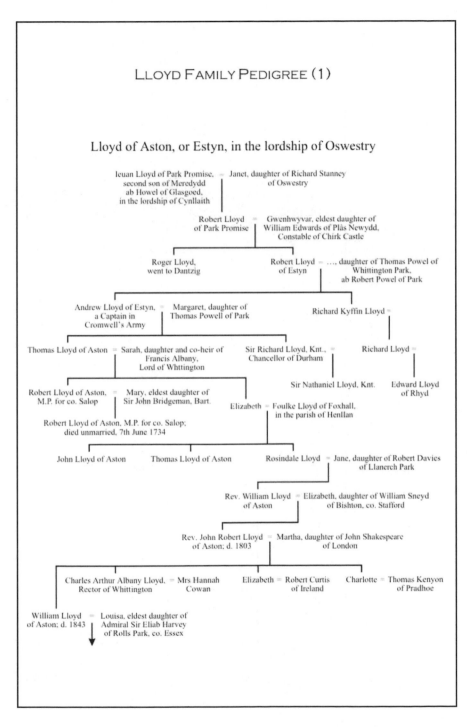

LLOYD FAMILY PEDIGREE (1)

Lloyd of Aston, or Estyn, in the lordship of Oswestry

Ieuan Lloyd of Park Promise, = Janet, daughter of Richard Stanney
second son of Meredydd of Oswestry
ab Howel of Glasgoed,
in the lordship of Cynllaith

Robert Lloyd = Gwenhwyvar, eldest daughter of
of Park Promise William Edwards of Plâs Newydd,
Constable of Chirk Castle

Roger Lloyd,   Robert Lloyd = ... daughter of Thomas Powel of
went to Dantzig   of Estyn   Whittington Park,
ab Robert Powel of Park

Andrew Lloyd of Estyn, = Margaret, daughter of   Richard Kyffin Lloyd =
a Captain in   Thomas Powell of Park
Cromwell's Army

Thomas Lloyd of Aston = Sarah, daughter and co-heir of   Sir Richard Lloyd, Knt., =   Richard Lloyd =
Francis Albany,   Chancellor of Durham
Lord of Whttington

     Sir Nathaniel Lloyd, Knt.   Edward Lloyd
of Rhyd

Robert Lloyd of Aston, = Mary, eldest daughter of
M.P. for co. Salop   Sir John Bridgeman, Bart.   Elizabeth = Foulke Lloyd of Foxhall,
in the parish of Henllan

Robert Lloyd of Aston, M.P. for co. Salop;
died unmarried, 7th June 1734

John Lloyd of Aston   Thomas Lloyd of Aston   Rosindale Lloyd = Jane, daughter of Robert Davies
of Llanerch Park

Rev. William Lloyd = Elizabeth, daughter of William Sneyd
of Aston   of Bishton, co. Stafford

Rev. John Robert Lloyd = Martha, daughter of John Shakespeare
of Aston; d. 1803   of London

Charles Arthur Albany Lloyd, = Mrs Hannah   Elizabeth = Robert Curtis   Charlotte = Thomas Kenyon
Rector of Whittington   Cowan   of Ireland   of Pradhoe

William Lloyd = Louisa, eldest daughter of
of Aston; d. 1843   Admiral Sir Eliab Harvey
of Rolls Park, co. Essex

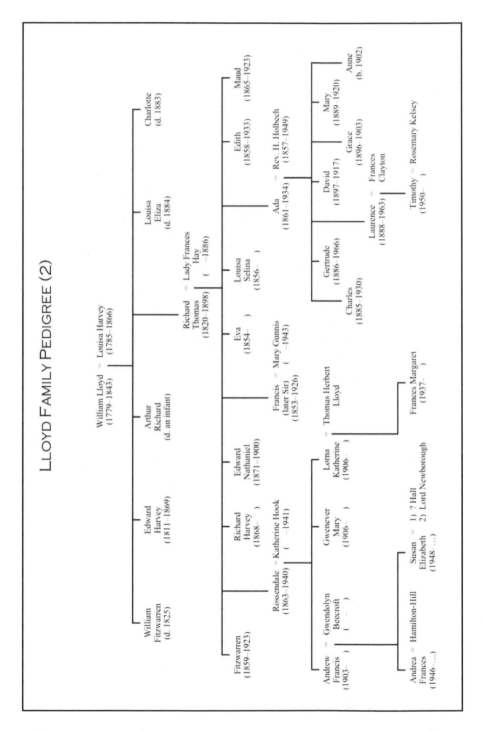

LLOYD FAMILY PEDIGREE (2)

Appendix:
War Memorials unveiled by Lieutenant General Sir Francis Lloyd GCVO, KCB, DSO

1. **Chigwell, Essex**

   (a) Memorial in St Mary's Church, unveiled 14 November 1920

   (b) Memorial adjoining Churchyard (Celtic Cross), unveiled 6 November 1921.

2. **Theydon Bois, Essex**

   Ionic cross in churchyard at St Mary's church, unveiled 20 February 1921.

3. **Waltham Abbey, Essex**

   Names of 183 men on marble slab, at west end inside Abbey church, unveiled 27 March 1921.

4. **Radwinter, Essex**

   Churchyard cross with crucifix at St Mary's church, unveiled 3 September 1921.

5. **Sydenham, Kent**

   Memorial tablet on north pillar of chancel screen at All Saints Church, unveiled 28 September 1921.(includes air raid on 19 May 1918).

6. **South Hackney Church, Middlesex**

   Cross in churchyard of St John of Jerusalem, unveiled 22 October 1921.

7. **Enfield , Middlesex**

   Cenotaph at Chase Green, unveiled 30 October 1921.

8. **Forest Gate, Essex**

   Screen at St James's church, unveiled 13 November 1921. The church was demolished in 1964, and it would appear that nothing from the memorial was saved.

9. **Beckton, Essex**

   Memorial tablet bearing names of 123 men in St Michael & All Angels Church, unveiled 11 June 1922. Church destroyed by air raid bomb in 1941 and not rebuilt.

10. **Enfield, Middlesex**

    Memorial tablet at Enfield Grammar School, unveiled 30 May 1922.

11. **Eastbourne, Sussex**

    Memorial tablet in All Saints Church, unveiled 20 July 1922. The original tablet was probably destroyed in a major fire in 1927, but replaced by a new one placed in the north aisle at the east end of the church.

12. **Manor Park, Essex**

    Cross with names of men engraved on dwarf curb wall, in City of London Cemetery, unveiled 23 September 1922.

13. **St Peter's Church, Cornhill, London**

    Four illuminated panels of names of the fallen at west end of church, unveiled 17 April 1923.

14. **Ballinger, Buckinghamshire**

    Tablet on outside of Memorial Hall unveiled on 7 June 1924.

15. **Pembroke, South Wales**

    Cenotaph in front of castle, in memory of men of Pembroke & Monkton, unveiled 28 June 1924.

16. **Wrexham, North Wales**

    Memorial to Royal Welch Fusiliers. Memorial consists of a fine group of statuary in bronze representing two Fusiliers. Unveiled 15 November 1924. Moved from original site in c1965, to site at junction of Park Avenue and Chester Street.

17. **Hempstead, Essex**

    Celtic Cross, opposite Bluebell Inn, unveiled 4 July 1925.

18. **Leytonstone, Essex**

Memorial in the form of an obelisk approximately 25 ft. high, at Harrow Green, unveiled 21 November 1925.

Memorials, the unveiling of which Sir Francis Lloyd attended, but which were unveiled by another person:

1. City of London

Memorial to London Troops in forecourt of Royal Exchange, unveiled by the Duke of York on 12 November 1920.

2. Kensington, London

Unveiled 1 July 1922, by HRH Princess Louise accompanied by Lieutenant General Sir Francis Lloyd.

3. Ilford, Essex

Unveiled on 11 November 1922, by Princess Louise, Duchess of Argyll, who was accompanied by Lieutenant General Sir Francis Lloyd.

References

1.   One source refers to Andrew Lloyd as a Colonel.

2.   Some sources refer to his father, Robert Lloyd, as of Estyn, which is probably an earlier form of Aston.

3.   Diaries of Sir Francis Lloyd. Note in diary for 1886, Archives of the Grenadier Guards.

4.   National Library of Wales: Aston Hall Correspondence, Letter No. 7830.

5.   Ibid, Letter No. 7837.

6.   Ibid, Letter No. 4563.

7.   Ibid, Letter No. 4564.

8.   Diaries, op. cit., 25 September 1924.

9.   Diaries, op. cit., 15 June 1912.

10.   *Oswestry Advertizer*, 19 August, 1874.

11.   Ibid, 10 August 1881.

12.   Ibid, 19 October 1881.

13.   Ibid, 1 March 1882.

14.   National Army Museum, MSS 7709-43, Gen. Sir Francis Lloyd Letters No.1-36.

15.   Featherstone, D. *Khartoum 1885: General Gordon's Last Stand* (Osprey 1993).

16.   National Army Museum, MSS 7709-43, Letter 13.

17.   Diaries of General Sir Francis Lloyd, October 1887, Archives of the Grenadier Guards.

18.   Diaries, op. cit., 23 August 1888.

19.   Diaries, op. cit., 21 February 1889.

20.   Diaries, op. cit., 20 December 1894.

21.   Diaries, op. cit., 28-30 September 1895.

22.   Diaries, op. cit., 3 April 1897.

23.   Diaries, op. cit., 31 July 1897.

24.   National Army Museum, MSS 7709-43, letters 37-49.

25.   There is a discrepancy between Lloyd's Diary which suggests they arrived at Fort Atbara on 9 August and the subsequent letter to his wife which indicates the 14 August.

26.   Asher, M. *Khartoum: The Ultimate Imperial Adventure* (2005).

27.   National Army Museum, MSS 7709-43, letter 46.

28.   Ziegler, Philip. *Omdurman* (1973).

29.   Charles Neufeld, a German engineer who had been the Khalifa's prisoner for thirteen years.

30.   Diaries, op. cit., 10 October 1899.

31.   Regimental Orderly Room.

32.   Judd, D, and Surridge, K. *The Boer War* (2002).

33.   National Army Museum, MSS 7709-43, letters 52-54.

34.   Ibid.

35.   Ibid, Letter 60.

36.   Ibid, Letter 61.

37.   Diaries, op. cit., 29 May 1900.

38.   Diaries, op. cit.

39.   Diaries, op. cit.

40.   Diaries, op. cit.

41.   Whitworth, Major-General RH. *The Grenadier Guards* (1974).

42.   De Wet, Christian. *Three Years War* (1902).

43.   National Army Museum, MSS 7709-43, Letter 70.

44.   National Library of Wales: Aston Hall Correspondence, Letter No. 7841, 31 May 1900.

45.   National Army Museum, MSS 7709-43, Letter 91.

46.   Judd, D and Surridge, K. *The Boer War* (2002).

47.   National Army Museum, MSS 7709-43, Letter 92.

48.   National Army Museum, MSS 7709-43, Letter 122.

49.   Diaries op. cit., 22 October 1901.

50.   National Army Museum, MSS 7709-43, Letter 164.

51.   Carver, Field Marshal Lord. *The Boer War* (1999). Lloyd's diaries give a lower number of killed and wounded.

52.   National Army Museum, MSS 7709-43, Letter 241.

53.   *The Border Counties Advertizer*, 12 November 1902.

54.   Diaries, op. cit., 1 January 1903.

55.   Diaries, op. cit., 26 January 1904.

56.   Diaries, op. cit., 2 February 1904.

57.   Diaries, op. cit., 9 February 1904.

58.   Diaries, op. cit., 19-25 April 1905.

59.   Diaries, op. cit., 22-31 July 1905.

60.   Diaries, op. cit., 21 October 1905.

61.   Diaries, op. cit., 17-31 December 1905.

62.   Diaries, op. cit., 10-12 March 1906.

63.   Diaries, op. cit., 27 June 1906.

64.   Diaries, op. cit., 13 April 1908.

65.   *The Times*, 1 July 1908.

66.   Diaries, op. cit., 28 October 1908 (original letter pasted into diary).

67.   Diaries, op. cit., 11 November 1908 (original letter pasted into diary).

68.   Diaries, op. cit., 21 December 1910.

69.   *Border Counties Advertizer,* 28 June 1911.

70.   Diaries, op. cit., 27 November 1912.

71.   Diaries, op. cit., 5 August 1913.

72.   Diaries, op. cit., 27 August 1913, name of newspaper not known.

73.   *The Times,* 27 February 1926.

74.   Diaries, op. cit., 11 March 1914.

75.   Diaries, op. cit., 14 May 1914.

76.   Diaries, op. cit., 25 May 1914.

77.   Diaries, op. cit., 2 August 1914.

78.   MacDonagh, M. *In London During the Great War (1935).*

79.   Diaries, op. cit., 1 October 1914.

80.   Diaries, op. cit., 15 October 1914.

81.   Diaries, op. cit., 16 January 1915.

82.   Dudley Ward, C H. *History of the Welsh Guards* p 3-4 (1920).

83.   *Western Mail,* 13 Feburary 1915.

84.   Diaries, op. cit., 12 February 1915.

85.   *Western Mail,* 13 Feburary 1915.

86. Diaries, op. cit., 2 March 1915.

87. *The Times* 13 December 1915.

88. National Army Museum, MSS 7709-43.

89. Weedon, B. *The History of the Queen Mary's University Hospital* (Roehampton 1996).

90. London and Metropolitan Archives, ref. H02/QM/A02/01.

91. London and Metropolitan Archives, ref. H02/QM/A01/01.

92. London and Metropolitan Archives, ref. H02/QM/A02/02.

93. *The Times*, 126 October 1918.

94. This time Lloyd may have been exaggerating.

95. Diaries, op. cit., 1 September 1915.

96. *The Times*, 1 October 1915.

97. National Library of Wales, Aston Hall Correspondence and Deeds.

98. Diaries, op. cit., 21 January 1916.

99. Stevenson, D. *1914-1918: The History of the First World War* (2004).

100. The total number of casualties, in and outside London, from the raid were thirty-eight killed and 124 wounded.

101. Diaries, op. cit., 13 October 1915. These are Lloyd's figures, which often differ slightly from those appearing in Press reports.

102. *The New York Times*, 26 February 1916.

103. Diaries, op. cit., 3 August 1916.

104. *Merchant of Venice:* Portia's answer to Nerissa's question.

105. Macdonagh, M. *In London During the Great War (1935).*

106. Diaries, op. cit., 12 December 1916.

107. Diaries, op. cit., 14 December 1916.

108. *Daily Express,* Saturday, 3 February 1917.

109. *The Times*, 3 February 1917.

110. Diaries, op. cit., 8 April 1917.

111. Diaries, op. cit., 20 June 1917.

112. House of Commons, 9 July 1917.

113. Macdonagh, M. *In London During the Great War.*

114. *The Times*, 9 October 1917.

115. *Illustrated London News*, 24 November 1917.

116. MacDonagh, M. *In London During the Great War.*

117.   *The Times*, 27 February 1926.

118.   Diaries, op. cit., 12 January 1918.

119.   Diaries, op. cit., 25 February 1918.

120.   Stevenson, D. *1914-1918*.

121.   Diaries, op. cit., 19 May 1918.

122.   Diaries, op. cit., 17 June 1918.

123.   MacDonagh, M. *In London During the Great War*.

124.   Lloyd George was in France on 30 August and did not return to London until the next day.

125.   Diaries, op. cit., 12 September 1918.

126.   Stevenson, D. *1914-1918*.

127.   Diaries, op. cit., 11 November 1918.

128.   Diaries, op. cit., 29 December 1918.

129.   Diaries, op. cit., 31 May 1919.

130.   *The World*, 28 June 1919.

131.   Diaries, op. cit., 27 September 1919.

132.   *Hansard*, 18 December 1919.

133.   Diaries, op. cit., 20 December 1920.

134.   Diaries, op. cit., 31 May 1920.

135.   *The Times*, 5 June 1920.

136.   Bonar Law had resigned earlier in the year due to ill health.

137.   Diaries, op. cit., 14 November 1923.

138.   Diaries, op. cit., 21 January 1924.

139.   Diaries, op. cit., 22 September 1924.

140.   Diaries, op. cit., 9 October 1924.

141.   Diaries, op. cit., 18 October 1924.

142.   *Essex Chronicle*, 10 July 1925.

143.   *The Times*, 30 September 1925.

144.   Diaries, op. cit., 8 November 1925.

145.   *The Times*, 27 February 1926.

146.   *Border Counties Advertizer*, 3 March 1926.

147.   *Border Counties Advertizer*, 3 March 1926.

148.   *Woodford Times*, 5 March 1926.

149.   *Border Counties Advertizer,* 10 March 1926.

150.   *Liverpool Daily Post,* March 1926.

151. Newman, J, and Pevesner, N. *The Buildings of England* (Shropshire 2006).

152. National Army Museum, NSS 7709-43, Letter 194.

153. Diaries, op. cit., 11 August 1910.

154. Diaries, op. cit., 2 April 1911.

155. Diaries, op. cit., 5 May 1914.

156. Diaries, op. cit., 3 May 1916.

157. Diaries, op. cit., 13 December 1917.

158. Diaries, op. cit., 3 September 1920.

159. *Oswestry and Border Counties Advertizer,* 15 June 1921.

160. Now in the collection of the North Carolina Museum of Art, USA.

161. Sold at Christie's in April 1997, purchaser unknown.

162. Still in ownership of a descendant of the family.

163. Ludlow, Briscoe and Hughes, Auctioneers and Valuers, Catalogue of Contents of Aston Hall, for sale by auction 2-12 July 1923.

164. *Border Counties Advertizer,* 11 July 1923.

165. *Border Counties Advertizer,* 8 June 1963.

166. *Border Counties Advertizer,* 7 August 1971.

167. Diaries, op. cit., 15 March 1920.

168. Diaries, op. cit., 24 May 1920.

169. Diaries, op. cit., 18 September 1920.

170. Diaries, op. cit., 26 January 1921.

171. Essex Record Office: D/CT 78.

172. Now the Loughton and District Historical Society.

173. The correct reference here should be to a bearskin cap.

174. This is probably a reference to the Debden estate, a mile away from Rolls Park, in Loughton Parish.

Index